OUT OF THIN AIR

OUT OF THIN AIR

A TRUE STORY OF IMPOSSIBLE MURDER IN ICELAND

Anthony Adeane

HarperCollins books may be purchased for educational, business,
or sales promotional use through our Special Markets Department.

HarperCollins Publishers Ltd
2 Bloor Street East, 20th Floor
Toronto, Ontario, Canada
M4W 1A8

www.harpercollins.ca

Library and Archives Canada Cataloguing in Publication
information is available upon request.

Typeset by CC Book Production

ISBN 978-1-44345-436-0

Printed and bound in the United States

LSC/H 9 8 7 6 5 4 3 2 1

CONTENTS

A NOTE ON NAMES

In Iceland, first names hold sway. The phone book is ordered alphabetically by first names, not surnames. This is due to Iceland's use of a patronymic naming system: surnames take the father's first name plus either –son or –dottir depending on whether the child is a son or a daughter. So if Aron is Jon's son, then he will be called Aron Jonsson. And Aron Jonsson's daughter Helga will be called Helga Aronsdottir.

In this book I follow Icelandic usage and refer to people by their first names throughout, unless there are two people with the same first name.

Icelandic spelling is anglicised and accents have been removed. This is to help the reader with words that include letters not in the English alphabet. The letter 'þ', for example, is written as 'th', and the letter 'ð' is written as 'd'. So the Icelandic newspaper *Alþýðublaðið* is written as *Althydubladid*.

KEY NAMES

Gudmundur Einarsson
Geirfinnur Einarsson

The suspects

Erla Bolladottir
Saevar Ciesielski
Kristjan Vidar Vidarsson
Tryggvi Runar Leifsson
Albert Klahn Skaftason
Gudjon Skarphedinsson

Key members of Keflavik investigation

Haukur Gudmundsson
Valtyr Sigurdsson
Kristjan Petursson

Key members of Reykjavik investigation

Orn Hoskuldsson

Sigurbjorn Vidir Eggertsson

Eggert N. Bjarnason

Karl Schütz

Gretar Saemundsson

The Klubburinn Four

Magnus Leopoldsson

Einar Bollason

Sigurbjorn Eiriksson

Valdimar Olsen

1

INTO THIN AIR

Today she has returned to the red hills.

More than four decades have passed since Erla went with police to the crumbling rock formations of Raudholar, but it is clear that the years have not dimmed her memory of the route. It is a journey she has made in her mind so many times that now she walks it unthinkingly, as if guided by invisible signs on the snow.

She brings us to a stop in front of a huge red rock. All is quiet except for the patter of snowflakes coating our backs. Peering into the wind, she points towards a trench cut deep beneath the rock face. 'There,' she murmurs. We lean in and the weight of our boots on the compacted ice makes the ground creak. 'There is where they told us we hid Geirfinnur's body.'

*

Imagine to yourself a country, which from one end to the other presents to your view only barren mountains, whose summits are covered with eternal snow, and between them fields divided by vitrified cliffs, whose high and sharp points seem to vie with each other, to deprive you of the sight of a little grass that springs up scantily among them.

These same dreary rocks likewise conceal the few scat-
tered habitations of the natives, and a single tree does no
where appear that may afford shelter to friendship and
innocence. I suppose, Sir, this will not inspire you with
any great inclination of becoming an inhabitant of Iceland;
and indeed at first sight of such a country one is tempted
to believe it impossible to be inhabited by any human
creature, if the sea, near the shores, was not every where
covered with boats.

When a young Swede named Uno von Troil wrote this account in
1772, the country was almost completely rural and the distances
between farms were long and treacherous. Life was fraught with
danger. Sudden earthquakes and volcanic eruptions could destroy
grazing land, bringing destitution to farmers and itinerant workers
around the country. Disease was rife and infant mortality high:
as late as the mid-nineteenth century, 35 per cent of babies died
before their first birthday.

Rural life was hard, especially during the long winters when the
household spent most of the working day inside. Farmhouses stank
from the livestock kept in the home, with particularly large animals
often placed below the bedroom to maximize heat. Bathing was
rare, spitting on the floor of the home was common, and head
lice were ubiquitous around the farm, so much so that many
people contracted a yellow fungal infection called favus, which
caused considerable hair loss. Sufferers kept their hats on indoors
to conceal their ravaged scalps.

But the winter darkness could also be beneficial. After the
livestock had been fed and milked during the few hours of daily

light, the rest of the day's labour was devoted to wool-working, the tedium of which was alleviated by some entertainment. This was part of the function of the widely practised tradition in rural society of the *kvoldvaka*, or evening wake, where the entire family gathered together for games, prayers and stories. Ensuring that every member of the household remained alert and focused while they carried out the monotonous task of working wool was how the farm sustained itself. The games played at the evening wake were underpinned by a serious purpose.

With everyone sat in the same room, the adults competed at composing verses, or tested the children on religious doctrine so that the local pastor would think highly of the family when he came to visit. Sometimes they read aloud from the Icelandic Sagas, the collection of stories written in the thirteenth and fourteenth centuries that vividly recount the legends and lives of the first generation of Icelandic settlers.

Not only did the evening wakes improve productivity, they also acted as an informal education for children who spent much of their childhoods working long hours around the farm. Eighteenth- and nineteenth-century education in Iceland was conducted by the family and supervised by the Church, so it was the evening wake that helped Iceland's peasant society to attain an almost universal level of literacy. For children working long hours in demanding conditions, explains Sigurdur Gylfi Magnusson in his social history of Iceland, *Wasteland with Words*, these ancient stories provided an escape from the exacting reality of farmland life into the realm of the imagination.

The 'natives' to whom von Troil refers in his account of Iceland may well have been invisible because of the island's bleak weather and unusual topography, but their response to the harsh winter conditions was perhaps not what he expected. While von Troil stomped around the vitrified cliffs wondering how anything could prosper in so brutal a landscape, Icelanders were huddled inside learning catechisms and reciting poetry.

Stories are central to the Icelandic way of life. That may sound banal – every society, culture, even civilization, is to some extent shaped and defined by its stories – but in the case of Iceland it bears emphasizing. This is a nation of reading and of story-telling, with a rich literary history of world renown, where it is a long-standing tradition to give books to each other as gifts on Christmas Eve, where the legends of the Sagas are writ large in public spaces, and where one in ten people see their words in print. When red-hot magma from a large volcanic eruption flowed towards a church at Kirkjubaer in southern Iceland in 1783, the Reverend Jon Steingrimsson is said to have uttered such an eloquent sermon that it brought the lava to a halt. In the late medieval age no Scandinavian court was complete without the presence of an Icelandic poet.

There is an Icelandic phrase, '*Ad ganga med bok I maganum*', meaning literally that everyone 'has a book in their stomach', to which the proliferation of biographies, autobiographies and historical accounts of daily life – most notably from a swathe of rural society that received little education outside of the home prior to the twentieth century – stands testament. What else is there to do in the dark winter months? The spirit of the evening wake endures. In Iceland, stories have long been told as a means of survival.

*

Every Icelander knows about the Gudmundur and Geirfinnur disappearances. They are a pair of criminal cases so embedded into Icelandic culture that they have become almost mythical, their details so commonplace that they have passed into idiom: 'He spent such a long time looking for his keys that I thought he would find Geirfinnur!' They are referenced in films, in political debates, and in the New Year's Eve sketch comedy television show watched by 90 per cent of the country. In an episode of popular comic cartoon programme *Hulli* from 2013, the bespectacled protagonist, based on the show's creator Hugleikur Dagsson, discovers a skeleton in the Icelandic wilderness and, identifying it as Geirfinnur, declares: 'This is the find of the century!'

Forty years on, they continue to fixate people. Teenagers born long after the disappearances are as knowledgeable about the particulars as their parents who lived through it. One journalist was drawn so deeply into the cases that he was tipped towards a nervous breakdown; another refers to them as a 'black hole'. Every Icelander knows what happened, but no one *knows* what happened. They are the most famous criminal cases in Icelandic history, ones that have, repeatedly, exposed the darkest parts of this safe and peaceful nation, and at their centre are absence, rumour and make-believe.

It all started when a young man went to a nightclub in January 1974.

Gudmundur Einarsson was eighteen years old. He had long dark hair and a porcelain complexion. A calm, quiet young man, he had recently finished school, and had already purchased the books he needed to help him become a mechanic.

At 8.00 p.m. on 26 January 1974, Gudmundur visited his friend Sigurbjorn Haraldsson's house. There he drank with some schoolmates, and at 11.00 p.m. they all left to attend a dance at a nightclub in Hafnarfjordur, a port town ten kilometres south of Reykjavik.

The nightclub was called Althyduhusid and had a reputation for being rough. Young men made the trip from neighbouring towns for so-called 'country balls' which, contrary to the genteel implications of the name, often descended into organized brawls. Fights careered through the tightly packed dance floor, and attendees had to shout into the ears of their companions to be heard.

Gudmundur got drunk, danced with his friends and then, after a few hours, stepped out into the night. It was two degrees above freezing with a strong wind, and the ground was slushy and grey with day-old snow. Gudmundur began to walk.

At 2.00 a.m. Gudmundur was spotted by some acquaintances of his. Two young women, named Elinborg Rafnsdottir and Sigridur Magnusdottir, saw him in the road near Althyduhusid. He was wearing a light chequered jacket, green trousers and brown shoes, and he was gesturing at cars to get them to stop. Elinborg and Sigridur slowed down as they drove past in order to give Gudmundur a lift, but when he saw them through the windscreen he thrust his hand into his pocket. He was not alone. There was a man with him wearing a yellow shirt.

The man in the yellow shirt was smaller and thinner than Gudmundur. He walked slightly behind Gudmundur, and he seemed very drunk. Just as the two women drove past, the yellow-shirted man suddenly threw himself across the hood of their Volkswagen and tumbled onto the other side of the car. They immediately hit the accelerator and drove off, the headlights punching through the blackness in front, while Gudmundur and his companion stumbled behind with their faces sheened red by the car's rear lights.

Between 2.00 a.m. and 3.00 a.m. Gudmundur was seen again. Sveinn Vilhjalmsson was driving with two others near Hafnarfjordur. They stopped at some traffic lights and saw by the side of the road a pale man with long dark hair and a chequered jacket. He seemed very drunk and had been trying to stop cars in front of them. He walked towards their stationary vehicle, but as he approached he slipped on the ice and fell to the ground. He stayed down for a second before getting back on to his feet and walking unsteadily away from the car. He appeared to be on his own.

The lights turned green and Sveinn drove off. He and his two companions may well have been the last people to see Gudmundur Einarsson alive. After that night, Gudmundur was never seen again.

When a person goes missing in Iceland it is the regular citizens who search for them. The call comes in and people from all walks of life assemble: lawyers, bankers, farmers and builders gather together to comb the landscape.

With no standing army and only a small coast guard, Iceland had no official organization to look for missing people until volunteers began establishing their own teams. The first were formed by women in fishing communities searching the coastline for their husbands and sons after accidents at sea, but it would not be until a remarkable rescue in 1950 that disparate groups around the country found cause to coalesce into a national institution.

On 14 September 1950, the *Geysir*, a silver Douglas DC-4 Skymaster flying from Luxembourg to Reykjavik for a refuelling stop and carrying the unusual cargo of a coffin containing the body of a forty-six-year-old American woman, no passengers, a pack of show dogs and a large collection of rare objects, including an ornate, lute-like instrument called a hurdy-gurdy, disappeared from radio contact. A substantial search for the missing plane ensued. Nothing was found. Pastors across the nation led their congregations in prayer for the *Geysir* and its crew.

Three days after the *Geysir* had vanished from the skies, the coast guard received a message: 'Position unknown – all alive.' The crew had managed to locate a transmitter and make contact with the outside world. They had subsisted on thirteen slices of rye bread, twenty-four bars of chocolate, a crate of Orangeade, and tea leaves boiled in melted snow in a makeshift coffee urn. The *Geysir* had crashed onto Bardarbunga, on the northwestern side of Vatnajokull, Iceland's largest glacier.

A rescue mission flew out from an American airbase in Iceland. The plane landed alongside the wreckage of the *Geysir* but soon became so submerged by snow that it was unable to take off. Now the rescuers needed rescuing. Marooned at an altitude of 1,800 metres atop the Vatnajokull glacier were three members of the American military, an aviation inspector, the six exhausted Icelandic crew members of the *Geysir*, a dozen surviving dogs, two planes, and a few tonnes of very cold antiques. The flight attendant located some bolts of cloth and festooned the wreckage with plush red fabric to retain warmth. A particularly vicious bulldog was locked in the lavatory.

Twenty-three Icelandic civilians, all experienced mountaineers, banded together and scaled Vatnajokull themselves, a group of them trekking in excess of thirty kilometres across the glacier to reach the wreckage. All ten survivors from both planes, as well as one of the dogs, were saved, and the death-defying rescue made headlines across the nation. Where members of the American military had been thwarted, Icelanders, with little in the way of specialized training, had succeeded. Inspired by this epic feat, a network of teams sprang up around the country. ICE-SAR, or the Icelandic Association for Search and Rescue, was born.

Staffed by volunteers who undertake two years of rigorous training to qualify as members, and part-funded by firework sales at New Year's Eve, ICE-SAR teams are renowned worldwide for their expertise and are called into action in crises of global concern. When a large-scale earthquake hit Haiti in 2010, a team of thirty-seven Icelandic volunteers were among the first international rescue groups to touch down in Port-au-Prince and haul survivors from the rubble.

Trips abroad, though, are rare. ICE-SAR teams are more often tasked with finding people caught out by Iceland's sudden changes in weather and terrain. Despite the country's reputation for extreme natural processes such as earthquakes and landslides, when disaster strikes it is usually less dramatic. There are likely to be warnings before fierce storms or major volcanic activity, but it is more difficult to prepare for gale-force winds that surge in from nowhere, or black ice that sends cars skating off the road.

The defining trait of Icelandic weather is unpredictability. When Icelanders talk of weather they often say that it comes in 'samples', changing so suddenly that, even on sunny mornings, it is advisable to wear a thick jacket. Step inside a café for lunch on a clear, bright day and by the time you re-emerge the whole of Reykjavik might be coated in white.

On the night that Gudmundur disappeared, a storm swept unexpectedly through Hafnarfjordur and the surrounding towns. While Gudmundur was inside the nightclub, the sky was largely clear, with patches of light drizzle, but come midway through the next morning, the grooved surface of the nearby lava fields had been rendered smooth and featureless by snow.

After a day had passed without Gudmundur returning, his parents placed an advert in the local newspaper to ask if anyone in Hafnarfjordur possessed information about where their son might be. It was the first time he had stayed away from home overnight without telling them where he was. The following day Gudmundur's father, Einar Baldursson, reported his son as missing.

On 30 January 1974, Njordur Snaeholm, the inspector in charge of the investigation, received a phone call from Elinborg Rafnsdottir, one of the two women who had seen Gudmundur from their car on the night he disappeared. She told Njordur about the man in the yellow shirt. Njordur spoke to the three friends who had been with Gudmundur that evening: none of them had been wearing yellow.

Known among his schoolmates as an easy-going young man who liked a drink and never lost an arm-wrestle, Gudmundur would sometimes spend nights out testing his strength against men from neighbouring villages. When he didn't reappear after the nightclub, his friends assumed he had either gone home with a woman or got into a drunken altercation with someone he had beaten in an arm-wrestle. By the next morning, they feared he could have been accidentally killed in a fight.

There was a likelihood, also, that he might have wandered into the lava. Walking at night from Hafnarfjordur towards Blesugrof, where Gudmundur lived, is challenging enough in the present day, but in 1974 it was a trip freighted with greater danger, especially if taken at night and under the influence of alcohol. Hafnarfjordur is located atop a sprawling, 7,000-year-old lava field, its houses built wherever the solidified magma allows. If Gudmundur had failed to flag a lift, then his most likely route home would have been a shortcut across an uninhabited area where the uneven ground is pocked with deep trenches.

The police organized nearly a dozen rescue squads to look for him. The ground was hidden beneath more than half a metre of snow, making a thorough search challenging, but the rescue party, around two hundred in total, was undeterred. They spread out across the lava fields with thermoses of coffee in their backpacks and ropes slung over their shoulders.

Knowing where to look was difficult. The area was large and the fresh snow meant there were no footprints or tracks to follow. Some teams scoured the landscape around Hafnarfjordur, while others worked their way north towards Reykjavik. When they tried to dig through the snow their spades hit ice.

A few days later the snow began to melt. On 3 February the rescue teams, by now joined by Gudmundur's father, raced back out in minivans to renew their search, scrambling around in caves and crevices to uncover any clue of the missing boy's whereabouts. The lava fields, their brain-like pits and fissures exposed once again, yielded no answers.

*

On 19 November 1974, Geirfinnur Einarsson finished his day's work and went home to Keflavik, a town nearly fifty kilometres southwest of Reykjavik. He had wavy fair that fell past his ears and he smoked a red and black pipe. His cigarette brand of choice was Raleigh.

Some ten months had passed since Gudmundur Einarsson had disappeared and, despite sharing surnames, the two men were unrelated. They shared no friends in common, lived in different towns, and were at contrasting stages in their lives. While Gudmundur was barely an adult when he vanished, Geirfinnur was a thirty-two-year-old man with a wife and two young children.

He was usually employed at power plants throughout Iceland, travelling long distances across the country to heap coal in remote areas, such as along the western boundary of the Thjorsardalur valley, or to work at the Sigolduvirkjun power plant in the country's southeast. But during November 1974 Geirfinnur was employed closer to home. He had a construction job near Keflavik, labouring for his friend Ellert Bjorn Skulason.

After work, Geirfinnur ate dinner with his wife Gudny Sigurdardottir. They finished their food and Gudny went out to the library. Geirfinnur read his book in bed.

By the time Gudny returned home, some time between 8.30 p.m. and 9.00 p.m., Geirfinnur's friend Thordur Ingimarsson had come round and the two men were watching television and drinking coffee. At around 10.00 p.m. Geirfinnur said he was leaving to meet some people, and asked Thordur for a lift in his car. Geirfinnur was not specific about who he was going to meet. He told Thordur that he had been asked to come alone.

While in the car, Geirfinnur told Thordur that he should have left for the meeting armed. Thordur took it as a joke. He dropped Geirfinnur off at the Hafnarbudin café near Keflavik docks and drove away.

It was a cold, clear night and the streets were quiet. Geirfinnur went inside the café but the people he was due to meet were not there. He bought some cigarettes and walked back to his house.

Geirfinnur arrived home at a quarter past ten. He took off his jacket. Shortly after he came in the front door, the telephone rang. Geirfinnur's son answered it. The voice on the other end asked to speak to Geirfinnur Einarsson and used his full name. The voice was deep and male, and the boy did not think he had heard it before. He passed the phone to his father. There was silence as Geirfinnur listened and then he said, 'I already came.' He paused. 'OK, I'm coming.' He grabbed his jacket and his pipe and headed for the door. The boy ran after his father and asked where he was going but he did not receive a response. He asked if he could come and he was told that he could not. Geirfinnur got into his red Ford Cortina and drove to the café.

Geirfinnur Einarsson did not return home that night. The next morning, his car was found unlocked and parked near to the café, his keys still in the ignition.

Like Gudmundur ten months before him, Geirfinnur had vanished.

Gudmundur's disappearance could have been a tragic accident, but Geirfinnur's bore the hallmarks of a criminal case. So many questions remained unanswered. Who had he gone to meet? Who had phoned him and asked him to return? And where was he now?

Serious crime was practically unheard of in Iceland in 1974. The last major murder investigation, of a taxi driver discovered in the front seat of his car with a bullet through his head, had finished, unsolved, nearly seven years previously. Murder was extremely rare, let alone in a town like Keflavik where most people knew each other. It was a baffling crime in a place where baffling crime didn't happen.

Most disappearances in Iceland involved someone getting lost or committing suicide, but it seemed unlikely that Geirfinnur had done either. The circumstances were too strange, the details too suspicious. Despite police requests, no one came forward to say that they had gone to meet Geirfinnur. This bolstered the suspicion that the people Geirfinnur planned to see at the café were complicit in his disappearance. A police tracker dog picked up Geirfinnur's scent and proceeded to run around in circles outside the café. Investigators deduced that Geirfinnur did not walk away from Hafnarbudin but entered another vehicle.

In the days that followed, the Keflavik police began to map out the details of Geirfinnur's life. Leads were difficult to come by, not because his personal affairs were particularly complicated, but because it was almost impossible to imagine why anyone would hold a grudge against him. He was not in financial difficulty and, in the years leading up to his disappearance, his income had been slightly higher than usual and he had been able to buy a home. He was comfortable enough to get by, but he did not have enough money to cause resentment.

Those who knew him said that he was quiet and restrained. He had few friends and no apparent enemies. When the police checked whether he had received any unusual parcels or phone calls in the months prior to his disappearance, they found nothing. His most consistent correspondence was a once-yearly letter from his father.

Valtyr Sigurdsson, an investigative lawyer assigned to the case, was told a story by an acquaintance of Geirfinnur's that helped to explain an important aspect of his character. The two men had been colleagues at a power plant but they had not been close, in part because Geirfinnur made little effort to befriend those he worked with. Each night after his shift had finished, Geirfinnur took the money he had earned and put it under his pillow. Private space was in short supply in the dormitories and unusual behaviour quickly drew attention. The concealment of his wages did not go unnoticed.

Late one evening, looking for a means of entertainment other than cards, some of Geirfinnur's fellow workers decided to play a prank on him. While Geirfinnur showered, one of his colleagues reached under the pillow and took the money he had stowed there. Hiding their smirks, they waited in poses of studied indifference for Geirfinnur to return. He came into the room, went to his bed, and surreptitiously peered beneath the pillow. Finding nothing there, he lifted up the duvet, wafting it up and down to make sure his money had not become lodged inside.

'Hey, Geirfinnur,' one of the men called out, 'are you looking for something or what?' Laughter broke out across the dormitory. Geirfinnur said nothing. He smiled slightly, took back his money, climbed into bed and turned to face the wall.

The police interpreted this story as a sign of Geirfinnur's equanimity. If Geirfinnur had been violent, he might have lashed out, but instead his response was calm and reasonable. He smiled because he was easy-going and he could see the funny side. Here was a man with an even temperament. Such a man, the police concluded, was unlikely to be drawn into a confrontation.

This assessment tallied with how Geirfinnur's wife, Gudny, described her husband. He was not like the headstrong young men at the nightclubs around Hafnarfjordur who sought out fights for their own entertainment. From a decade of marriage, Gudny could only recall seeing Geirfinnur get angry once. Even in this instance, he did not lose his temper but instead went silent, withdrawing inside himself until the emotion passed.

There was a genuine concern among the investigators that Geirfinnur might just be in the middle of a particularly heavy drinking session. It was not unheard of for people to disappear for a few nights on long drinking sprees, especially during the winter months. None of the Keflavik police officers had ever worked on a murder case before and were more accustomed to dealing with accidents, break-ins and the occasional small-time drug bust; petty crimes that required investigative skills far removed from those needed for a murder inquiry. After all the work put into the investigation, they could imagine nothing more embarrassing than Geirfinnur returning home unharmed and reeking of alcohol. They would be the laughing stock of Iceland.

Three days after the disappearance, the Keflavik investigators received their first major lead. In front of the café, housed in a small booth, was a public telephone. At around a quarter past ten on 19 November 1974, at exactly the time Geirfinnur would have been returning home following his first visit to the café, a man in a brown leather jacket had made a call from the payphone. He hadn't needed to consult the phone directory.

The police decided this was surely the deep-voiced man who had spoken first with Geirfinnur's son and then with Geirfinnur. Perhaps he had arrived late to the café, phoned Geirfinnur from the payphone, and met Geirfinnur at his car upon his return.

Two teenagers, Asta Elin Gretarsdottir and Sigridur Helga Georgsdottir had been inside the café, as well as an employee behind the counter named Gudlaug Jonasdottir. None of the three women had seen the caller before. In a town like Keflavik this was strange. Gudlaug, in particular, was adamant she would have recognized a local. The man in the leather jacket had passed over a twenty-kronur piece to pay for the call. That was the Reykjavik price. In Keflavik it only cost fifteen kronur. This detail implied the caller had been an out-of-towner. Everything seemed to indicate that a stranger had come to Keflavik that night and committed murder.

Keflavik detectives summoned the witnesses from the café, flicking through police identikit booklets to match up mouths, noses and eyes into bewildering configurations in an attempt to conjure an accurate representation of the caller's face. The investigators took the unusual step of commissioning a bust to be made. Perhaps, the police reasoned, it might be easier to capture the man's likeness in three dimensions rather than two.

A sculpture of the phone caller's head was cast in clay. It could be held comfortably in the palms of both hands. It was dark-brown in colour, with a bouffant of hair and a clear, penetrating gaze.

Just over a week after Geirfinnur had gone missing, the Keflavik investigators took the clay head, or 'Clayfinnur', to the capital in a brown paper bag to show to the Reykjavik police. After considerable deliberation, the unusual sculpture was shown on RUV, the state broadcaster.

The strange effigy was beamed into people's living rooms, bringing news of the mysterious disappearance to the furthest reaches of the country. 'We had been so sheltered,' said Sigridur Petursdottir, a journalist who, at the time, was a young girl living in the small town of Husavik on the north coast of Icleand. 'The only thing we knew about crime was from Enid Blyton books, then we see this creepy statue on the television and we were convinced that it was coming for us.'

Suddenly the entire Icelandic population seemed to hold vital information about what might have happened to Geirfinnur. The police received so many calls that they were forced to appoint an extra officer to man the telephone. An engineer who read about the investigation in the newspaper sent in a homemade Dictaphone to the police station so that the detectives could record phone calls. They wrote up the different sightings of 'Clayfinnur' lookalikes from all around the country. The pile of tip-offs relating to what people had seen in their dreams was nearly half an inch thick.

'I have the name of the murderer on my desk', read one headline on the front page of a daily Icelandic newspaper, accompanying a picture of a Keflavik police officer leafing through a phone book with the names of every resident of Iceland in front of him.

The 'Clayfinnur' man had spoken on the phone in Icelandic and so was very likely to be an Icelander. It was unsettling for people to imagine that one of their own might have committed murder. Killing had been something historical, a tale to tell children as a reminder of the country's Viking past, like something from the Sagas. The Geirfinnur disappearance felt like the moment a generation of Icelanders realized they, too, could kill and be killed.

Each time there was a phone call providing the police with new information, the investigators would show a picture of the accused to one of the witnesses from the café. One name that arose was that of Magnus Leopoldsson, a well-known figure in Reykjavik who bore a striking resemblance to the clay head.

Magnus was the manager of a nightclub named Klubburinn, one of the few places that stayed open late in Reykjavik. Two nights before his disappearance, Geirfinnur had paid a visit to Klubburinn. The friends who had accompanied Geirfinnur that night told police he had been talking with a man at the club. This man had been between twenty-five and thirty years of age and had dirty blond hair that reached the bottom of his ears. On the journey home that night, Geirfinnur had not mentioned this man or what they had discussed.

Rumours had long circulated around Reykjavik that the men who ran Klubburinn were also involved in smuggling alcohol to sell at the nightclub. Beer could only be sold in Iceland if it was less than 2.25 per cent in strength and there was (and still is) a state monopoly on licensed sales, making alcohol very expensive. Reykjavik nightclub owners were rumoured to circumvent the high price of liquor by brewing vats of homemade moonshine in bathtubs or collecting illegal imports thrown from ships by Norwegian sailors. Police already suspected that Geirfinnur, too, was linked to local smuggling operations. Investigators had spoken to a man who said he had asked Geirfinnur to distil sixty litres of alcohol for him, but that Geirfinnur had disappeared before he had the chance to come good on any agreement.

The police began to suspect Geirfinnur's disappearance was connected with a plan to smuggle bootleg alcohol with the man he had met at Klubburinn.

On 25 January 1975, the police brought Magnus Leopoldsson in for questioning. He was released without charge that same day. It would not be the last time that he was brought in for questioning in connection with the case.

In the following months, the investigators continued their work, but the trail had gone cold. On 5 June 1975, the Geirfinnur case was formally closed. It was almost one and a half years since Gudmundur had disappeared from a nightclub in Hafnarfjordur, and over six months since Geirfinnur had driven to a café and never returned, and there was no substantial evidence relating to the whereabouts of either man. Gudmundur's disappearance was not being treated as a criminal incident, while the most promising leads in Geirfinnur's case concerned the two men he had seemingly been in contact with prior to his vanishing: a man in Klubburinn two days before he disappeared and a man in a leather jacket making a phone call from a Keflavik café.

These phantom men, half glimpsed by witnesses, moved in the margins of events; the details about them vague, their outlines indistinct. The 'Clayfinnur' with its half-smile and vacant stare was one of the few pieces of tangible evidence among the swirl of rumours about smuggling and Klubburinn and Magnus Leopoldsson.

Both cases might well have stayed closed if it weren't for the

arrest of one woman and her boyfriend on an unrelated embezzlement charge six months later. That woman was twenty years of age
with strawberry-blonde hair and gold-framed aviator spectacles.
Her name was Erla Bolladottir.

2

BY THE RED LIGHT

I approached Mosaic Films, a London-based production company, in autumn 2014 with the idea for making a documentary about the Gudmundur and Geirfinnur disappearances. The managing director at Mosaic, Andy Glynne, liked the idea and sent filmmaker Dylan Howitt and myself to shoot some interviews for a teaser that could subsequently be pitched to commissioners. Over the course of two years I went back and forth to Iceland accompanying Dylan, and then for another year and a half, when the filming had finished and I was gathering more research, on my own.

At first the cases seemed impenetrable. Each morning Dylan and myself would set out early from our rented flat in central Reykjavik optimistic about discovering more than we already knew, but by evening our heads spun, the clarity we thought we had attained now obscured by new information and conflicting stories. One Icelander, who is obsessed with the disappearances, describes learning about them as being akin to 'going into the woods', and only after more than a year of research were we able to carve a path of sorts through the trees.

There can be few places easier to make a documentary than Iceland. An online database contains the phone number of every Icelandic citizen, including the President and the Prime Minster, and markers on a map indicate where each person lives. Almost everyone we interviewed spoke near-perfect English and proved courteous and approachable, even when talking about highly sensitive topics, and many welcomed us into their homes with trays of food and drink: grey tongues of pickled herring on buttered bread, pastries with pink-and-yellow icing and black coffee by the jug. Most Icelanders live in and around Reykjavik, a city you can drive the breadth of on a traffic-free day in ten minutes, and when snow falls the roads are cleared before it can settle.

A population of less than 350,000 creates the impression that everyone knows everyone. If you need to be introduced to someone, then there is a chance the person you just interviewed has a cousin who can put you in touch. The sense of community is uncommonly strong. You do not take a surname, you are a –son or –dottir of Iceland. When an Icelander dies, no matter if they are not well known outside of their circle of friends and family, the nation's biggest newspaper *Morgunbladid* publishes an obituary.

Filming an interview with someone is, obviously, different to talking to them beforehand. Interviewees are more inclined to speak naturally when faced with a small microphone or a notebook, but once a camera is trained upon them, no matter who they are or how the interview is conducted, the awareness of being filmed affects the way in which they answer. Some interviewees become more cautious, hedging their responses with qualifying statements that, whether they realize it or not, will probably make much of what they say unusable in a medium that prizes the pithy soundbite. Others, though, become even more adept at expressing themselves with concision and emotion when the lights are shining in their eyes.

Erla Bolladottir falls into the latter camp. She has talked about her life in court, in news packages and in documentaries. She has written a book. This frequent retelling has made her skilled at narrating her own life, the parts where she might once have been hazy now clarified through repetition. It is something we all do. From the people, things and experiences that have populated our lives, we build narratives about our origins and who we are. But Erla is a unique case. For her, being a specialist in the details of her life has become a matter of survival.

When we arrived in Iceland, Erla's was the first home we visited. We took off our shoes at the door and shuffled into her well-appointed basement flat, hanging up our coats and scarves on hooks along the corridor. As we sat with cups of coffee warming our hands and listened to her speak, I was grateful that Dylan was there to gently steer the conversation. I felt young and ill equipped to be handling the raw materials of someone's life, and it would not be until years later, when my immersion in the bewildering specifics of the cases was far greater, that I would feel capable of trying to put down in writing an account of the disappearances and their aftermath.

Sitting at the kitchen table while Erla spoke, I was secretly glad it was not me who would be in the editing suite and have the final responsibility of condensing so much detail and pain into something accurate.

*

Born in Reykjavik on 19 July 1955, Erla was the middle child, with three sisters and a brother. Her mother Thora cared for her children full time. She had been a great beauty in her youth, modelling for fashion shoots at home and abroad, and in the sharp arches of her cheekbones was the haughtiness that the very beautiful sometimes possess, a certain hardness when her face was at rest that made her expression sterner than she intended.

Thora took pride in dressing her daughters in matching clothes for birthdays and Christmas celebrations. Family photos look like the von Trapp children on holiday. Four blonde girls in red dresses, white shirts buttoned up to their throats and ribbons in their hair, with their mother, dressed in identical attire, lipsticked and beaming over them.

An exuberant and outgoing child, Erla's voice would carry across the street when she played. Thora was the disciplinarian of the two parents, the one whom Erla feared as a child, and would reprimand Erla for disturbing the neighbourhood with her noise.

Erla's father, Bolli, was a softer touch. He was a station manager for Loftleidir Icelandic at Idlewild Airport, now known as Kennedy Airport, in New York, which led to the family relocating to Long Island for five years when Erla was a child. Working for an airline was a glamorous occupation in the early days of mass-market travel, and on languid summer evenings, the sofas would be pushed to the corners of the living room and men and women in their finery would descend upon the family home to dance. Sociable and charismatic, Bolli was always Erla's favourite.

Some of Erla's earliest memories are of watching the quintessentially American TV shows *Gunsmoke* and *Bonanza*, and cycling with her sisters on the boulevards by the water. This American influence lent her an exotic quality when she returned to Iceland in 1962 as a seven-year-old. It was a feather in her hat to show off to her new schoolmates. Children would ask her whether she had seen The Beatles while in America and she would reply that, yes, John Lennon and Paul McCartney lived on her street and she saw them every day.

And this made sense. For Icelandic children, the outside world was distant and remote. Iceland was home and the people who lived there one big family. When politicians from rival parties argued on television it was like siblings squabbling with each other. Erla knew the name of every road in Reykjavik. Foreign imports were expensive and rare. At Christmas time certain fruits arrived in the country in bulk and for a month the streets of Reykjavik smelled of fresh apples.

Sometimes in the summer Erla and her siblings would be sent to farms around Iceland. This has been a tradition in Iceland for centuries. In the past, these trips were motivated by a need for money: children went to pursue seasonal work at farms and brought their modest earnings back to their families. But by the time Erla was a child, the value of these summer trips was no longer financial. What mattered was the cultural experience. Children could only truly understand their country by living out in nature for a few months. Editorials in the national papers extolled the importance of young Icelanders witnessing first-hand the rhythms of labour that had kept the nation supplied with meat and wool for centuries.

Erla was sent to stay at a farm in a small village in the northwest of the country. Only three families inhabited it, there were no other farms for miles, and it could only be accessed by boat or by air. One day, when Erla was helping the farmer collect eggs in the chicken shed, he forcibly kissed her and touched her all over her body. When Erla told the farmer's wife, she said she would speak to her husband to ensure it did not happen again. Erla should not tell anyone.

Erla returned home changed. Unable to talk to her family about the incident at the farm, she felt like an outsider. She would watch her parents and siblings engrossed in some activity and feel so apart from them, so uninvolved in whatever it was they were doing, that she started wondering whether she had been picked up from the hospital by the wrong family as a baby. She began to spend more time alone. Hours would slide past as she sat in her bedroom, transfixed by daydreams about being reunited with her real parents.

She stole money from her father's wallet and purchased a pack of cigarettes. She took them to a hill overlooking the apartment building where her family lived and lit up. From where Erla sat she could see her mother through the kitchen window preparing the evening meal, and as she watched her she dragged on the cigarette, pulling harder on it, and thought, "This serves you right." Somehow what had happened at the farm was her mother's fault. Smoking a cigarette, sat high up on a rock, watching her mother as she moved, oblivious, around the kitchen, gave Erla back a feeling of control that had been largely absent since her return from the farm.

When Erla was still young, her father embezzled money from the sales office at Pan American Airlines, where he now worked in Reykjavik. He started small, considering himself to be borrowing money he would pay back in the future, but in 1966 he stole 400,000 kronur, the equivalent of a little less than £60,000 today. The following year he took twice as much. The annual audit showed the deficit and he was caught. Bolli had been a success at the company and they did not want to press charges, but he lost his job.

The heady days in the airline business proved to be a high-water mark in Erla's father's career and his subsequent positions were decreasingly lucrative. With every change in job the family moved house, each home becoming progressively smaller, until Erla and her siblings bunked in the same bedroom while her parents slept in the sitting room. The lavish parties of her childhood were over.

The financial strain eventually took its toll on Erla's parents and they separated when Erla was fourteen. 'There had been difficulties at home,' says Erla, 'but it had always looked great on the outside. That is a part of living in a small community. It is really important that no one knows that anything is wrong.'

When she was approaching her sixteenth birthday, the last barrier before independence from her family, her mother told her she needed to be home before midnight. After Erla repeatedly flaunted the curfew, Thora confronted her. They argued. Suddenly Thora slapped Erla in the face. Before she knew what she was doing, Erla slapped her back. They stood in silence. Erla's hand burned with a curious sensation that was not unpleasant.

She turned sixteen a few weeks later and went to live with her father in Reykjavik.

At the crest of a small hill in downtown Reykjavik is a monument of a Viking gazing out to sea. Created by Einar Jonsson, a sculptor whose works decorate city parks throughout the country, the statue is of Ingolfur Arnarson, commonly recognized as the founder of Iceland.

Chronicles of voyagers visiting Iceland before its settlement are scant. In 400 BC, the Greek explorer Pytheas discovered an island far north in the Atlantic Ocean where the sun could be seen throughout the night. Over a thousand years later, travelling Irish monks arrived at a strange country, located in a similar part of the Atlantic, where the sun was so bright they could pick the lice from their shirts at midnight. Then, in the ninth century, the Vikings arrived.

Although the exact year of the settlement of Iceland is still contested, the most popular origin story takes place in 874 when Ingolfur Arnarson and his followers left Norway in search of new land, sailing northwest until they arrived at Iceland's southern flank. Seeing a distant shore on the horizon, Arnarson threw the wooden columns from his chieftain's seat into the ocean and declared that he would build his home wherever they washed up. The pillars settled on a small bay (or 'vik'), which, due to the nearby hot springs, was shrouded by steam (or 'reykja'). He named it Reykjavik and from there Iceland was founded. Much of the terrain was inhospitable and there were few land animals to hunt, yet it was not without potential: the freshwater rivers teemed with fish and in the valleys along the coast the grass grew long and lush.

Did Ingolfur and his companions feel trepidation at setting foot upon an alien land whose entrails smouldered with smoke? Iceland sits upon the faultline of the Mid-Atlantic Ridge and its rock formations are only sixteen million years old, a blink of the eye compared to the four-billion-year life spans of some of the earth's oldest land masses. More so than perhaps any other country, the landscape seems to be visibly in the process of its creation. Steam emanates from the ground and geysers leap upwards like exclamation marks. Volcanoes erupt underwater and create new islands.

Like founding stories around the world, elements of it are apocryphal. When a hundred wooden columns were thrown in the water in the summer of 1974 to mark the 1,100-year anniversary of the settlement, none of them washed up anywhere near Reykjavik. But the idea at its heart, that a group of independent men and women broke away to forge a new society on a barren and hitherto uninhabited piece of rock, remains the integral part of the Icelandic origin story.

Iceland's independence was short-lived. In the thirteenth century, Icelandic chieftains swore allegiance to Norway in order to have access to trade and to bring stability to the country after decades of bloodshed during the so-called Sturlung Age. When Norway became a dependency of Denmark, Iceland was subjected to Danish rule.

Centuries of hardship fostered resentment towards Denmark. Famine and disease blighted Iceland but scant aid was sent from Copenhagen. When, in 1627, pirates from North Africa flipped Viking legend on its head and kidnapped nearly 250 citizens from Iceland's Westman Islands to sell as slaves in Algiers, the Danish King barely raised a finger. In fertile fishing grounds a few kilometres off the southern coast, the British hauled out bulging nets of Icelandic cod with impunity. Pious Danish rulers banned dancing for more than a century.

The misery of subjugation reached its nadir with a huge volcanic eruption in 1783 in southern Iceland that caused poisonous gas, lava and ash to belch from the ground for eight successive months. It was an explosion of such gargantuan proportions that it holds the dubious honour of being not only Iceland's worst natural disaster, but also Britain's. Livestock perished and a large-scale famine resulted in the death of around a fifth of Iceland's population, leaving less than 40,000 people alive. Due to the harsh terms of the Danish trade monopoly, Iceland was compelled to export a significant proportion of its remaining supplies of food at the same time as thousands of its citizens were dying of hunger.

Independence was increasingly viewed as the antidote to the destitution and indignity of half a millennium under foreign rule. During the nineteenth century, a group of Icelandic intellectuals led by scholar Jon Sigurdsson became the figureheads of a growing movement. They argued that Iceland did not lawfully surrender its independence in medieval times. Therefore Norway, and by extension Denmark, had never actually had any claim over Iceland.

The independence movement vaunted the Sagas, the stories that powerfully portray the lives of the first generations of settlers, as representing an era when Icelanders had lived in triumph and plenty, a golden age before foreign interference. Although the essence of these tales is largely fictional, taken together they constitute perhaps the most intricately detailed depiction of a functioning medieval society found in Europe in the Middle Ages. The courage and pioneering spirit of the Vikings were held aloft as characteristics innate to the Icelandic people. By casting off the yoke of the Danes, everyday citizens could live in their own land just as the heroes of the Sagas once had. The first stirrings of nationalism could be discerned in Icelandic public life.

Denmark gradually ceded power to Iceland. In a bid to propel Iceland towards urbanization, Danish authorities granted municipal charters to Reykjavik and five other towns. Having been little more than a farm for centuries, Reykjavik soon attracted some of the institutions common in cities across Europe: there was a prison, a bishopric, a library, and a school. The Icelandic parliament, known as the Althing and founded in Thingvellir valley around 930, was moved to Reykjavik and held its first assembly on 1 July 1845. In 1874, one thousand years after Ingolfur Arnarson supposedly threw his wooden pillars towards Iceland, the Danish king allowed the country its own constitution. The number of people living in Reykjavik grew from a few hundred to more than a thousand.

Iceland's quest for self-rule was accelerated by Reykjavik's rapid growth. Two major innovations in the fishing industry caused the city's population to boom. First, decked boats replaced rowing boats during the last decades of the nineteenth century. Decked boats held larger quantities of fish and operated in deeper waters. Part-funded by investment from the newly founded national bank Landsbanki, Iceland's first major enterprises with more than a hundred employees were formed. It was the birth of capitalism in Iceland. Second, fishing boats started to use engines. In 1902 a boat called the *Stanley* was fitted with a Danish two-horsepower engine, which enabled it to undertake multiple fishing trips in a day as opposed to one. Trawler companies proliferated along the coast. Iceland's industrial revolution had arrived, the catalysts not trains and coal but boats and fish.

Reykjavik, a city with, prior to the expansion of commercial fishing, little industry to attract economic migrants from around

Iceland, found its population growing by nearly 10 per cent year on year between 1897 and 1908. The capital was home to 5.5 per cent of the total population in 1890, and by 1930 that figure had risen to 25.8 per cent. Iceland's economic growth boosted its claim to independence and, aided too by changing global attitudes to colonial rule, sovereignty was confirmed in a 1918 treaty and officially declared in 1944. By then, fish constituted around 90 per cent of the country's exports.

Despite the pre-eminence bestowed upon Reykjavik by the country's founding story, Iceland's national identity has always been, and in some ways still is, rooted in the countryside. You learn how to speak 'real' Icelandic in the rural parts of the country as opposed to 'on the gravel', as larger towns and cities in Iceland used to be disparagingly labelled. A considerable electoral imbalance in favour of the rural regions remained long after citizens had drained from countryside to coast.

When Erla moved out of her mother's house in 1971, however, a process that had been sparked by technological advances in the fishing industry had turned Reykjavik and the surrounding area into Iceland's political and economic hub, the place where not only parliament and the majority of employment opportunities now resided but also nearly half the population. Novelists had traditionally depicted the city as a den of iniquity, the place where the protagonist's morality was tested before they returned to the safety of rural life. The 1970s, though, were arguably the first decade wherein a greater number of works of Icelandic fiction were set in Reykjavik than in the countryside.

It was an exciting time to be a young person in Reykjavik. Airlines such as Loftleidir Icelandic, colloquially termed the 'hippie

airline', had made travel to America and Western Europe considerably more affordable and, from 1950 to 1970, the number
of Icelanders who flew abroad rose more than sixfold. Young
Icelanders travelled to London and San Francisco and brought
back with them new music and fashion tastes, and Icelandic flight
attendants stuffed their luggage with Cream and Moody Blues
vinyls to play to their compatriots back home. In the city centre
a shop called Karnabaer, modelled on London's Carnaby Street,
sold new clothes to the Reykjavik youth.

On 22 June 1970 Led Zeppelin played the Reykjavik Arts Fes-
tival. The popularity of the gig caused the reporter on RUV, the
state broadcaster, to remark that ticket sales had been unlike
anything seen in the capital since overshoes were sold for ration
coupons during the Second World War. The band, for their part,
were so taken by Iceland that it inspired the lyrics to one of their
most famous tracks, 'Immigrant Song'. As Led Zeppelin passed
through the city centre, police lined the pavements to protect
the band, but it didn't stop teenagers from reaching their hands
through the gaps in the barriers to brush Robert Plant's coat. A
new world was in touching distance and young Icelanders were
not going to miss the opportunity.

Young people in Reykjavik were aligning themselves to ideol-
ogies and ways of thinking that were anathema to their parents.
They were the first generation to have grown up free from Danish
rule and, as such, found alien the more nationalistic impulses of
their elders. The drug-taking, free-loving, socially conscious hippie
broke from the conservative farmer culture that had defined Iceland
for centuries. Protests over Iceland's NATO involvement ended
in bloodshed when the police clashed with the young anti-war

peaceniks. Soviet Boris Spassky and American Bobby Fischer went head to head in the World Chess Championship in Reykjavik in 1972 and, much to the chagrin of the ruling Progressive government, many Icelanders vociferously supported the Russian.

In autumn 1970 the first Department of Social Sciences was established at the University of Iceland in Reykjavik, and courses in political science and sociology soon proved popular with long-haired students living in the capital. Communes appeared around Reykjavik where young people went to take drugs and put the world to rights. 'The pill had just arrived too,' says author Halldora Thoroddsen, who lived in the city in those years, 'so lots of people just went there to fuck.'

Erla haunted the communes by Reykjavik harbour, where she smoked hash and listened to Jefferson Airplane and Icelandic progressive rock bands such as Trubrot. 'Authorities suck, capitalists are swine – all of that,' she says of her mindset back then. Getting high at parties with friends gave her that same satisfying, secretive feeling she had enjoyed while she smoked stolen cigarettes and watched her mother from the hilltop.

It was at one of these parties that Erla saw Saevar Ciesielski. They had met before, as children, on a summer trip that Erla had taken to Saevar's grandparents' farmhouse. She remembered him showing her a secret spot in a barn from where they could jump without getting hurt, and they spent a long afternoon leaping from the windowsills into bundles of hay. Now here he was, almost a decade on, standing a little apart from the rest of the group at the party, a slight smile on his face.

'I found him very interesting,' says Stefan Unnsteinsson, a journalist who remembers encountering Saevar at a number of the communes in downtown Reykjavik. 'He was young then, maybe seventeen or eighteen, and he had this raw intelligence. Amongst hippie circles people thought he was interesting. He was foreign-looking, very delicate, but very sure of himself. He could speak about anything and he was a nice presence to be around. You soon learned, of course, that he had a bit of a reputation.'

Born on July 6 1955 to an American father of Polish origin and an Icelandic mother, Saevar's surname Ciesielski (*Sees-yell-ski*) immediately marked him out as different. In a country of -sons and -dottirs, where patronyms are commonplace for the majority of the population, Ciesielski's sliding sibilance made him an outsider from birth. It is unsurprising, perhaps, that in what was one of the most homogenous societies in Europe, in which over 95 per cent of residents were born-and-bred Icelanders, Saevar, a young boy of foreign extraction with unusual origins and an even more unusual surname, should become one of the country's most legendary bogeymen.

Saevar grew up in one of the poorer neighbourhoods in downtown Reykjavik. Michael, his father, was strict, especially towards his son, and at night he would sit, drunk, and lecture Saevar on how the world was full of liars and cheats. Sometimes he would instil discipline in his boy by beating him. Saevar's sister Anna recalls one occasion in which her father removed his belt and folded it in half so that he could strike his son without using the buckle.

School did not suit Saevar. Opinionated and headstrong, he often argued with classmates and teachers, and his small stature meant he was an easy target for schoolyard bullies. Before long, Saevar was stealing from shops and being moved from school to school. One former teacher remembers him being 'impossible'.

When Saevar was fourteen, a psychiatrist judged he had difficulty adapting and recommended he be sent to Breidavik, an institute in northwest Iceland for delinquent boys. A row of symmetrical, starkly white buildings located in one of the remotest corners of the country, Breidavik occupies an unsettling space in the Icelandic psyche. Children of the fifties and sixties recall how its name would be used as a threat – 'If you don't finish your homework then you'll be packed off to Breidavik' – and even today, the spectre of its former existence still casts a shadow over those sent there. For parents it was a place that brought results: their boys went to Breidavik and returned changed.

It was not until years later, decades after its closure, that the truth about Breidavik came into sharper focus. Claims of ritual humiliation and rape, often at the hands of a particularly sadistic director, became too numerous to ignore. An institution founded with the intention of instilling discipline in troubled boys, instead fostered an environment in which many of them were maltreated. Breidavik was shut down in 1979, its legacy dozens of damaged and broken men whose chances in life were hampered by the abuse meted out to them. A study conducted by professor of forensic psychology Gisli Gudjonsson with boys who had attended Breidavik between 1953 and 1970 found 75 per cent were convicted in court for criminal activity later in life.

This was the environment from which Saevar returned to Reykjavik as a teenager. For many of the children who came from Breidavik, the place would continue to haunt them for the rest of their lives, but for Saevar it simply appeared to confirm everything he was already learning about the world: at home, at school and at Breidavik, those in positions of authority would try to break you. Saevar turned to petty crime, making ends meet by picking pockets and selling drugs at parties.

With his shoulder-length brown hair, slender physique and big leather jacket, Saevar could not have looked more different to the butch blond studs that starred in the American television shows Erla watched as a child. But he possessed a magnetism that any number of bland gunslingers lacked. When he was in a room, people were drawn to him.

At a party in December 1973, Erla's drink was spiked with LSD. As soon as she felt the drug take grip she endeavoured to retreat somewhere and ride it out in peace. Away from the din of the party, she found a door that led through to an unlit room. A red light was emanating from a stereo system in the corner and she groped towards it, knocking into furniture hidden in the gloom, until she tripped over someone lying on the floor in the dark. It was Saevar. His drink had also been spiked.

The pair lit a match and went through the records by the stereo – Frank Zappa, Pink Floyd – and talked about everything there was to know about one another. 'He made so much sense to me,' says Erla, 'I felt like I had met one of the most incredible human beings ever, and he felt the same way.' They left the house the next day a couple. 'The world maybe wasn't so different,' says Erla, 'but boy were we.'

Erla had never met anyone like Saevar. His mind whirred with different projects and plans and he would be swept along by ideas he wanted to pursue. He was always inquisitive, restless. He loved art and Erla remembers evenings spent together where she would watch him translate his thoughts into impressionistic paintings. When a friend introduced him to cubism, he stayed up all night covering the walls of a commune with imitations of Picasso.

Filmmaking was another passion and he became a figure in Reykjavik's incipient film scene. Local documentarian Vilhjalmur Knudsen taught Saevar how to use a Super 8 camera and there were nights at Vilhjalmur's where budding filmmakers squeezed into his sitting room to compare ideas and discuss films by François Truffaut and Jean-Luc Godard. Tax on imported goods was extremely high, and they used their contacts in the shipping business to smuggle into Iceland film equipment such as Bolex cameras and 75mm Yvar lenses. Saevar worked on a film about slaughterhouses and the hypocrisy of eating meat. Later, he made a short using a Super 8, wherein he created a mask of Erla's face from wax and filmed it in a cemetery.

Erla's family did not approve of Saevar. She brought him to her mother's home for a meal later that month and when he excused himself from the dinner table Thora needled her daughter about her new boyfriend. Once she learned that Saevar had been at Breidavik her worst fears were confirmed – this boy was trouble. After another awkward social visit in which Thora inferred that Saevar was feeding drugs to Erla in the bathroom, she banned Saevar from visiting her home. Erla told her mother that if Saevar could not come round, then neither would she.

In December 1973 she moved from her friend's house to live with her father in his new flat in Hafnarfjordur, one month before

Gudmundur Einarsson went on a night out there with some friends and was never seen again.

From outside it looked like a doll's house, its white walls offset by a red roof and red piping around the frames of the windows. But the police photos taken much later suggest that the tidiness stopped at the front door. The bedroom floor was covered in clothes and the storage room crowded with junk. It was a basement flat that Erla moved into, comprised of two rooms and a bathroom, on a road called Hamarsbraut, door number 11.

Hamarsbraut 11 was located a short walk from the centre of Hafnarfjordur and with its empty car parks and silent streets the area near the flat felt like no-man's-land. These were difficult months for Erla. It was a bitter winter with frequent storms and Erla would drag herself in the morning darkness to her job as a telegraph clerk at Ritsimi Islands, the state-run telegraph service. She dropped to less than fifty kilos in weight.

Her father was in hospital having suffered a stroke and she felt alone, isolated from her family and former friends. Dark moods approached, took hold of her and refused to let go. The sun rose at 11.00 a.m. and would disappear again by 4.00 p.m., and each morning, when Erla awoke in the darkness, she felt as if a hand were pushing her down. From the apartment above she could hear the sound of her neighbours walking back and forth on their wooden floor. Sometimes she would lie on her bed and think to herself that she wanted a cigarette. Her pack would be on the table and all she would have to do was reach over to them. But then she would think, 'What does it matter?' and remain where she was. A large tree blocked the view from her window and she would stare at it from her bed and wait for the time when she could return to sleep.

Exhausted by work, the weather, and her ongoing struggle with her mental health, Erla could find Saevar overbearing. 'Everything was about his ideas,' she says, 'people were fools and my friends were fools too. His reasoning was logical – I couldn't argue with the things he said – but I didn't have the strength to discuss things at the same level as he did. He would somehow not allow me to. He would set it up so if I didn't agree with him then I was the same fool as everybody else.' Worse, she suspected he was cheating on her. Sometimes he would disappear from her life for days at a time without notifying her of his whereabouts.

He spoke to Erla about how he wanted to commit the perfect crime. Fascinated by Al Capone, he fantasized about robbing banks on horseback or introducing LSD into the water supply to give the citizens of Reykjavik an unforgettable experience. What brought him satisfaction was the idea of the police and customs officers knowing he had done something and being unable to pin it on him. He stole candlesticks, alcohol, bags of old chequebooks, and a 100-kilo halibut from a fisherman at Reykjavik harbour. At the communes he sold drugs he had smuggled into Iceland in film canisters. But although he was one of Reykjavik's best-known criminals, it was Erla who masterminded a plan that outwitted the authorities.

To rob a post office in 1970s Iceland you needed a fake ID and an unusually thorough knowledge of the country's telegram service. Erla's job at Ritsimi Islands and an identification card that Saevar had stolen put them in position to make a lot of money.

On 23 August 1974, Erla phoned the National Phone Company's telegram reception centre and stated that she worked for a post office in Grindavik in southwest Iceland. She and Saevar had tampered with their telephone by unscrewing the mouthpiece and thumbing in some cloth in order to muffle Erla's voice and create the impression she was phoning long-distance. Erla read out the text for five different telephone money transmissions totalling 475,000 kronur (worth approximately £22,500 today). She was sure her colleague would recognize her voice, but no, they spoke about the weather and the transaction was confirmed.

A friend of Saevar, who bore a resemblance to the woman on the ID card, collected the money. The friend received 100,000 kronur and Saevar and Erla kept the remaining 375,000. Saevar lent 300,000 of their share to documentarian Vilhjalmur Knudsen in exchange for access to his filmmaking equipment.

They did it again. On 18 October 1974, Erla repeated the call and pretended to be from Grindavik post office. But this time, they did not use a friend to collect the money. Instead, Erla went. Grindavik had been chosen because it was busy and thus lessened the likelihood of attracting attention. However, when she arrived, it transpired the cheques had been sent to the incorrect branch. On 22 October she travelled to a much smaller, quieter post office in the town of Selfoss.

To disguise herself, Erla borrowed clothes from Saevar's sister and daubed her face in heavy make-up, something that she hadn't done since before she had become friends with the hippies at the communes. It wasn't a convincing disguise and, as she tottered towards the counter, she was certain her scheme would be uncovered.

One of the women behind the counter said to Erla, 'Oh, so you're the one who is collecting a lot of money today!' and the other people in the post office immediately turned to look at her. Erla waited for the clamp of a hand upon her shoulder and the click of cold steel around her wrist. But instead she was directed to the bank next door where the clerk counted out the money. Erla put it into a cloth bag and left.

At home with Saevar she unzipped the bag and poured the money on the bed. Inside was nearly half a million kronur. They laid the colourful bundles of notes flat upon their palms to feel the weight of 100,000 kronur. There was enough money to put down a mortgage on a house. Erla had an old dressing gown of her mother's and they put half of the money in the left pocket and the other half in the right. They did not touch the robe for a long time. It felt like having a monster in the closet.

Unsure of what to do with the money, Erla and Saevar checked into a posh hotel and pretended to be out-of-towners. They purchased art equipment and Saevar bought himself a fishing rod. They put down a payment on a white Mustang with green stripes and a tiger's head on the hood. They ate beef and only beef for three weeks.

But the police were closing in. Investigators visited Ritsimi Islands and began to interview employees to find out if anyone knew about the fraud. When they learned that Erla was in a relationship with Saevar Ciesielski, their suspicions were confirmed.

In December 1974, shortly after Geirfinnur disappeared, they went on the run from the embezzlement. Erla and Saevar bought one-way tickets to Copenhagen. There was still plenty of money left, so they exchanged it for Danish kroner and taped the money to Erla's legs. She wrapped some gauze around the wads of cash and pulled on some high boots. There were restrictions about how much foreign currency could be taken out of the country, but she walked through customs undisturbed.

They lived together in Christiania, the self-governing society in the heart of the city, and frittered away their remaining money, eventually having to resort to stealing apples from fruit stalls in Copenhagen in order to eat.

It felt like Christiania's heyday had passed. The utopian vision set out by the neighbourhood's founders was beginning to sour. Erla worked as a cleaner at hotels around the city and the smell of the bleach made her throw up into the same toilets she was scrubbing. She took a pregnancy test and discovered she was carrying her and Saevar's baby.

They returned to Iceland and moved into a flat in a new build in the Kopavogur neighbourhood on the outskirts of Reykjavik, just weeks before Erla was due to give birth.

On 24 September 1975, Julia was born. 'She looked like what I had seen in a dream,' says Erla. 'I was twenty years old and I was so young and naïve and so unaware of so many things. I wasn't even really aware of the process of giving birth – the act itself shocked me. They laid her on my shoulder and I was going to lick her, it was such a natural instinct because she was covered in slime and blood, but then I realized that is probably not what you are supposed to do. I loved her beyond everything and nothing was going to get in my way. She was now my life.'

Saevar wanted to find a means to provide for them. He undertook another smuggling mission in the autumn of 1975 and in December brought back 3.7 kilos of cannabis from Rotterdam on the ocean liner *Reykjafoss*. Meanwhile, Erla lived a life of quiet domesticity. She tidied her new home and stretched out the freshly cleaned nappies over pots and pans to dry. She and Saevar decided that, although they would live together, they would no longer be a couple. As she pottered around the new flat with her baby on her hip she felt a calm she had not felt in years.

On 12 December 1975 Saevar was arrested on suspicion of embezzlement. The next day, so was Erla.

3

NIGHTMARE AT HAMARSBRAUT 11

You can tell if the Icelandic economy is thriving by the amount of cranes throughout the capital. During the boom years of the noughties, when Iceland's financial sector became a player in the global economy, the city was dense with construction, as upmarket hotels and restaurants were built to cater for financiers swooping in for long weekends. When the crash hit in 2008, the cranes disappeared, leaving behind half-finished buildings, some of which still remain in various states of completion throughout the city, each one an Ozymandias.

It is September 2016 and I am halfway through a lengthier stay than usual in Reykjavik. Previous visits had been busy with meetings and interviews and I had only formed a fleeting impression of the city. It felt like a warm-up act before the main event, a place where visitors bought overpriced knitwear and ate good food before driving into the snow-capped hills beyond. But after staying in Reykjavik for a longer stretch of time, the city began to work its peculiar charm on me.

Nestled beside the more touristic shops in the centre are the places that have been quietly attracting locals for years: a 1950s coffee shop called Mokka, all low-hanging lights and wood panelling, which serves very strong coffee and waffles so big they droop over the sides of the plates; a musty second-hand clothes shop in the basement of Laugavegur 25 run by a twirly-moustached, pagan priest called Jormundur; Bokin, a labyrinthine bookshop on the corner of Klapparstigur, heaped high with boxes of paperbacks that overflow into the street. Between the primary-coloured corrugated iron houses and austere public buildings can be glimpsed the mountains in the distance or the edges of the bay. The totemic Hallgrimskirkja church looms above the skyline like an all-seeing-eye, a flagpole planted in the centre of the city.

Away from the criss-cross of busy streets downtown, the neighbourhoods are quiet and residential. Neatly printed on the front door of every home is the name of each occupant. Geothermal heating means that it is cheap, not to mention green, to keep homes well heated, and even when it is snowing almost every window is ajar to let the air in. Along the still roads the silence is disturbed by burblings of radio and snatches of conversation emanating from within unseen kitchens.

Dylan and I walk through the downtown area at dusk. We wend our way past the picturesque pond in the city centre. Around the perimeter are many of the nation's most important buildings: parliament, the national museum, the city library, the Supreme Court. Scores of people are ice-skating on the frozen surface of the water and across the pond a woman spins perfect pirouettes while her boyfriend films on his phone. In the dwindling light the snow-encrusted pavements are pink, and then, when the sun dips below the horizon, blue.

Erla is already outside the restaurant when we arrive, a phone in her right hand and a cigarette in the other, and her head is wreathed in smoke. Her dyed blonde hair has dark lines running through it. She has large brown eyes behind a pair of rimless rectangular glasses and her fingers are covered in rings. Sometimes when she speaks her phrasing bears traces of her younger years in the Reykjavik hippie communes: 'I see myself as a spiritual being before I am a human being,' or 'If this is all there is of this physical existence, then man have I been cheated.' She seems younger than sixty-one and I find it difficult to look at her without seeing the face of the girl from nearly forty years ago who sat in the Supreme Court, her chin cupped in her hand as she awaited her fate.

She is fun to be around. There is an openness and warmth about her personality that is immediately engaging. She likes people, draws energy from them, and throughout all the time I spend with her I see numerous small interactions with strangers, often ending in a joke or a smile, that speak to me of someone who takes a natural enjoyment from being with others. But her vivaciousness is also tempered by a wariness, especially when getting into the details of the cases, that although not instinctive to her, has proved a necessary defence in a life chequered with disappointments. Naturally unguarded but compelled to be cautious, she can make for contradictory company.

We enter the restaurant, Erla in front of me, Dylan behind, and as we cross the threshold I see Erla flinch. I follow her gaze and see a table of five immaculately dressed women in their mid-thirties openly gesturing towards Erla and whispering to each other in such a poorly executed attempt at being subtle that it is almost laughable. The five women aren't trying particularly hard to be discreet. As any schoolyard bully can attest, the whole point of gossiping about someone in the playground is not to be covert but to be caught in the act of being covert. If it was someone other than Erla, then I might try to say something consoling, but she wouldn't like this. In fact, it would probably irritate her. Although she wants people to empathize with her, overt pity, even if sincerely intended, makes her bristle.

The look at the door changes Erla for the evening. If she is feeling vulnerable, then this sort of unpleasant interaction makes her feel embarrassed and she becomes quiet and withdrawn. But when she is in a good mood, like tonight, the attention makes her defiant. She meets people's stares with an impudent grin, becomes a more outwardly confident version of herself. She seems to laugh louder, gesticulate more forcefully, aware that she is on show and taking the opportunity to demonstrate that she does not feel burdened by the role of notorious villain or, perhaps worse, downtrodden victim.

The next day, we drive away from Reykjavik, ostensibly with the aim of doing some filming in the countryside, but also so that Erla can show us around southwest Iceland. Aghast when she hears that no one in her company has ever tried dried fish, or 'hardfiskur', a foodstuff akin to fish jerky that is a popular snack in Iceland, she pulls over at a supermarket and buys three large packets and a tub of butter. In the car, as she drives, I make the mistake of trying to break off a chunk with my hands but each strip of fish is as strong as rope. Instead, I tear off a mouthful with my teeth, and chew, cow-like, on the tough strands of fish, now smeared with butter, until the sturdy flesh yields its surprisingly mellow taste.

One of the most striking things about driving around Iceland is the lack of man-made landmarks. Against the backdrop of its barren mountains and vast open spaces, all manner of strange creatures have been conjured over the centuries: trolls that live in the hills; elf-women who wait at crossroads to tempt men into madness; and monsters who tap at the window while you sleep.

In the absence of medieval churches, ancient palaces, and castles, it is mythological stories that tell the history of the landscape. At the vast Vatnajokull glacier, once traversed at great personal risk by farmers in the north of the country who needed access to the fertile waters in the south during fishing season, the ice is said to reverberate with the sound of hymns sung by those who fell through the cracks. When construction projects are forced to relocate because they might encroach upon the home of an elf, the reason for diverting the trucks is not to spare the life of a supernatural being but because these places have become cultural treasures.

It is a widely held stereotype that belief in the supernatural is high in Iceland, with one 1998 study conducted by Icelandic newspaper DV, and often cited by foreign journalists, finding that 54.4 per cent of those polled believed that elves exist. But the survival of these stories does not mean that Icelanders believe in supernatural phenomena in any greater numbers than the citizens of other nations. To bore a hole through a rock that is said to house a mythological creature is to destroy a relic from the country's past.

We drive east and as we put more kilometres between us and Reykjavik, the black hills grow larger, monolithic rock formations that block out more and more of the sky on either side of the car, until it feels like we are being funnelled towards our destination.

A few kilometres shy of the black beaches of Vik we hit something unexpected: a traffic jam. Every summer, farmers across Iceland release their sheep into the wild to fatten them up. The farmers put markings on their cattle. A fully grown ewe will have a nick on her horn to indicate her province, a label for her district, and a mark on her ear for her farm. The sheep roam the mountain passes, feeding on heather, until the day of the '*rettir*', or round-up, in mid-September when the cattle, now considerably heavier, are herded back to the farm, many to be slaughtered.

Erla lights a cigarette and leans against the bonnet of the car as hundreds of sheep pour past us. When one veers off into the trenches on either side of the road, farmers on horseback click their tongues and expertly guide them back into the pack. One of the farmers comes to a stop next to our vehicle. He is in his mid-fifties and powerfully built, and sits astride a large, brown horse with a mane of blond hair along its neck. The man calls over to some of his friends and they all ride over until there is a huddle of half a dozen of them sitting silently on their horses. It is clear that they all know who Erla is.

My thoughts are still coloured by the looks she received in the restaurant and in that moment I find it difficult to tell whether the tone of the situation is amicable. Then one of them shouts, 'We are all on your side!' and they all laugh and Erla laughs too, and she leaps from the car to join them. The farmer descends from his horse, gives his helmet to Erla and helps her into the saddle. 'I haven't ridden a horse since I was a little girl!' she calls, before throwing us her car keys and galloping off with the farmers down the road, her horse picking its way through the sheep.

Erla still lives in the country where she is infamous. Anywhere else in the world she would be unknown: there would be no second glance from the diners in the restaurant, no pause from the farmer on his horse.

A national celebrity for the wrong reasons, much of her adult life has been lived under public scrutiny. As is evident from the most cursory glance through the tabloids, women accused of serious crimes always hold a particular appeal for the press. There is no doubt that if Erla was a man, she would not be as well known as she has become. Abroad she is freed by anonymity and she can go about her daily life unnoticed. But in Iceland, almost everywhere she goes, she is recognized as the woman at the heart of the Gudmundur and Geirfinnur disappearances.

Back from the ride, she leaps down from the horse, her face flushed by the wind. The farmers ride off and we get back in the car to continue the drive east.

Saevar's recollection of his arrest is dramatic. In an interview filmed in 1996, he describes what he remembers from that day. Sat at my laptop, the rushes from the original tapes now digitized, I find myself oddly thrilled to be able to finally watch Saevar talk. He is dressed in a red jumper and a white shirt and his brown hair is cut to an inch above his shoulder.

Urgent and impatient, his style of speaking is staccato and machine-gun-like compared to the tripping musicality of most spoken Icelandic. Unable to disentangle himself from the minutiae of the case, Saevar's thoughts race off on tangents and he becomes fixated on details that seem superfluous to his overarching point. Sigursteinn Masson, the journalist who conducted the interview, used barely any of the footage in his film. In the rushes you can hear Sigursteinn asking Saevar to give certain subjects another try because his answers have deviated from the original question. At one point Sigursteinn says, 'Listen, let's have something clear – I ask the questions and you answer.' Saevar's head twitches slightly when he talks.

SAEVAR: Do I look smart like this? Quite smart.

CAMERA OPERATOR: I'm ready. It's rolling.

SIGURSTEINN: 1975. December. You are living with Erla in Kopavogur. And something happens. A short description like it appeared to you at that time. You become aware that police cars are driving to the house.

SAEVAR: No, no. I had no inkling anything would happen and there is a knock on the door. It was during lunch and there are two policemen there that I *didn't* know. [*Laughs.*]

Two strangers who said they were detectives and asked me to come with them. I asked if it was urgent and why they were there and they said that it would become apparent. I asked whether it was alright if I came later that day because I was busy and eating. They looked like they were going to barge in so I demanded to see a warrant and then I closed the door.

Then I didn't think anymore about that. I felt it was strange that they wanted to talk to me and I looked at Erla, like with a question in my eyes, but then I pushed it away.

It wasn't until I heard a scream in the hallway that I noticed that something was happening. By then Erla had taken the rubbish out after dinner and she was on the floor [in the corridor] and they were going to handcuff her. I asked them what the fuck they were doing and an older lady arrived from the next apartment and shouted, asking who these men were. Then they let her go. I told them to get out of the building.

We lived on the third floor in a block in Kopavogur and I looked out from the balcony and I could see that the house was surrounded with policemen. There were three police cars and I felt it was like, you know . . .

SIGURSTEINN: Let's do this question again.

SAEVAR: I look out on the balcony. I look out. And I see that there are police cars all around the house and I felt it was very strange and threatening. I called Jon Oddsson who is a lawyer [. . .] and told him that there were two policemen there and they had been very rude and that the house was surrounded by police. He asked me to wait and said he was going to come. But he didn't.

Then [the two police officers] came with a warrant and I didn't know them, hadn't seen them, they could have just been anyone, see. I didn't know who they were but they said they were detectives. They didn't behave like detectives. They started to search and I was handcuffed and they went through everything. I was moved away, still handcuffed. On the way I remember they said something on the radio about whether they should take me downtown or to the other side of town.

[. . .] I knew there was something big going on but they started with all kinds of insults and I was put in

front of a judge, Orn Hoskuldsson, who put me in custody because of the mail fraud case.

And I complained about how these men behaved,
how they attacked the mother of my child and insulted
me. Then he just laughed, and they laughed as well, in
a crazy manner. And then I knew something was going
on. And I knew it had nothing to do with the mail fraud
case either.

Erla and Saevar were taken to Sidumuli prison in Reykjavik and
consigned to individual cells to await questioning. Originally built
as a car wash for the police, in 1972 Sidumuli was converted into
the holding facility for criminal suspects prior to trial.

There was a window in the corner of Erla's cell and a light
that flashed on and off, intermittently coating the walls and sink
green. The floor was concrete, the walls were concrete, and the
bed was concrete. The only concession to comfort was a thin
rubber mattress. The door had a peephole through which the
police could observe her.

Erla longed to know what the investigators were saying to
Saevar. The pair of them had already agreed what to do if questioned about the embezzlement: deny, deny, deny. She reasoned
that too much time had passed since the fraud for the police to
prove anything. Mostly she thought about her baby's tiny feet.

The next day she was taken to an interrogation room in Sidumuli prison. Three investigators were working on the case. Orn
Hoskuldsson was the representative of the criminal judge and the
chief investigator. He was a large man with glasses, thinning hair
and an egg-shaped head. Sigurbjorn Vidir Eggertson was a little

younger at twenty-seven and had only been with the criminal police for a couple of years. He was slick, a smooth operator, and tended to be more sympathetic in his tone to counterbalance Orn's gruffness. Eggert N. Bjarnason was the third. Physically imposing, with a well-kept black beard and a big gold ring on the middle finger of his left hand, he was the oldest of the three at thirty-eight years of age. They all wore suits.

Iceland's legal system was inherited from Danish rule: it was an inquisitorial, rather than accusatory, legal procedure. In the accusatory system, as used in the UK and the USA, the prosecution and the defence both gather evidence and bring their case to court to present to the judge and jury. But in the inquisitorial system, judges are actively involved in the investigation and can interrogate witnesses and gather evidence themselves. When Erla was being interrogated by Orn Hoskuldsson, she was being interrogated by the person who held the power to decide how long to extend her custody.

She stated that she did not know anything about the embezzlement. She assumed she would be in custody for twenty-four hours, but this was then extended for another day. And another. And another. They told her that they had a warrant to hold her for thirty days. She broke down. A period of days and nights passed where, alone in her cell, she thought about how she needed to tell the investigators everything, not just relating to the embezzlement, but every bad thing she had ever done, so that she and her baby could have a fresh start.

On the sixth day of custody, 18 December 1975, over the course of a six-and-a-half-hour interview, Erla told the investigators everything she knew about the postal fraud. In the corner of the room a police officer tapped up the statement on a typewriter using only his index fingers, as if he were a toddler playing the piano. The investigators read back the statement to her and she confirmed it was true. On 19 December, she signed it.

Erla felt renewed and optimistic. The investigators had helped her. They told her that she had done well and patted her on the back. After confessing to a crime such as fraud, suspects were usually released. She could already feel the physical sensation in her breast at the thought of returning to her baby.

Just as she was heading to get her coat, Erla says that one of the investigators stopped her. 'Oh, by the way, we have one more question we want to ask you.' Erla felt impatient. She wanted to get home. 'Do you know a guy by the name of Gudmundur Einarsson?'

Erla knew a few Gudmundur Einarssons. It was not an uncommon name. Erla says that the police showed her a photo of the Gudmundur Einarsson who had last been seen in the early hours of 27 January 1974.

She knew him. They had met each other a couple of times. The first occasion had been in Reykjavik. She had caught a lift with a friend and Gudmundur had been in the car. The second time had been at a party. She remembered him from that night because she thought he might have been interested in her.

The investigators were not asking Erla on a whim. A police report specified that the reason for questioning Erla was that the detectives had heard that Erla's partner could possibly be involved in the disappearance of Gudmundur Einarsson. Kristjan Petursson, a customs officer in Keflavik, claimed that, a week after Gudmundur disappeared, Saevar had told him he possessed valuable information about a major crime. Saevar, claimed Petursson, had bragged he knew about a big case, and that Petursson would give millions of kronur to find out what it was that Saevar knew.

The investigators found it strange that Erla had not heard about Gudmundur's disappearance. But Erla wasn't surprised. If anyone in Iceland were going to have missed the story during those winter months, it would have been her. She had barely been able to summon the strength to get out of the flat, let alone become interested in local news. She would watch from bed as her cigarette extinguished itself in the ashtray, centimetre by centimetre, until all that was left was a drooping finger of ash. Above her the footsteps paced back and forth and the branches of the tree tapped at the window.

She says they pressed her for more information, asking her what she was doing on the weekend of 26 January 1974. Specifics didn't leap out at her but she could easily summarize those months. She would go to work, visit her father in hospital, go to sleep, and then go to work again. She felt embarrassed to admit that she was lonely, but eventually she told them that too. They asked her about everything: what she had been eating, who she had been speaking to on the phone. And then, after hours of interrogations, she told them about her nightmare.

Erla's distinction between a nightmare and a bad dream is interesting. For her a bad dream is where you wake up and realize you were just dreaming, but in a nightmare you wake convinced something terrible is still happening.

On the evening of the nightmare she went to a nightclub. She did not want to go but her friend insisted. They went to a party afterwards and then her friend drove her back to Hamarsbraut 11.

Erla asked to be let out before they reached the flat. She was worried Saevar would be upset if he saw she had been out with people he didn't approve of. But then she remembered he was in Denmark. She said goodbye and walked from the car to the flat.

It was late, somewhere between 3.30 and 4.00 in the morning. She entered the flat. There was no one home. Everything was dark. Outside there was a storm and the tree bucked and shook and dragged its branches across her window. Snow was falling so heavily it was almost horizontal. The wind made the walls creak. She fell asleep.

In her nightmare, Erla was in bed in Hamarsbraut 11. As she lay there, she heard a sound. It was coming from outside her window. The window was two metres from where she slept. She lay still and listened. She could hear whispering. She looked over to the window. Silhouettes moved against the blinds. There were people outside her bedroom and they were whispering to each other.

She knew who they were. It was Saevar and two of his friends. These were violent people. They had visited the house once before, a few weeks prior to the nightmare, and Saevar had warned her that they were dangerous. She listened closer.

Amid the noise of the wind, it took a while for her to pick out what they were whispering. But then she realized what it was. 'Is she awake?' And again: 'Is she awake?'

Erla woke up. She had found the nightmare profoundly disquieting. Then she did something she had never done before. She pulled down her pyjama bottoms and defecated in her bed. She went back to sleep.

When she woke the next morning, the shame was intolerable. It felt like the culmination of the depression that had hung over her for months. She took the sheet off the bed, carefully bundled it up, and threw it into the bin outside.

In the interrogation room, Erla felt too ashamed to tell the police about her moment of incontinence. But she told them the rest of the story, including, after further questioning, the detail that the next morning she went out to the dustbin and found a bed sheet inside.

Erla recalls that the investigators were very interested by her nightmare. She says Orn Hoskuldsson, the chief investigator, leaned over the desk and put his face up close to hers. He said to her: 'Something really bad happened that night and you need to go back into your cell to think about it.'

After the interrogation was over, Erla was returned to her cell. She thought about how listless she had felt during that winter at Hamarsbraut 11. A seed of doubt began to take root. Was she hiding something from herself? Maybe she *had* witnessed something awful. That night in her green cell she lay in bed and tried to remember what had happened that weekend.

A memory came to her now. On Sunday, the day following the nightmare, her sister Helga had visited. It was the same morning she had put the soiled bed sheet into the bin and her sister's unexpected presence had made her feel uneasy. Helga asked Erla about Saevar and she replied that he was in Denmark.

'Oh really?' said Helga. 'How can he be in Denmark if I just saw him downtown?' There was a pause. Erla told Helga that she must be mistaken. 'No', said Helga, 'he was wearing a leather jacket and carrying a briefcase. I saw him standing at the bus stop talking to another man.'

Erla could see that her sister was not lying to her.

That same night Saevar came to Hamarsbraut 11. He said he had just come from the airport. When Erla asked him how he could be in Denmark and in downtown Reykjavik at the same time, he laughed in the way that he always did when he was in trouble. He said that he had been conducting some business downtown but hadn't wanted to tell her.

Alone in her cell in Sidumuli prison Erla began to wonder whether perhaps she was being interrogated about whatever it was he had tried to hide from her.

Saevar was not a violent man but some of his friends could be. One of the men in Erla's nightmare was Kristjan Vidar Vidarsson. Kristjan's upbringing had been tough. His father died in a trawler accident off the coast of Newfoundland when Kristjan was four years old and by eleven he was regularly sniffing turpentine to induce hallucinations. He was expelled from school for arguing with teachers.

While Saevar was slight, fully three centimetres shorter than Erla, Kristjan was hulking and well built, with pale skin, big cheeks and a mop of brown hair. When other children bullied Saevar at school, Kristjan intervened. Sometimes they met up to drink alcohol and inhale petrol fumes, but where Saevar drew the line at huffing thinner and glue, Kristjan did not.

Physically they were a little-and-large double act in the mould of Asterix and Obelix or, perhaps more accurately, George and Lennie from *Of Mice and Men*. Saevar was the more contemplative of the two, the one who devised the schemes, and Kristjan was his willing co-conspirator, easily influenced by his smaller, smarter friend.

The day after Erla was first questioned about Gudmundur, she says the investigators zeroed in on her nightmare. They tried to establish whether the weekend Saevar had invited Kristjan and another friend to Hamarsbraut 11 and warned Erla that they were dangerous was, in fact, the night of 26 January 1974.

Erla remembers the interrogation as being a series of possibles. It was possible that it had been the same weekend. It was possible that there had been people in her flat on the evening of her nightmare. It was possible that she had repressed something that she had witnessed.

On 20 December 1975, after a week in custody, she gave a witness statement implicating Saevar and Kristjan in the disappearance of Gudmundur.

There were no lights on anywhere. Inside the flat the door to the storage room was open. I thought I had closed it before I left in the morning. It seemed like someone had been in the apartment. Also, the sugar I had left in my bedroom had spilled on the floor.

I was tired and went straight to bed in all my clothes. When I lay on the bed I noticed that the sheet was missing, which was odd. I fell asleep but woke up again because I thought I heard a noise outside of the window. Then I fell asleep again.

Then I heard someone in the house. I thought from the sound that there was more than one person and that they were carrying something heavy. I got out of bed and saw that the [bedroom] door was now half open – I had closed it when I came in.

I didn't turn on the light or make any sound. I stood on the side of the door so I could see into the hallway. I heard people – either in the laundry room or in the storage room. I was sure that there were more people because I could hear them speaking. I heard two voices I knew – Saevar and his friend Kristjan.

Then I heard a third voice but I didn't know who it was. The voices came from the storage room but I didn't hear what they were saying. There was something going on there. I came closer and I could see Saevar and Kristjan and a third person I didn't recognize in the storage room carrying something heavy. Kristjan was holding one end and that end was in a knot, and Saevar was at the other tying another knot.

I didn't see what was in the sheet but I was sure that it was a body.

I couldn't move. I made a noise and Kristjan Vidar turned around and noticed I was standing there. He cursed and asked me what I was doing there. Saevar looked up and told Kristjan to stay calm. I stood there like I was nailed to the floor – I couldn't move. I was cold but at the same time it felt like I was sweating.

They carried the body – Kristjan held one end and Saevar the other, the third one in the middle. They walked towards the door where I was standing – it was the only exit from the room. Saevar pushed me out of the way. I fell to the floor and lay there for a while but still couldn't move. Later Saevar took me by the arms and put me to bed. He asked me if I saw anything and I said I was going to deny everything. Then he left the house.

I think I woke up before it was bright but I didn't dare to go outside. I was devastated for a few days and I couldn't focus. I never talked to Saevar about it.

After she signed the statement, Erla recalls that the investigators consoled her and told her how brave she had been. The police dropped her off at Thora's home. When she saw her baby, perfect and oblivious, she began to cry.

On 22 December 1975, two days after Erla's confession, a statement was taken from Saevar. The statement implicated two men Erla had not mentioned, one called Tryggvi Runar Leifsson and another named Albert Klahn Skaftason.

The police report says Saevar told them that Gudmundur Einarsson, Kristjan and Tryggvi had all come to the apartment at Hamarsbraut 11. A fight had broken out and resulted in Gudmundur's death. Saevar called his friend Albert, who had driven to Hamarsbraut 11 in his father's car. They put Gudmundur's body in the car and later buried it in the lava fields south of Hafnarfjordur.

On 23 December 1975, the day after Saevar had made his statement, Kristjan, Tryggvi and Albert were summoned to Sidumuli prison in Reykjavik.

Kristjan was serving a six-month sentence for theft at Iceland's largest prison, Litla-Hraun, located approximately fifty kilometres southeast of Reykjavik, but he was brought to Sidumuli for immediate questioning. He denied any involvement. He said he knew Gudmundur Einarsson as they had been at school together, but that he did not know anything about his disappearance. Tryggvi, too, said he knew nothing.

Albert Skaftason, however, told a different story. He was a sleepy-eyed stoner who had been friends with Saevar since they were children. He could remember something from the night in question.

On 23 December, a statement was taken. Albert remembered sitting in his father's yellow Toyota outside Hamarsbraut 11. Saevar emerged from the house, walked over to the car and asked Albert to open the trunk. Saevar returned inside and when he re-emerged he was accompanied by Kristjan and Tryggvi. Albert watched them approach in the left rear-view mirror. The three men were carrying something. It looked like a large bag. They heaved whatever it was into the trunk of the Toyota and the car dipped with the weight.

Albert started the car. Saevar sat in the passenger seat and Kristjan and Tryggvi in the back. They drove south out of Hafnarfjordur, past the blackness of the sea and sky beyond the harbour, and onwards to the red-and-white striped silos at Straumsvik aluminium plant. Saevar instructed Albert to park the car where it could not be seen from the road. Saevar, Kristjan and Tryggvi lifted the bag from the trunk and walked into the lava fields. Albert remained in the vehicle. It was silent. The three men returned to the car. The bag was gone. Saevar told Albert that inside the bag had been a body.

A few days later, Kristjan, the strapping young man who had been friends with Saevar since school, also confessed. With Albert, it was like looking at what had happened through a keyhole: the Toyota dipped with the weight, the men carried the body in the rear-view mirror. But Kristjan's account, although imprecise, inched the door open a little wider. On 28 December 1975, a statement was taken from him over the course of six hours.

Kristjan told police he had gone to Hamarsbraut 11 with Saevar, Tryggvi and a man he didn't know. This man, referred to as a stranger throughout the statement, was presumably Gudmundur. Kristjan did not think that Erla had been at home. There was a fight but he could not remember who it involved: he could only assume that it must have been between Tryggvi and the stranger because Saevar was not much of a fighter. The altercation started in the bedroom. Punches were thrown. The fight spilled out of the bedroom and into the living room.

Kristjan was on doctor's orders not to consume alcohol, but on that night he was drunk, very drunk, and perhaps this is why the statement feels so fragmented, as if some of the vital information is taking place in the blurred margins of Kristjan's recollection. People appear and disappear seemingly at random and his attention is attracted by details of little apparent interest. Suddenly, almost in the middle of his description of the fight, they are driving. There were three of them in the car and the stranger was gone. They drove around Hafnarfjordur and, by the time they returned, Erla was there. Saevar and Tryggvi began to 'do something' in either the laundry room or the storage room but Kristjan couldn't see what it was. On Saevar's instruction, Kristjan took Erla away.

The next thing Kristjan remembers is being in Albert's car. It was 'yellow, a small sedan and made in Japan'. Saevar and Tryggvi put something heavy in the trunk and then they drove off. They exited town to the south, drove past the towers of the aluminium plant, and along a bumpy road. The car stopped and Saevar and Tryggvi took out whatever they had put into the trunk and went away from the car for around fifteen minutes. In Albert's statement,

Kristjan had gone with them to dispose of the body but in Kristjan's statement he depicts himself as a bystander. Saevar and Tryggvi returned to the car without the bag.

There were still a lot of gaps in the timeline of the night, particularly between Gudmundur leaving the Althyduhusid nightclub and arriving at Hamarsbraut 11. None of the statements gave more information about how Gudmundur, a boy with no hint of a criminal past, had found himself in the company of Saevar, Kristjan and Tryggvi. Years later, Kristjan would say in a statement that the reason for the conflict at Hamarsbraut 11 was because Gudmundur had referred to them as 'junkies'. There had been an argument about alcohol and Gudmundur had been killed, by mistake, in a fight.

As soon as Kristjan's interrogation was over, he was taken to the lava fields to look for the body. It was 1.42 in the morning. He was returned to Sidumuli at 3.00 a.m. Nothing was found. The investigators were on the trail of something big and they wanted to capitalize quickly on the statements being made to them. While people all over Iceland were entering into the festive spirit, they had barely taken a day off. They came into Sidumuli on Christmas Eve and worked late into the night on weekends.

On 3 January 1976, a further statement was taken from Kristjan. This time he gave a more detailed description of how he thought the fight at Hamarsbraut 11 had played out. Kristjan's role in Gudmundur's death seemed to be becoming more prominent with each passing interview. Now he recalled that Saevar was losing a fight with Gudmundur. He called for help. Kristjan came to his aid. He held on to Gudmundur's leg to incapacitate him and Saevar kicked him in the head, repeatedly, until he stopped moving.

On 9 January 1976, Tryggvi, too, made a statement that put him at Hamarsbraut 11 on the night of Gudmundur's disappearance. He said he had thought a lot about the case since his arrest on 23 December, and could now say he had been at a house with Saevar, Kristjan and someone else during the weekend in question.

Tryggvi was four years older than the others. His teenage years were strewn with criminality and substance abuse. He went to school in Reykjavik but left when he was fourteen, and by the time he was seventeen he was stealing cars and forging cheques. Listed on his criminal record was the longest juvenile sentence ever handed down in Iceland: nine months for car theft. Tryggvi and his friends would take amphetamines, and drive around in stolen cars for days partying at different locations around Reykjavik. A small, muscular man, his red hair sprouted out of his head in tight knots like the coils in a light bulb.

On Sunday, 11 January 1976, Orn Hoskuldsson summoned the defendants to court and interviewed all of them individually. Saevar's custody was about to expire. Now it was extended, to sixty days, with him ordered to undergo psychiatric evaluation. The statements suggested that this group of misfits, with Saevar the mastermind, Kristjan and Tryggvi the muscle, and Albert the driver, had nearly pulled off the perfect murder. They had left no clues and had remained undetected for two years.

What had begun as a fraud investigation had spiralled into a series of confessions relating to the disappearance of a man that few people thought had even been murdered.

After she was released from custody on 20 December 1975, Erla lived at her mother's flat in Storagerdi 29 in central Reykjavik.

Days later, Erla says that she received a phone call from the police. They told her that Saevar had given a statement that matched, in detail, the one she had made about Gudmundur.

This is when everything changed for Erla. When she had confessed, she had not been convinced that it was true. But when she heard what he had said, it provided confirmation that it did happen. Her nightmare had been real.

Memories of Saevar's odd behaviour came to her now. She remembered him coming home upset, which was unusual for him, with his shoes and socks sodden. They put the wet clothing in the bath to dry and Saevar said he had been taking a shortcut through a nearby valley when somebody had shot at him and narrowly missed. He had run home and splashed through a river. But had this story been a cover-up for something else? When she peeled off his wet socks had he been laughing into his sleeve? The doubts that had crept into her relationship with Saevar were beginning to coalesce into a sickening realization.

She thought about her sister seeing Saevar with a briefcase in town when he had said he was away. She thought about the times that he had cheated on her with other women. She started picturing all the different moments in her life when he had been holding the baby or meeting her friends or lying on the floor painting pictures. Had this been the real Saevar? Or had he just returned from killing someone? He had been in her life without her ever really knowing him. Now she was finding out.

Her paranoia was compounded when she started to receive anonymous phone calls at her mother's home in mid-January 1976. When Erla answered, the person on the other end did not say a word. Down the phone she could hear breathing. On one occasion he spoke, asking her if she 'had not said enough'. The voice then warned her that she should be careful.

The police took the threats made against her seriously. Two armed officers, Magnus Magnusson and Haraldur Arnason, were sent to stay at her mother's flat.

Although Saevar was only a five-minute drive away in Sidumuli prison, it was like he was in another country. In the midst of a tumultuous few weeks, she began to rely on the investigators. Erla says that they would drive to her mother's house to share cigarettes and cups of coffee, and to quiz Erla about multiple details relating to Gudmundur's disappearance.

Erla says that during one of those visits she was driven to the flat at Thverbrekka in Kopavogur where she and Saevar had been arrested. It had been sealed off as a crime scene but there were some items Erla needed to collect for her baby. Sigurbjorn Vidir, one of the investigators, escorted her to the apartment because they wouldn't allow her to go there by herself. The younger of the three investigators, Sigurbjorn Vidir's easy charm and sympathetic manner were increasingly a source of comfort for Erla.

While they were in the apartment the conversation turned towards the subject of Geirfinnur Einarsson. Erla told Sigurbjorn Vidir about a conversation that had taken place at Saevar's mother's house when the disappearance of Geirfinnur was in the news. Saevar was listening to his mother speculating about the case and then he interjected, saying, 'I mean it is obvious that this guy was just opening his mouth when he should have kept it shut.' Erla explained to Sigurbjorn Vidir that this was typical of Saevar – he was always acting like he knew more than he did. Sigurbjorn Vidir was listening intently.

Erla says that the next day Orn Hoskuldsson (the representative of the judge) and Sigurbjorn Vidir paid her a house call and began to ask her more questions about Geirfinnur.

The police version of the story is different. They say they interviewed Erla only after she complained about threatening phone calls. Police notes written by investigator Eggert N. Bjarnason on 10 March 1976 state that Erla told them she was afraid of certain men. When the police asked her who these might be, she mentioned her half-brother Einar Bollason and some individuals affiliated with nightclubs in Reykjavik. She said that it was in connection to the disappearance of Geirfinnur.

The police interrogated Saevar. They asked him what he knew about Geirfinnur. Police reports state that Saevar was told Erla was scared of some people but there was no indication of who they were. Then Saevar mentioned some of the same men Erla had.

Erla says she was coerced into giving these names, but the police say she gave them of her own volition. Now that Saevar had confirmed some of the names, it hardly seemed to matter. The man who had confessed to killing Gudmundur appeared to know something about what had happened to Geirfinnur.

On 22 January 1976, Saevar provided a witness statement in which he confessed to seeing Geirfinnur on the night he disappeared.

Saevar said he went for a drive with some men. They intended to collect Geirfinnur at a café and drive to the dry dock in Keflavik for a smuggling job. The plan was to pick up some kegs of alcohol that had been dropped a little way out from shore. They were running late and by the time they arrived Geirfinnur wasn't there. One of the men went to a café and phoned Geirfinnur, who then came to meet them before being brought to the dry dock on the other side of Keflavik.

The dry dock was a large expanse of gravel, coal-black and strewn with bigger shards of rock, which sloped downwards from the road to the sea, where there were two boats moored for repair work. It was quiet there except for the metallic jangling of cords left unloosened on the boats and the gentle wash of the waves. Piles of rotten wood were stacked upon the ground. There were no streetlights but across the water the snow-capped peak of Mount Esja gleamed in the moonlight.

The men went out to sea in a small boat to pick up the alcohol. In his statement, Saevar said he did not join them. He drove off in his car for a while. But when he returned, it was apparent something had gone wrong. There had been an accident. Geirfinnur had fallen off the boat and drowned.

A statement was taken from Erla the following day, on 23 January 1976. According to Erla and Saevar's statements, they had both been at the dry dock with Kristjan that night. Einar Bollason, Erla's half-brother, had also been present. And so too was Magnus Leopoldsson, the manager of Klubburinn, who bore an uncanny resemblance to the clay head.

4

THE NIGHTCLUB AND
THE POLITICIAN

In 1974 residents of Reykjavik were not allowed to keep dogs as pets, own lizards, or watch television on Thursdays. But perhaps the most challenging nationwide prohibition of all was on beer.

Alcohol was banned in Iceland on 1 January 1915 following a public vote. Wine was legalized in 1922 when the Spanish threatened to stop buying salted cod if they could no longer sell their Rioja to Iceland, and by 1935 spirits were legal too, but beer of more than 2.25 per cent concentration remained forbidden.

'Icelanders,' said socialist politician Sigurjon Olafsson in 1934, 'are not able to use alcohol like civilized people: their nature is still very much of the Viking kind and they get too excited and brutal.' Denying workers access to beer was intended to prevent them from using it as a 'gateway' drink to harder liquor. Prohibition was also a way of defining Icelandic drinking habits in opposition to their beer-swilling Danish overlords in the years before independence. To drink beer was considered unpatriotic. But by the 1970s Icelandic sovereignty had long since been achieved and the demand for beer was such that bartenders mixed vodka with non-alcoholic ale to create so-called 'ghost beers', a grim cocktail that only the most blind drunk of clientele would ever mistake for a lager.

For those willing to take the risk, smuggling could be very profitable. Fishermen were legally permitted to import small amounts of beer for private use, which they sometimes sold on, and merchant sailors brought in larger quantities by throwing overboard buoyant kegs bound together with rope. Associates set out in dinghies from harbours along the coast, scanning the dark waters with their torches before towing the stash back to shore.

There weren't many nightclubs in Reykjavik. Before it burned down in 1972, Glaumbaer, next to the pond, was the best in town; nearby Glaesibaer was a low-lit venue for older clientele; and Rodull, on Skipholt, was where the sailors and wives of absent fishermen went to drink. An old lady owned Rodull and she sat at the entrance in full national costume selling tickets. When the live music got too loud she would go onstage and furiously whip the drummer with a wet towel.

And then there was Klubburinn, the nightclub managed by Magnus Leopoldsson, which had three floors, capacity of a thousand, and, like most nightclubs in town, was rumoured to be overflowing with smuggled drink. The investigators believed there was a link between Geirfinnur, smuggling and Klubburinn. The statements made by Saevar and Erla began to knit together these different ideas.

The confessions had the ring of truth, not least because they included Magnus, the man who had been associated with the disappearance from the start, but also because Keflavik, where

Geirfinnur lived, was the entry point for a large proportion of the smuggled goods that came into the country. If the men who worked at Klubburinn needed a large quantity of alcohol, then Keflavik was a likely place through which to smuggle it. An extensive alcohol-smuggling operation had been uncovered at Sudurnes near the Keflavik docks during the same month that Geirfinnur disappeared. There had been so many criss-crossing lines of rope to catch the bobbing containers of alcohol that local journalists had likened it to a giant spider's web.

Geirfinnur could not have disappeared from anywhere that more acutely resonated with Icelanders about what their nation had become. Since the Second World War, Keflavik, and specifically the airbase constructed there, had needled at neuroses about the changing state of the country.

Floating on its own in a vast swathe of the ocean, Iceland may not seem like a prize asset during a worldwide conflict. But as the likelihood of a Second World War grew, both the Allied forces and the German Reich rushed to establish a presence in neutral Iceland so they could control the waterways on either side of the island.

Iceland intrigued the Nazis. In March 1939 Heinrich Himmler sent genealogical experts to chart the purity of the country's racial make-up. Hermann Goering, too, had an interest, albeit a more strategic one, and in the years prior to the Second World War his men could be seen wandering through the lunar landscape in the south as they searched for locations that might be suitable for a military base. From there they would be able to monitor enemy submarines and attack Allied supply lines. Goering cloaked his intentions by claiming that underlings were working on his behalf to study the flight paths of falcons. In 1936 the poets W. H. Auden and Louis MacNeice even bumped into Goering's 'rather academic'-looking brother during breakfast in a hostel in Holar, presumably while he was purporting to track birds of prey for his high-ranking sibling.

Both the Allied forces and the German Reich had their requests to build a base rejected, but the British persisted. At 5.00 a.m. on 10 May 1940, Icelanders awoke to see around half a dozen warships moored in Reykjavik harbour. The identity of the new arrivals was not apparent until foreign soldiers swept ashore, affixing notices written in broken Icelandic around Reykjavik to inform the general populace that the British had arrived. They took control of key sites around Iceland and arrested the German consul general, Werner Gerlach, at the exact moment his wife and children were setting fire to his secret documents in the bathtub.

The Icelandic government formally protested the presence of the British, but in private there was a reluctant acceptance that it was better to have the Brits than the Nazis, and a deal was struck to keep Allied forces in Iceland until the end of the conflict. The Prime Minister instructed the nation over the airwaves to welcome the British as guests. It was a major strategic boon for the Allies: Winston Churchill reportedly dubbed Iceland 'the unsinkable aircraft carrier'. The occupation of Iceland had begun.

Having been an isolated nation in comparison to the rest of Europe, the arrival of British soldiers and, a year later in July 1941, tens of thousands of American troops, was a watershed moment. The Americans constructed an airfield and large military base at Keflavik from where operations could be conducted and aircraft refuelled. A delivery man from Keflavik, quoted in Thor

Whitehead's *Iceland and the Allied Military Presence*, said: 'Before the occupation you knew everyone, even the cars by the sound of their engines. There was an unhurried feel to life in town. Then the army arrived, and everything looked different. The old times were gone and they never came back.' For better or worse, Iceland had opened itself up to the rest of the world.

Both Keflavik and nearby Reykjavik were transformed by the arrival of foreign troops, and in particular the Americans. Iconic buildings in Rekyjavik like Hotel Borg in Austurvollur Square and the imposing National Theatre of Iceland were converted into makeshift headquarters for the occupying forces. Eateries serving exotic foods like hot dogs and burgers were established to cater for the off-duty GIs, and at bars in downtown Reykjavik the arrivals taught the locals how to dance the foxtrot. A new cinema opened to play films from abroad and attendance tripled. Chewing gum became readily available in shops, and the fridges at the local stores now had cans of fizzy drinks stacked alongside rural staples like blood pudding and sheep head. Icelanders tried Coca-Cola and many of them liked the taste.

Icelanders had far more courtships with the virile Americans than with the buttoned-up Brits. Even the gifts given by the Americans were better. Iceland's unforgiving terrain meant fruit was a rarity, so some soldiers would give their rations as presents to locals they had befriended. A British soldier might bring an orange, or maybe an apple. An American GI, though, would bring a whole basket of assorted fruit, as well as a box of chocolates. Their confident approach often tipped over into brashness. Many Icelandic women recall being catcalled so often by soldiers walking through town that it helped them to learn English.

The response from the authorities was heavy-handed. Young women suspected of having relationships with foreign soldiers were sent to do penance on specially designated farms around the country. They were medically examined to ensure that they had not picked up infectious diseases. The Chief Medical Officer declared it necessary to monitor sexual relations between the occupying forces and Icelanders in order to stop the nation from 'losing its identity'.

After the Second World War, the American government decided that, actually, they rather liked having such a well-placed base and they requested permission to stay. This put the Icelandic authorities in a difficult position. They took pains over their response. After centuries of Norwegian and Danish rule, Iceland's hard-won independence had only been made official on 17 June 1944. Naturally, having thousands of American troops stationed in Keflavik was not ideal for a country whose recently minted constitution held neutrality as a central tenet. The US ambassador to Iceland complained about the country's 'peculiar independence complex'.

But the US presence also gave Iceland something it had never had before: wealth. In that sense, it had been a good war. Thousands of Icelanders had flooded to Keflavik and Reykjavik to work in the now booming services industry, and local farmers hit pay dirt by selling meat to hungry troops. Investment by US forces and a large sum from the Marshall Plan had made Iceland rich. Between 1948 and 1952, Icelanders received more money per capita from Marshall Aid than any other country, with each Icelander receiving on average 209 dollars. Holland, which had suffered far greater damage during the war, came in second, with a per capita rate of 109 dollars. The Americans wanted to keep their influence in Iceland, and they were prepared to pay large amounts of money to do so.

Here, then, was the existential dilemma: keeping the base at Keflavik brought prosperity yet also a desertion of the values enshrined in the constitution. By having American forces at Keflavik, Iceland would no longer be neutral, yet the financial security might lead to greater freedom in the long run. It was independence with strings attached.

Halldor Laxness, the great twentieth-century chronicler of Icelandic life who would win the Nobel Prize for Literature in 1955, articulated the distrust of the base in his 1948 novel *The Atom Station*. In the book the fictional Prime Minister rejects criticism of his decision to allow the Americans to build a power station in the country with the words: 'What is Iceland for the Icelanders? Nothing. Only the West matters for the North. We live for the West; we die for the West; one West. Small nation – dirt. The East shall be wiped out. The dollar shall stand.' Every single copy of Laxness's book sold on its first day in print.

In their bid to persuade the Icelandic government, US military representatives emphasized the possibility of a Soviet invasion. Their argument was helped by the Communist *coup d'état* in Czechoslovakia in late February 1948. Iceland's only defence against a possible Soviet attack was 120 lightly armed police officers. In spring 1948 a large fleet of Soviet fishermen was spotted lurking in Icelandic waters. They were there to catch herring. But the timing of their visit, the first to the Icelandic coast, did little to quell concerns about a potential attack.

In March 1949 the founding treaty of NATO was submitted to parliament and Iceland were formally invited to join. Thousands of protesters demanding a referendum on NATO membership gathered outside the Althing and threw eggs and stones through the windows. While the politicians debated inside parliament, projectiles and shattered glass rained down upon them. The Socialist Party fiercely opposed the motion but on 30 March 1949 it passed by thirty-seven votes to thirteen. Later, the protests outside became so violent that Icelandic police used tear gas for the first time and fifteen people were left requiring medical attention.

Thousands of Icelanders walked the fifty kilometres from Reykjavik to Keflavik to demonstrate their displeasure. Roger Boyes explains in his book *Meltdown Iceland* that the protests were 'not just about war, about the loss of neutrality, the branding of a proud community as a mere garrison. Rather, it was the touchstone of modernity. How much were they willing to change; how much of their identity could they surrender? No one wanted to live in the Middle Ages, go back to turf cottages – but was the price of progress Americanization?' Early in the morning on 7 May 1951, while it was still dark, American aircraft began to land at Keflavik airport, and soon around four thousand soldiers were stationed in Iceland, mostly at the new NATO base in the town.

Not only did the airbase undermine the country's neutrality and open up the possibility that Iceland might be annihiliated in a nuclear conflict, it further unleashed American culture on a populace that had, until then, been largely insulated from its effects. Having the airbase in Keflavik was like having a mini America, with its own bowling alley and Wendy's, next to one of the largest towns in Iceland.

For many Icelanders, exposure to the American way of life was thrilling. There were venues where visiting music groups could perform and the sounds filtered through the gated perimeter into the emergent rock scene in Keflavik. Iceland's unusually short growing season meant that cannabis had to come from overseas and Icelandic kids with long hair and baggy clothes would go to Keflavik to pick up marijuana from soldiers. Legislation was passed allowing beer to be drunk within the confines of the base.

Organizations linked to the past, such as the Icelandic Folk Dance Society, dwindled in popularity, while consumption of American programmes broadcast for the soldiers skyrocketed. In neighbouring towns, people picked up the signals from the base by bending their aerials towards Keflavik. Heroic American television stars transfixed a new generation of youngsters just as stories of brave Vikings once had in darkened farmhouses across rural Iceland.

But the Americans were also a source of unease. In the wake of independence, now was the time for the country to celebrate its own unique culture and history, not become enamoured with another's. Apprehension about the impact of the outside world was felt more keenly, of course, on an island inhabited by only a couple of hundred thousand people. There was a very real fear that the Icelandic language, which remained largely unchanged since the days of the Sagas, might die out if Icelanders began to abandon their mother tongue.

Editorials in newspapers discussed the importance of not letting the words 'banana' and 'coffee' slip into common parlance. In the small town of Hofn in the country's southeast a farmer is said to have heard an Elvis imitator singing down the radio from a station based in Keflavik and died of a heart attack as a result. Foreigners were only permitted to live in Iceland if they renounced their own surname in favour of one that could decline with Icelandic grammar. This was the case until 1995.

It is an anxiety that has existed in Iceland for centuries – invasion always represents the biggest threat for an island nation. Pirates raiding the west coast, rival fishing boats plundering the Iceland catch, and two plagues in the 1400s that wiped out thousands all had one thing in common: they came from overseas. During the eighteenth century, farmers in the north occasionally found they had to protect their land from polar bears that arrived on blocks of ice from Greenland. For centuries, foreigners weren't even allowed to spend the winter in Iceland. They had to leave by September.

Measures were taken to counter the perceived encroachment of American influence. Aircraftmen were restricted from leaving the airbase so they could not scandalize locals with their lewd behaviour. Moreover, the government banned black soldiers from being stationed in Iceland at all, mainly so there would be no chance of them sleeping with Icelandic women. This policy remained a secret until the racial ban was publicly disclosed in 1959. An annual Icelandic song competition was established in order to dilute the concentration of English-language pop songs on the radio – it was a situation that had become, in the eyes of the organizers, 'dangerous for our tastes, mother tongue and nationality'. A television channel, RUV, was set up by the state in 1966, in part to dissuade Icelanders from watching the American programmes broadcast at the base.

It was an unease that found expression in popular culture. When a controversial singer named Soffia Karlsdottir performed a song called 'Dating a Soldier is a Dream' on the same day as

Iceland's National Day of celebrations, she provoked widespread condemnation from the country's media. She later renounced her singing career and burned the clothes she had performed in. In the iconic Icelandic film *The Girl Gogo* (based on the 1955 Indridi Gudmundur Thorsteinsson novella *79 from the Station*) a man called Ragnar from the country's rural heartland has his heart broken by a woman who he believes is faithful to him but who actually spends her nights in the arms of numerous broad-shouldered GIs.

Iceland's growing exposure to the outside world produced a decidedly ambivalent response. 'The war finished ages ago but they're still here molesting our women,' says disgruntled, drunken Grettir in the 1996 film *Devil's Island*, set in the years after the American occupation, as he watches a soldier dance with his wife. 'I'm not complaining,' replies his friend, 'they're buying up all our land.' For every politician declaring that Icelandic culture would be corrupted, there was a family at a Keflavik farm making more money than they ever thought possible. For every NATO protester, a rock band.

From almost the moment that Geirfinnur disappeared, the case and its outcome was tied to this larger narrative about the changes taking place in Iceland. For Geirfinnur to disappear from Keflavik was fitting. It was the place where the outside world clamoured to get in: not just music and strange tastes from abroad, but now serious crime too. There was no clearer sign that Icelandic society had gone to seed than a group of young drug dealers confessing to a murder.

For those who felt that corrupting influences would infect the younger generation, these cases had a significance that went beyond two disappearances. This is what happened when a country lost touch with its roots. Our small country will never be the same again, declared an editorial in the newspaper *Morgunbladid*; 'changes in our society' have brought about these wrongdoings, wrote another. A homogenous nation with little crime now had a bizarre double murder to contend with. 'All of a sudden the big, bad world was knocking at our door,' says journalist Halldor Reynisson. 'Our innocent little door!'

'It was the morning, 26 January 1976, a date I will never forget. I was fast asleep with my wife – my daughters were in the next room – and I woke up to the sound of footsteps in my garden. There was a knock on the door. I went to answer and there were all these people outside. They drove me to a building that I had never seen before. I was in a room and there were more people standing around me. They asked me take off my belt. Only then did I realize what was going on.'

Famous in Iceland for an illustrious sports career during the 1960s, Einar Bollason, Erla's half-brother, was arrested at six in the morning and thrust into the middle of a murder investigation. 'I felt paralysed,' he says. 'Naturally, I had read about Geirfinnur's disappearance like everyone else so I thought it was a joke. I just tried to stay calm and keep on telling myself there had been a misunderstanding.' Later, he would learn he had been too calm. As one of the country's most famous sports stars, the investigators assumed that if he were innocent he would fight them with the same tenacity as when he competed. Instead, Einar, known as a gentle giant by pupils at the education centre where he worked, meekly acquiesced to police demands.

In his mid-seventies now, he still has the towering frame befitting a former basketball player. His body is stooped, slightly, from age, and when he talks about that time in his life a different weight seems to push down upon him and he becomes slow and ponderous, in marked distinction from the breezy cordiality with which he welcomes us into his home.

Magnus Leopoldsson, by contrast, recounts the morning of his arrest with what can best be described as energetic irritation. The more he speaks, the more aggravated he becomes, until his answers stretch on for eight, nine, sometimes ten minutes. It is hard to tell whether his visible frustration comes from delving into a part of his life that riles him or because he is sick of talking about something he has discussed with Icelandic media outlets almost as much as Erla has.

I spend some of the interview comparing his face with the 'Clayfinnur's'. I have seen pictures of Magnus before, but in the flesh the resemblance is more striking: he shares the brown bust's strong jawline and sunken eyes.

At 6.00 a.m., the same time as Einar was being taken into custody, Magnus awoke to find three police officers standing at the end of his bed. His nine-year-old daughter had let them in because the ringing of the doorbell hadn't roused him. The police instructed him to get dressed and come with them.

In the car on the way to the station, Magnus could tell from the way the officers were talking that it was not just him who had been arrested. Two further men were taken into custody following Erla's and Saevar's statements: Valdimar Olsen, the brother of one of Erla's friends, and two weeks later Sigurbjorn Eiriksson, the owner of Klubburinn. Even though Magnus and Sigurbjorn Eiriksson were the only two of these men with an affiliation to Klubburinn, they would come to be known as the Klubburinn Four.

Saevar, Kristjan, Tryggvi and Albert had all committed petty crimes in the past. They fitted the profile of people who might become involved in a violent assault. But the Klubburinn Four were different. They were respectable members of society with full-time jobs and young families. Omar Ragnarsson, a journalist at the state broadcaster RUV, says: 'I remember the atmosphere when we heard that Einar Bollason and Magnus had been put in prison. We sank down in our chairs and said to each other, "Wow . . . what the hell is going on?!" Einar Bollason was our country's best basketball player. I knew him very well. Now he is a criminal? Him?! *He* killed Geirfinnur?!'

If Einar Bollason could be involved in smuggling and murder, then that suggested a moral degradation in Icelandic society far more profound than the random violence of a few dropouts. 'These men who were arrested were gentlemen!' says journalist Sigtryggur Sigtryggsson. That was what was so chilling. It felt like your next-door neighbour, someone whom you trusted and whose house you let your children play at, had just been exposed as a murderer.

Newspapers have always wielded powerful influence in Iceland. Editorial sheets in the 1800s helped rouse opposition to Danish rule and the major broadsheets articulated the national debate over the NATO base for decades. One of them, *Morgunbladid*, had a circulation in 1976 of around a fifth of the population. Its front page was generally reserved for foreign news, but now there was a home-grown story ripe for in-depth coverage.

Every newspaper had a political affiliation. *Morgunbladid* was loyal to the Independence Party, *Althydubladid* was associated with the Social Democratic Party, and the newspaper *Timinn* was a mouthpiece for the Progressive Party. *Visir* was the nation's tabloid of choice but it was also linked to the Independence Party. There was a gap in the market for a tabloid where journalists could take aim at the establishment without being hauled in front of their paymasters for not toeing the party line. In September 1975, a few months before Erla and Saevar were arrested, *Visir* split in two following an advertising dispute, and a newspaper called *Dagbladid* was born.

Not beholden to any political party, *Dagbladid*'s existence meant that, for the first time, there was an attempt at an entirely independent paper in Iceland. For young journalists hungry to make their names in the profession, the newspaper's forceful attitude towards the political elite was intoxicating.

'It was a glorious time,' says Omar Valdimarsson, a former journalist at *Dagbladid*. 'We worked like animals and then after work we drank like animals. Most of us gave everything we had to this paper because we believed in the idea that the media needed to be free from political control.' The motto among the writers was that the paper's only interests were those of their readers. 'We had the attitude "We won't take any shit",' says Omar, 'and it made no difference to us whether you ran a kiosk downtown or whether you were the Prime Minister – here is the question and we would like you to answer it.'

Dagbladid was a hit, and brought about a decline in sales for some of the traditional newspapers with the notable exception of the right-leaning *Morgunbladid*. For Omar and his colleagues at *Dagbladid*, as well as the journalists at the other tabloid *Visir*, it often felt like they were a step behind the rival broadsheet. It took a while for Omar to discover how the journalists at *Morgunbladid* stayed ahead. 'They simply called the police up and got given the stories! We never had that privilege at *Dagbladid*. We would call the police, and often they would just take the phone and throw it against the wall.' Sigtryggur Sigtryggsson, a journalist at *Morgunbladid*, confirms the arrangement, saying, 'We simply contacted the Reykjavik criminal court to get news. They made sure not to give us anything that would spoil the investigation.'

Morgunbladid would break a story in the morning and then the journalists at the tabloids would hit the phones to get a new angle before they went to press in the afternoon. A battle was emerging between the establishment broadsheet *Morgunbladid*, the traditional tabloid *Visir* and the emergent *Dagbladid* to get the best scoops on Iceland's biggest story.

On 26 January 1976, the same afternoon that the Klubburinn Four were arrested, an article in *Visir* under the headline 'Can it be kept secret any longer?' sent the cases, and the country, into meltdown.

The article, written by a young firebrand called Vilmundur Gylfason, who had recently returned from his studies at the University of Exeter in the UK to energize the flagging Social Democratic Party, contained two accusations. Both of them were made against Olafur Johannesson, a politician from the rival Progressive Party, who was also the Minister of Justice and one of the most well-known figures in the country. Alongside the article was a cartoon of Olafur with a leering expression on his face, his body bloated by greed.

Accusation number one was that Olafur had interfered with a historical investigation of alleged fraud at Klubburinn. The article claimed that in October 1972, when Klubburinn had been closed down on suspicion of tax evasion, Olafur had ordered the club be reopened.

Accusation number two was more severe. Vilmundur suggested Olafur had actively hindered the investigation of the Geirfinnur case.

In January 1975, a year before the Klubburinn Four were all taken into custody, the Reykjavik detectives had brought a certain man in for questioning. Although Vilmundur did not name the man, it was obvious he was referring to Magnus Leopoldsson. Vilmundur contended that a letter had been sent by Olafur and the Ministry of Justice instructing the police to stop investigating the men from Klubburinn.

Vilmundur was accusing Olafur of twice having protected a nightclub whose manager had now been rearrested under suspicion of killing Geirfinnur.

State television broadcast live from the Althing as Sighvatur Bjorgvinsson, another young MP from the same party as Vilmundur, accused Olafur of interfering with the investigation. Harsh and outspoken in his tone, Sighvatur showed none of the deference a figure of Olafur's stature might expect and accused him of cronyism. On the balconies above the main auditorium of the Althing, spectators swung their legs through the railings so more people could squeeze into the space behind them to watch.

Taking to the stand to defend himself, the barrel-chested Olafur came out swinging. Over the course of an impassioned speech, mostly directed towards the top of Sighvatur's head as the young

MP feverishly took notes, Olafur robustly denied any involvement. He said he had not nixed the closure of Klubburinn in 1972, that his opinion on the matter had never been requested, and that he had not interfered with the Geirfinnur investigation. At one point he fixed Sighvatur with a furious stare and declared, twice, 'This has nothing to do with me!' *Dagbladid* reported that 'it was the most dramatic exchange anyone could remember and the town spoke of nothing else afterwards'. Olafur Johannesson, one of Iceland's most prominent politicians, was mired in accusations that he had meddled with a murder investigation to protect his own interests.

Vilmundur and Sighvatur continued to pillory Olafur Johannesson in the newspapers. The Progressive Party newspaper *Timinn* leaped to the defence of Olafur with a front-page article on 3 February 1976, insisting there had been nothing suspicious about the Ministry of Justice's involvement in Klubburinn's affairs. Olafur accused the right-leaning tabloid *Visir*, where a number of the accusations had been printed, of being run by gangsters who should be held accountable for publicly threatening him. (A litigation suit would later have this statement declared null and void.)

But when the Ministry of Justice disclosed its correspondence, some of Vilmundur's accusations were shown to be true. The Ministry *had* responded to complaints made by the men from Klubburinn in relation to the Geirfinnur investigation. The Ministry had asked investigators whether 'other solutions might be sought' in lieu of putting more pressure upon Magnus and Sigurbjorn Eiriksson.

This was perfect fodder for tabloid journalists looking to make their mark. Not only did these cases possess all the intrigue and moral panic of a murder investigation, but they had also sucked in some of Iceland's leading political figures. For the first time since the days of the Sagas, politics and murder were compellingly intertwined in an Icelandic news story. A missing person case was now political.

Circulation of newspapers rose. On 3 February 1976, the day of Sighvatur and Olafur's showdown in parliament, *Visir* reported record sales of more than 14,000 copies. From 1975 to 1976, *Dagbladid*'s sales doubled from 8,000 to 14,000, partly because it was a new publication finding its audience, but also aided by their extensive coverage of the disappearance of Geirfinnur. Many of the newspapers had solemnly vowed in editorials that they would not release the names of those arrested until guilt had been proven, but the temptation became too much to resist. Soon Sigurbjorn Eiriksson, the man who owned Klubburinn and who at that time was still yet to be arrested, found his name hinted at in the press in connection to the case, and in some instances being printed. Spurred on by competition with one another, newspapers were making hay from what was turning out to be the story of the century – and let the consequences be damned.

Criminals were often thought of as good-natured and bumbling. In one widely shared story, an Icelandic thief, while burgling a house, found a book of Steinn Steinarr's poetry and became so distracted by it that he fell asleep at the crime scene and didn't wake up until the police came to arrest him. Reykjavik police didn't need to keep meticulous records because serious crime barely registered as a major social ill. Annals that detail minute fluctuations in weather and fish tonnage can be traced back decades, but records of murder rates in Iceland in the fifties and sixties are patchy. Murder was barely an annual event. In Reykjavik people still left their doors unlocked.

But of course every society, no matter how safe, has its dark side. The accusations made in parliament revealed the photo negative of a picture-perfect society. Iceland's close-knit community appeared to have been harbouring a murderous cabal of politicians, bootleggers and thugs. The mix of politics and nightclubs, smuggling and the Reykjavik underworld, seemed to herald the arrival of a new and troubling social ill to Iceland's shores: organized crime.

Viewed as so dangerous that their prison wardens checked their food packages to ensure that weapons weren't being sent to them, the Klubburinn Four sat in custody in Sidumuli prison.

Einar was not physically suited to the confines of his cell. Standing at nearly two metres tall, he could touch both walls with the tips of his fingers, and when he lay in bed his feet stretched over the end. Exhausted by the long days in custody, Einar developed a system to keep his mind sharp. He had never thought of himself as particularly religious, but he now found himself praying every night. A trip to the criminal court was a welcome excursion akin to going on holiday. He would have as many showers as the prison guards would allow him. He did twenty-five push-ups three times a day. He did sit-ups.

The police's conviction in Einar and Magnus's involvement seemed grounded upon a solid source, but the scenarios they put to them kept on changing. First Geirfinnur fell overboard and drowned; then he was assaulted on a boat and thrown in the sea; then he was killed on land – all of these scenarios with an ever shifting cast of co-conspirators: men whom they knew, men whom they didn't, men who were stout, or slim, or smoked cigars.

The investigators continued to look for clues. Einar told police that, on the night Geirfinnur disappeared, he might have been playing basketball in Ireland with his team, the Reykjavik-based KR basketball club. But when the investigators looked into this they discovered that the team only went to Ireland on 22 November, three days after the night in question.

Magnus, too, had no one to vouch for him. On the night Geirfinnur disappeared, a group of student nurses attended a party at Klubburinn. When the Reykjavik investigators interviewed them, they said they had only spotted Magnus early on in the night. Likewise, a police officer who had been on duty at Klubburinn that night said he thought Magnus had been absent. At the exact moment a phone call was being made at the Hafnarbudin café in Keflavik, a forty-minute drive away, Magnus was nowhere to been seen.

On 26 March 1976, at half past three in the afternoon, Orn Hoskuldsson, the investigating judge, held a meeting at the criminal court. Orn phoned a reporter from each of the major newspapers to invite them personally, so they would not realize it was a press conference until they arrived.

Orn stood before the assembled journalists and explained what the investigators had learned in the two months since the Klubburinn Four had been taken into custody. He spoke slowly and calmly with only one or two interruptions from reporters. The testimonies of the three witnesses to Geirfinnur's disappearance – Erla, Saevar and Kristjan – were put forward as the basis for the arrests.

He stated that after Gudmundur's killers had been arrested, Erla Bolladottir had complained of disturbances in the form of anonymous phone calls. The voice at the other end of the line threatened her due to her knowledge about the Geirfinnur case. This had left her extremely afraid and she told the police the names of men who were, according to her, involved in the case.

When Saevar was interrogated about whether he knew about Geirfinnur's disappearance, he named the same men. Later, so did Kristjan. Saevar and Kristjan told the police about a trip to Keflavik with Erla and a fourth man who drove the car. That man had been Magnus Leopoldsson. The purpose of the trip was to pick up some illegal homebrew for distribution.

During the journey to Keflavik, Magnus and Saevar talked about a certain man who was 'always making trouble'. They thought it best if they could get rid of him for good.

They drove to the dry dock in Keflavik where the rest of the Klubburinn Four and some other men were waiting. While the men went out to sea in a boat, Erla ran away and hid in a red house. Out at sea an argument broke out. The men from Klubburinn beat Geirfinnur to death. His body was taken back to land. Saevar and Kristjan were told that, if they didn't keep their mouths shut, they would be killed.

Naturally, the assembled journalists wanted to know how confidently these assertions were being made. Orn was careful to say that nothing had yet been proven, but that the statements made by Erla were solid and justified keeping the Klubburinn Four in custody for longer. Orn referred to her as the 'perfect witness'.

The attorneys of the Klubburinn Four were furious. The day after the press conference they met at noon to compare notes and then published a joint statement, accusing the police investigation unit of not disclosing key information pertaining to the cases. The attorneys were insistent that they had a number of witnesses who could discredit the testimonies of Erla, Saevar and Kristjan. They accused the police of incompetence, claiming that, despite more than two months having passed since their clients' arrest, the investigators had not managed to find any evidence whatsoever.

These complaints did little to subdue the extensive media coverage. Someone had been at the docks that night and seen what happened; 'She panicked and hid in an abandoned house', read the headline of an article in *Althydubladid* that gave a detailed summary of Erla's testimony. Omar Ragnarsson, the news anchor at the state broadcaster RUV, says: 'I looked into the eyes of all Icelanders and said, "This is how it is." They killed Geirfinnur in Keflavik. I felt like I was finally telling the nation the truth.' Across the country people talked in hushed tones about what the men from the nightclub had done.

Three days after the press conference, Einar Bollason was fired from his job at the Hafnarfjordur education centre. The Supreme Court confirmed that the custody of the Klubburinn Four would be extended while they were interrogated further.

After nearly three months in custody, Einar remembered that on the night of Geirfinnur's disappearance he had been watching television.

The investigators took Einar to the television station and showed him three short clips from the programme he had viewed. 'It was one of the happiest moments in my life. I realized that I remembered everything. I told them right there on the spot about what was in the rest of the programme. It was a television show about these guys in Scotland – they were throwing around these big tree trunks.'

While Geirfinnur drove to meet someone at a café, Einar was at home watching a programme about the Highland Games.

Further police investigation bolstered Einar's alibi. Other members of the KR basketball team said that Einar had helped them with fundraising for the Ireland trip on the night of the nineteenth. Einar had hired a babysitter for his children and when police spoke to her she showed them an entry in her diary which mentioned that Einar had returned home around 10.00 p.m.

Einar's wife, Sigrun Ingolfsdottir, had been at a sewing class, and she had a receipt for the materials she had bought. She returned home at midnight and had an argument with Einar about why she was back so late. In the intervening two hours between seeing the babysitter and his wife, Einar had watched television and gone to bed.

Magnus, too, had an alibi. Lara Hannesdottir and Thuridur Gisladottir both worked in the Klubburinn cloakroom. They had seen him at the club on the night Geirfinnur disappeared. According to Lara and Thuridur, Magnus had been at Klubburinn until at least midnight. Their testimony was more plausible than either the student nurses or the police officer: Lara kept a detailed log where she registered the events of each working shift.

The two men's emerging alibis confirmed what the investigators were already beginning to realize themselves: the Klubburinn Four were innocent. For them to be grouped together as a criminal gang whose tentacles reached into the highest echelons of society was absurd: some of them had never even met.

Magnus remembers Orn Hoskuldsson coming into his cell one evening. 'I am sitting on my bench and Orn is standing over me. I'm looking at him from the side – in profile – and he is not looking at me. Then he tells me that he knows that I am innocent.'

Magnus asked whether he could leave, to which Orn replied, 'What am I supposed to tell my superiors?' Magnus says Orn told him everything would be done to make his time in custody shorter. There were just some formalities that needed to be dealt with.

He remained in custody for another month.

In early May 1976, the Klubburinn Four were released. Reporters camped in front of the prison. The road was lined with the parked cars of people who had come to witness their release. At ten in the evening the doors opened and Magnus Leopoldsson stepped into the night air. 'It was a wonderful feeling to get into that car – just to be able to open a car door.' He had been told not to speak to the media until noon the next day because of a war between the newspapers: the police didn't want the afternoon tabloids to get the story first.

In thirty-minute intervals, Einar, Sigurbjorn Eiriksson and Valdimar were also released. They were forbidden from speaking to anyone else about why they had been set free and they were still under police surveillance. Restrictions were placed upon their travel. That night the newly freed men spoke on the phone to each other about what they had been through. Then they sat till dawn with their families and watched the sun come up – three of them, *Dagbladid* reported, hadn't seen it since January.

Einar, Magnus and Valdimar had been in solitary confinement for 105 days. At one stage, Einar says he sat in his cell for 45 days without being interrogated. No evidence had been found to connect any of them to Geirfinnur's disappearance. In fact, their only connection to Keflavik dry dock was an array of statements made by Erla, Saevar and Kristjan.

The reporters who had condemned the Klubburinn Four as criminals now became their cheerleaders. *Morgunbladid* and *Dagbladid* were quick to print editorials laying emphasis upon every person's right to be treated as innocent until proven guilty. In *Althydubladid* the editor demanded the journalistic profession review its position: reputations had been destroyed and innocent people had been convicted. 'Never has public opinion in this country been as unanimous in giving the guilty verdict to anyone as to the four men who were released from custody the night before yesterday,' intoned an article written in *Visir* on 12 May 1976.

Einar Bollason was interviewed at home by the state broadcaster RUV. With his wife Sigrun by his side, he explained what he had been through in a plain, dignified manner. He had been fired from his job. He had nearly lost his house. Here was a good man, an Icelandic sports hero no less, whose vilification in the court of public opinion had caused him and his reputation serious damage. Einar told the interviewer of his struggle to keep his sanity while in custody, describing how he had been unable to eat because he was so anxious. Nationwide, the enormity of the situation was beginning to sink in. These men had suffered and it had all been for nothing.

'I was around forty at the time,' Styrmir Gunnarsson, the former editor of *Morgunbladid* tells me, 'and I had never experienced such an atmosphere in this small country. There were no theories put forward that didn't catch on. People believed absolutely everything.' The whole nation had seemed in the grip of hysteria.

Everyone felt responsible somehow. The Klubburinn Four had been dragged through the media, declared guilty by the public, and crushed by the machinery of the state. Einar Bollason was holding back his tears on a sofa while calmly explaining that he had nearly gone mad in custody. 'Suspicion and distrust of a kind that we have never known before prevails,' thundered *Morgunbladid*.

Orn Hoskuldsson had assured the nation's media the statements forming the basis of the Geirfinnur investigation had been 100 per cent accurate. Erla, he said, was the 'perfect witness'. But if the Klubburinn Four were innocent, then what did that say about the people who had accused them?

It had taken weeks in custody before Magnus and Einar realized where all this information about them seemed to be coming from. Magnus remembers it well. He was taken in handcuffs to the criminal court. He had never been put in cuffs before. At court there were lawyers and police and a woman he says he had never met before. Later he discovered this woman was Erla Bolladottir.

She was asked about a trip to Keflavik that was supposed to have taken place. She described it in detail. Two cars had driven to Keflavik and it was clear who was in which car and what time it was. She said that Magnus grabbed Geirfinnur's arm to stop him and Kristjan then took Geirfinnur and strangled him to death. Magnus recalls this description being so detailed it lasted an hour.

Einar, too, had a similar experience, made all the more difficult because the accusations were coming from his half-sister. Although he and Erla were not particularly close, only seeing each other at family events such as weddings and Christmas parties (and even less after she began a relationship with Saevar), it was still a shock to see she was one of the people accusing him. He says she was trying to convince him he was there with them when Geirfinnur was being killed. She asked him to tell the investigators the truth. That would be best for everybody.

That was why the scenarios put to Einar and Magnus kept changing: there *was* no factual foundation to the Klubburinn Four's involvement. The whole thing had been cooked up in someone's imagination.

'She is really incredible,' says Magnus of Erla, 'this woman is exceptional and she will be remembered in the history of our civilization . . . At the time I didn't realize exactly why she was doing what she was doing, but I think I was mature enough to realize that people do not lie unless they are hiding something. I want to point out that wrongfully accusing someone is very close to killing someone. This changed my life. I'm sitting here now in front of you going through this and I am reminded of this every single day.'

Einar had spent a lot of time in custody pondering why they might have done this to him: 'I used to think about this a lot back in the day. What have I done? What did I do?' He thought it must have been something to do with Hamarsbraut 11. 'Erla and Saevar stayed in my father's flat and he asked me to sell it. So I had somebody change the locks there. That was the only thing that I could think of that they had against me.'

He could not understand how she could accuse her own flesh and blood. 'In those first years,' says Einar, 'I would not have shed one tear if she was run over by a bus – I hated her. Of course! That is only human.'

5

KOMMISSAR KUGELBLITZ

Erla is picking her way over the uneven ground towards the hills at Raudholar and we are walking in her wake. Dylan has his camera mounted on his shoulder and I am further behind, awkwardly stretching an umbrella over his head to protect the lens from the snow.

Raudholar is an unusual-looking place in a country not lacking in unusual-looking places. Hollywood producers love setting science fiction films in Iceland because they can convey outer space without recourse to special effects: it is the inhospitable Mann's planet in *Interstellar*; the alien moon in *Prometheus*; and the endless black deserts in *Star Trek: Into Darkness*. Its rock formations are so similar to those found on the moon that NASA arranged for Neil Armstrong and Buzz Aldrin to train in Iceland before the Apollo Missions. Raudholar, though, is not lunar in appearance: its cratered, dust-red hills look like the surface of Mars.

'There is only one reason for my brother and my friend's brother Valdimar being involved,' says Erla, 'and it was never my idea.' She says the police already had the story in mind. They pressured her into it. 'My sisters tried to ask me "What did our brother do?" and "Do you mean to say that our brother was involved in Geirfinnur's disappearance?", and I had to tell them "Yes". That was the situation.'

The police maintain that these statements were made willingly; and that they were designed to throw the investigators off the scent. The months that followed the Klubburinn Four's release bore out this theory. Erla was taken back into custody on the evening of 3 May 1976 and, as with Gudmundur, statements that she made about Geirfinnur were confirmed by Saevar.

Saevar, Erla and Kristjan appeared to know a great deal more about Geirfinnur's disappearance than they had first let on.

With the blizzard howling around us, we shoot a quick interview. 'We are here in Raudholar,' says Erla, 'which is a very well-known place to everyone in this area. This is the place Geirfinnur's body is supposed to have been got rid of.'

It is freezing and Erla returns to the car to warm up. The snow-covered landscape is a kind of heaven for Dylan. I hold the umbrella and he continues filming until there is ice in his beard, his fingers so cold he can barely work the buttons. We find our way back to where the car is parked and Erla has wound the windows down for a smoke. The vehicle throbs with the banshee wail of Janis Joplin's greatest hits.

By May 1976, the investigation needed an outsider.

The Klubburinn Four fiasco had put the police under immense pressure. They had leaned heavily on Erla's testimony and buttressed it with information from the most unreliable source possible: the people who had killed Gudmundur. Now their testimonies had been exposed as false, four innocent men had sat in custody for a hundred days, and the investigators had been publicly humiliated.

Articles in the press demanded help be sought from abroad. 'It might be better to ask foreigners to take over the investigation,' wrote *Althydubladid*. 'Thankfully we are not used to dealing with cases such as this one.' A foreign investigator would be more experienced and, crucially, their separateness from Icelandic society guaranteed neutrality in a case that had become political in its dimensions.

It was an idea that appealed to Olafur Johannesson, the Minister of Justice. The sudden release of the Klubburinn Four had benefited him, rendering his involvement in the nightclub's affairs altogether less suspicious, but he still wanted to bring the case to a quick and decisive end.

On 11 May 1976, the day after the release of the Klubburinn Four, Olafur called a meeting with the investigators. He stressed the Ministry of Justice's desire that the examination of the case be sped up. No expense would be spared, he said, to accomplish that aim.

Olafur's desire for an expedient resolution was intensified by developments in Iceland's territorial waters. While the printing presses hummed with accusations about murders and nightclubs, British and Icelandic fishing trawlers were ramming into each other in the North Atlantic Ocean. The so-called Cod Wars, a long-running dispute between Britain and Iceland over fishing rights off the Icelandic coast, were reaching their climax.

Each Cod War followed a similar pattern: the Icelandic government legally extended its fishing lines, the British continued to fish there, confrontations between Icelandic and British boats ensued, and eventually the British conceded.

Like most geopolitical disputes, money and self-interest lay at its heart. The fertile fishing grounds off Iceland's coast were highly prized by Britain, and although their economy was not as reliant on fishing as Iceland's, fish caught in Icelandic waters made up around half of the total catch of Britain's distant-water fishing fleet. Added to this was an imperialistic motivation. If Iceland succeeded in expanding its fishing limits, then it might embolden other countries to take similar action and inhibit the Royal Navy from projecting power across the world.

The stakes were higher for Iceland. The economic advantages were considerable, as was the need to prevent foreign boats from depleting stocks in Icelandic waters, but the Cod Wars were not just about fish: this was a test of the country's newly acquired status as an independent nation. The leaders of the major political parties in Iceland repeatedly appealed to nationalistic sentiment by conducting negotiations with the British in a hard-nosed and occasionally counterproductive fashion, sometimes rejecting favourable agreements so as to push for greater concessions. Iceland had not fought for independence for centuries in order to be bullied from its own fishing waters by distant powers.

Not that this stopped the British from behaving as if they were Iceland's imperial masters. When Iceland expanded its fishing lines from ten kilometres to twenty in 1958, the Royal Navy was sent to protect the trawlers that remained in Icelandic waters. Requests made by the Icelandic Coast Guard asking the British boats to leave were met with blasts of 'Rule, Britannia!' over the radio. There were demonstrations outside the British embassy in Reykjavik and Ambassador Andrew Gilchrist's ludicrous response was to crank up the volume on his gramophone in order to taunt the gathered protesters with a series of bagpipe solos and military marching tunes.

The UK's high-handed approach to the dispute infuriated Britain's allies. Iceland's perennially advantageous geographical position made it a key asset during the Cold War. A US admiral, quoted in David Fairhall's *Cold Front: Conflict Ahead in Arctic Waters,* described the Keflavik airbase as being 'the most valuable piece of real estate in NATO'. Losing an outpost of such strategic significance might tip the balance of power in the North Atlantic over to the Soviets. By continuing to fish in Icelandic waters, the British were putting this vital strategic outpost in jeopardy.

In turn, the Icelandic government knew the Keflavik airbase was a valuable bargaining chip. Whenever the British became too belligerent in their approach, Iceland threatened to leave NATO and eject US forces from Keflavik unless a suitable solution could be found. Henry Kissinger was fascinated by the conflict, writing in his book *Years of Upheaval* that it spoke 'volumes about the contemporary world and of the tyranny that the weak can impose on it'.

The Soviets spotted an opportunity to gain leverage. The British enforced a landing ban that prevented Iceland from selling fish, their biggest export, to the UK, their biggest market, and so the USSR rapidly began to purchase the unsold fish. The USA, concerned that they might not be buying enough, induced other European countries to buy Icelandic fish and help fight Communism.

While Olafur defended himself in parliament against accusations of political corruption, the final Cod War was thundering towards its conclusion. Icelandic fishermen used an ingenious device called a trawl-wire cutter to cut the cable that dragged trawler nets behind British boats. Live rounds were exchanged. At one point, an irate British fisherman threw an axe at the Icelandic Coast Guard. In February 1976, Iceland halted diplomatic relations with Britain, the only time that a country has taken such action against a fellow NATO member.

There were vociferous protests at the NATO base in Keflavik. The Cod Wars were seen as another example of foreign powers meddling in Icelandic affairs. Organizations that were opposed to NATO, such as the left-wing Samtaka Herstodvarandstaedinga, found their membership was growing, while rival political parties capitalized on the rise in the base's unpopularity by promising to withdraw from NATO in their election manifesto. The leaders of the free world were watching events in Iceland with interest.

At a NATO cabinet meeting, Einar Agustsson, the Icelandic Foreign Minister, told his counterparts that the Icelandic government was on the verge of collapse. The Cod Wars showed no sign of abating, a ruinously expensive general strike threatened the country's economy, and Olafur Johannesson, the politician in charge of thrashing out negotiations with the UK, was being accused of covering up a murder. Domestic difficulties had become entangled with international ones.

The British press scented weakness and sought to denigrate the Icelandic negotiator whose hardline position was causing such consternation in the fishing ports of Grimsby and Hull. The *Guardian* ran a piece on 4 February 1976 about the Cod Wars claiming that 'Johannesson has recently been playing hard to the gallery to protect his own position, after allegations of a cover-up [. . .] in a case involving one of Iceland's rare murders'. The *Sunday Times*, meanwhile, declared that Olafur's party was implicated in 'an extensive criminal case dealing with drug trafficking, murder and fraud'.

The collapse of the Icelandic government was not an option. NATO leaders could not risk having a rival party elected to power on a ticket that promised to shut down the airbase. Private discussions took place between Joseph Luns, the Secretary General of NATO, and US President Gerald Ford. Crisis meetings were held between the foreign ministers from Iceland, the US and West Germany.

In the summer of 1976, the Icelandic Ambassador Petur Eggerz and the director of West Germany's Ministry of the Interior met each other. They discussed the Geirfinnur disappearance and the pressure upon the government to find a solution. The West German Criminal Police were not permitted to investigate abroad, but they were able to recommend someone. The person they had in mind had retired from the West German secret service a few months earlier with the intention of spending his winters skiing and his summers travelling by boat, but he was happy to delay his retirement to take over the cases as a consultant. His appointment was organized and then confirmed by Olafur Johannesson.

Enter Karl Schütz.

Known in his home country as Kommisar Kugelblitz or 'Inspector Ball Lightning', Karl Schütz travelled to Iceland for one week in June 1976 to familiarize himself with the Geirfinnur case and returned on 2 August to establish a twelve-person-strong task force. The investigative protocol in Iceland was smaller and more disorganized than Schütz was accustomed to in West Germany and the name of his task force was never actually finalized: reports were signed using various names, including the Reykjavik Investigation Committee, the Investigation Committee of Reykjavik, and the Investigation Committee in Reykjavik.

A former member of the West German secret police, Schütz's credentials were impressive. When Germany's leading political magazine, *Der Spiegel*, was accused of treason, it was Karl Schütz who smashed through the office doors to arrest journalists and to seize papers. When the Baader-Meinhof gang, a far-left terrorist group, set department stores on fire, Schütz was one of the investigators who shaped police strategy to catch them. When Willy Brandt, the Chancellor of the Federal Republic of Germany, was accused of harbouring Communist sympathies, Schütz moved behind the scenes to bring about his resignation. Highly experienced in overseeing pressurized investigations with a political dimension, he was exactly what the Icelandic government had been looking for.

Almost as soon as Schütz arrived in Iceland, he solved a murder. A female cleaner had been killed in Miklabraut in central Reykjavik and within days Schütz had apprehended the killer. A well-known television personality named Asgeir Ingolfsson had been caught unawares by the cleaner in the act of stealing jewellery and a valuable stamp collection. He bludgeoned her with an iron bar and made his escape, but not before unwittingly leaving behind some of his hair by bumping his head on the staircase. Schütz enlisted a laboratory in West Germany to examine the forensic evidence and Asgeir was arrested. By coincidence, Asgeir could speak German. He wanted to make his confession to Schütz, and Schütz alone, because he thought so little of the Icelandic police.

In the month preceding Schütz's arrival, newspapers had gushed about the expertise of the West German policeman brought in by Olafur Johannesson, and now here he was, unravelling mysteries he hadn't been hired to solve.

Schütz presided over his task force with absolute authority. He was a small, chubby man with blue eyes and closely cropped grey hair, and his controlled demeanour commanded respect. Schütz had strong opinions about both the case and the undeveloped state of the Icelandic police force, frequently telling the media that the Ministry of Justice should invest in more technology, both for the benefit of its officers and to keep up with other European countries. Although Schütz could barely speak a word of Icelandic, he would sometimes reprimand his translator if he thought they were misinterpreting him. He kept three biros clipped to the top pocket of his tweed jacket.

Schütz was given an office at the criminal court on Borgatun in the city centre from which to conduct his work. The back wall was covered with aerial maps of Keflavik. On a long table were a circular ashtray, two silver jugs of coffee and the 'Clayfinnur'. The phones rang constantly with journalists from *Morgunbladid* looking for copy for the morning editions, and *Dagbladid* and *Visir* for the afternoon. The energy was frenetic.

Schütz was systematic in his approach. Police officers were given individual tasks and had to report back to Schütz on their completion: there was little indication this had taken place in the early stages of the investigation. He assigned different members of the task force to each suspect and introduced a card system for collating information. For the first time in Iceland's history a computer was used to help assist the detectives in their work.

With his unswerving confidence in his investigative abilities he was a different animal to the Icelandic police officers, none of whom had worked on a case of similar complexity or magnitude. Members of the task force seemed awestruck by him.

Schütz's powerful personality was not confined to his dealings with the task force. An interview with *Althydubladid* shows how he dealt with the press. In a square box in the middle of the page, where a photo would usually feature, there was a small note. It read:

> When Karl Schütz was interviewed, he requested that no photos were taken of him. That wish was granted, but if and when his cases have been solved, he said that he would allow himself to be photographed if the press wished.

Before Schütz's arrival, the investigators had been mocked for failing to do their jobs properly, their names and faces splashed across the front pages in articles denouncing them as incompetent. But Schütz changed the dynamic: no photos would be taken of him without express permission. It wasn't just the task force that was in awe of him – sections of the media were, too. These were 'his cases'.

The article continues: 'We couldn't help but notice that Schütz kept looking at the clock more and more often, so we concluded the interview.' Obstinate? Perhaps. Impatient? Definitely. But Schütz seemed to offer a genuine chance of finally bringing the cases to a conclusion.

Psychiatric evaluations were taken. With Erla rearrested in early May, there were now three people in custody suspected of involvement in Geirfinnur's disappearance: Saevar, Kristjan and Erla. Tryggvi was still being held under suspicion of killing Gudmundur, and Albert, who had confessed to transporting Gudmundur's body, had been released from custody on 19 March.

Saevar, wrote psychologist Gylfi Asmundsson, was able to relate to other people on a superficial level, though it was not possible to forge any deeper connection with him. The assessment recorded how: 'He was constantly trying to manipulate [the psychologist], is rather talkative, tries to avoid taking the psychological tests, and uses a slick tone or threatens legal action. His behaviour and reactions are typical for a psychopathic personality.' This chimed with what a juvenile psychiatrist had concluded when Saevar was sent to the children's home at Breidavik. They believed that his garrulous charm masked something much darker.

Saevar did not take drugs and he rarely drank. The investigators thought his sobriety sinister. While Kristjan and Tryggvi were perceived as brutish and violent, stumbling drunkenly into a fight with Gudmundur almost without realizing, Saevar was clear-headed and driven onwards by some other compulsion. He was in control of himself, and also of them.

The psychological assessment of Erla implied she, too, was under Saevar's influence. According to Gylfi Asmundsson, the answers she provided in the test were not consistent with reality, and were self-centred and tainted by her own experience. She is described as being so compliant that it bordered on masochism.

Susceptible to manipulation by a more powerful personality, the assessment suggested Erla made for an ideal partner in crime. Saevar was the small, mysterious Svengali figure, amoral and in possession of strange capabilities, Charles Manson-like, and Erla was the compliant girlfriend ready to obey his every command.

We have to stay vigilant at all times, Schütz urged journalists at a conference he had called, because Kristjan, Saevar and Erla have, on numerous occasions, tried to confuse us. Schütz described them as 'cunning': they were trying to mislead the investigators with conflicting statements.

In June 1976, a few weeks prior to Schütz's arrival, the press discovered that Saevar and a seventeen-year-old inmate had been exchanging letters while in custody. Written with toothpaste on strips of foil and then folded around a comb, they used string to cast their letters to one another across the corridors of Sidumuli prison. Saevar had asked that his letters be delivered to the Ministry of Justice, but instead his new pen pal took the missives to the national newspapers and attempted to sell eight of them for 100,000 kronur. Eventually a deal was made, with *Samuel* – a gossip magazine – agreeing to buy them for 40,000 kronur, but the police intervened before the letters could be made public. Most of them were confiscated.

Newspapers deplored the leaky custody situation in Sidumuli. Jon Oddsson, Saevar's lawyer, told *Althydubladid* that he believed the prisoners were not being kept in complete isolation and that messages could be passed between the cells. This was supposed to be the finest custodial prison in the country and yet the prisoners were able to communicate with one another far too easily.

The implication was that the suspects were coordinating their lies to the police through secret messages. Their failure to pin the blame on to the Klubburinn Four had left them only one option: to mire the investigation in misinformation. They continually retracted their statements, and, when they did confess, their stories were wildly contradictory: in one, Geirfinnur was killed by a rifle; in another, he was drowned; and in another, he was beaten with a plank. New doorsteps were installed in Sidumuli so that notes could no longer be slipped beneath the doors.

For Schütz, there were enough similarities in the suspects' confessions to start to pin the story down. Despite the swirl of conflicting accounts, some of what they said could be corroborated independently. Schütz commissioned comparative reports from his task force to match up consistencies across the testimonies. From these he discovered a few fixed points from which he could begin to piece together the evening of Geirfinnur's disappearance.

That night, Erla and Saevar had been at the Kjarvalsstadir cinema in Reykjavik watching *Eldur i Heimaey*, a documentary about a volcanic eruption on the Westman Islands in 1973. Vil-hjalmur Knudsen, the documentarian who had once welcomed Saevar into his home to teach him filmmaking techniques, came forward to say that, after the showing was over, he had heard Saevar say he was going to drive to Keflavik. Another witness was found who said they had seen Kristjan heading towards Vatnsstigur, a road in central Reykjavik, at a time that tallied with when Erla and Saevar could have met Kristjan there, picked him up, and driven to Keflavik in time to phone Geirfinnur at 10.15 p.m.

All of the suspects mentioned a 'foreign-looking' driver who had been with them that night. Kristjan said this man had handed a piece of paper with Geirfinnur's name and number to Saevar, and then Saevar had given it to Kristjan. Kristjan confessed it had been he who had gone into the café to make the phone call. He said a child had answered the phone and called out 'Daddy,

Daddy' before passing the receiver to his father. In a statement made the same week, Saevar confirmed he had told Kristjan to go into the café and phone Geirfinnur. Saevar was able to remember the digits '31' from Geirfinnur's phone number. The police checked if he was right, and he was.

Geirfinnur was collected from the café and brought to the dry dock. A fight broke out after a disagreement over alcohol pricing and Geirfinnur was knocked violently down to the ground. 'Kristjan touched him,' said Saevar in a statement, 'then looked at me and shook his head.' Geirfinnur's body was dragged into a van, driven by another man, so it could be disposed of.

Suddenly they realized Erla had disappeared. They drove around looking for her but they could not find her. She had run up the black gravel track sloping away from the sea and broken into an abandoned building. She remained there for several hours in the dark.

The next day Erla hitched a ride home in two different cars. Both drivers were found. They said they thought they could remember driving her home on the morning after Geirfinnur's disappearance. One man said he thought he had picked Erla up near Grindavik and driven her part of the way home. In a police line-up he successfully identified her.

Schütz needed two more things to fall into place. Firstly, he wanted to find a corpse.

Scouring such a vast landscape was a daunting task. Schütz took the unusual step of authorizing prison guards to leave their posts and join the operation. On trips from Sidumuli prison, often accompanied by Saevar, Kristjan or Erla, the investigators and prison guards searched for Geirfinnur's body. They donned Russian-style fur hats and tinted glasses to deflect the gleam of the snow. Their long black coats flapped in the wind.

They looked in the lava fields near Grafningur at a spot where Saevar said he hid the body in a crack. They searched the lake at Thingvellir, near the seat of Iceland's first parliament. They searched a football pitch. They went to a beach at Alftanes, hired an excavator and then dug up the sand until they hit solid rock.

They also tried to find Gudmundur's body. The investigators searched the lava fields south of Hafnarfjordur and near the aluminium plant at Straumsvik. In early October 1976 they drove to Fossvogur cemetery and Saevar pointed to where Gudmundur's body might have been moved. When the cemetery's foreman investigated, no soil had been excavated from the area in question.

The German detective became increasingly certain that Geirfinnur's body was hidden in the Martian landscape of Raudholar. Over and over again the suspects were taken to the crumbling red hills. The investigators studied aerial images in an attempt to identify any obvious disturbances in the topography. Erla pointed to a location fifty metres from where Saevar had also indicated, but the subsequent excavation dug up only red soil.

When the first frost set in, the bulldozers were called off. Schütz had not found a body. Yet he was more successful with his second wish: to discover the identity of the 'foreign-looking' man who had driven to Keflavik. It had become an obsession for Schütz. A police report written by Schütz shows him narrowing in on the man's identity during an interrogation of Erla on 30 October 1976:

She became silent again, started crying and hid her face with her hands. Finally she claimed to be afraid of the man. She was told that her testimony was strictly confidential and it would be treated as such. Nevertheless, she didn't want to say anything else, except that he was a very dangerous man. He was rich, and that explained it. He was a man who had done such a thing before and he would do it again without hesitation.

She named a man called Gudjon Skarphedinsson. This corroborated what investigators had already heard from Kristjan in May 1976 and Saevar on 27 October. Although not exactly 'foreign-looking', his rangy physique and neatly trimmed handlebar moustache lent him a striking appearance. He wore a fine gold chain around his neck. In his statement, Saevar said that Gudjon had helped him and Kristjan beat Geirfinnur to death.

I had phoned ahead to remind Gudjon that I was paying him a visit, but when I arrive on his doorstep he sounds baffled. His voice, faint over the intercom, asks, 'Who are you?' I explain. 'Well I suppose you better come up then.'

I reach the top floor and remove my shoes, and he welcomes me into his home. Now in his mid-seventies, he moves slowly around his flat in his slippers and dressing gown and brews me a fruit tea. The corners of his eyebrows arch upwards in a way that makes him look ever so slightly bemused by everything he hears.

He makes for curious company. At first I find him aloof, either ignoring questions or replying to them disinterestedly, the expression on his face suggesting that talking about a case from decades ago is unimaginably tedious. It is in noticeable contrast to, say, Magnus, whose indignation courses through him when he speaks.

But over the duration of the afternoon, and subsequent visits, I realize I am mistaken, and what I interpreted as dismissiveness is, in fact, a sense of humour so deadpan I'd failed to detect it. With barely any change in his facial expression or tone of voice, he denounces Schütz in a drawling monotone as 'an old Nazi', his lips curling into a smile when he sees that his purposefully exaggerated barb has hit its mark.

Gudjon had once been Saevar's teacher. They had first encountered one another at Reykjanes School in the Westfjords in the northwest of Iceland during the autumn of 1971. This student–teacher relationship had only lasted a couple of months because Saevar was soon expelled.

In 1975 Gudjon met Saevar again, by chance, on a ferry. Saevar wanted to smuggle some cannabis from Holland to Iceland in Gudjon's car. He promised Gudjon that he would pay for the transportation of the car and give him a further 100,000 kronur once the cannabis had been sold. Gudjon found that he didn't have the power to say no. They stuffed 3.7 kilos of cannabis into the doors of Gudjon's brown Citroën. When they arrived in Iceland the police were waiting for them at the docks.

After Saevar had confessed in both the Gudmundur and Geirfinnur cases, Gudjon was interviewed by the police. They wanted him to provide a character assessment of his former pupil. On 10 February 1976, Gudjon told officers that Saevar had said it was easy to kill people in Iceland because bodies could be disposed of and never found again. Saevar told Gudjon that he knew a lot about the Geirfinnur case, but he did not elaborate any further.

On 12 November 1976, Gudjon was arrested at his mother's flat. In his room was a briefcase containing a diary. Written inside were notes about the case taken from newspaper reports in the days after Geirfinnur's disappearance. On the first page of Gudjon's diary were the words 'Written at Laugavegur 28, on June 6th, with Saevar's new pen'.

The link between Gudjon and Saevar was stronger than the investigators had originally thought. Not only was Gudjon using Saevar's stationery to make notes about what the media knew about Geirfinnur's disappearance, but there also seemed to be an interesting power dynamic between the two men, one that suggested Gudjon might have been the dominant figure in the group that travelled to Keflavik.

In a statement made after Gudjon had been arrested, Saevar told the police that the reason why he hadn't immediately answered the door when the police had come to arrest him at his flat in Kopavogur was that he had needed to call Gudjon. With investigators at the door and a squadron of police cars outside the flat, Gudjon told Saevar to shut up about what he knew about Geirfinnur's disappearance.

The police had been convinced Saevar was the ringleader, the schemer who manipulated the others; but, from what Saevar was saying, it was Gudjon who was in control. The dynamic of Gudjon and Saevar's former relationship offered up a tempting comparison: was Saevar the pupil and Gudjon the master?

For Schütz, what was most important was that Gudjon had a credibility the others lacked. The investigators had already been excoriated in the press for relying upon the untrustworthy testimonies of Erla, Saevar and Kristjan, and for putting four innocent men in custody. Gudjon was more than ten years older, better educated, did not have an extensive criminal background, and, crucially, he did not seem to be attempting to mislead the police. According to the prison guards in Sidumuli, he conducted himself like a young professor.

Karl Schütz was Gudjon's confessor. For the first three weeks that Gudjon was held in custody, he denied all involvement. But Schütz began to direct more and more of his questioning towards him, the two of them conducting long conversations in German.

Gudjon told Schütz he hardly knew the people involved and that he had never met Kristjan. But in an identification line-up at the end of November 1976, Kristjan picked out Gudjon from a group of eight men. Kristjan told investigators that he was 'quite sure' Gudjon was the other man who had been at the dry dock that night. Two weeks later, Gudjon confessed to Schütz that three of them had beaten Geirfinnur to death.

When he was asked why he hadn't confessed earlier, he told the investigators that in 1974 he had become very depressed and he could not recall certain events clearly. But there were some things he could. He could remember a drive to Keflavik. He could remember that Saevar and Kristjan had been present. And he could remember that, when he drove them back to Reykjavik, Saevar had punched him on the shoulder and said, 'So, now you are an accomplice to murder!'

Schütz had found the final culprit.

Most families in Iceland have the same New Year's Eve routine today as they did in 1976. To begin with there is a bonfire, next a big dinner with extended family and friends, and then, just before fireworks light up the skies at midnight, everyone gathers in front of the television to watch a sketch comedy programme called *Aramotaskaupid*. First broadcast in 1966, the programme parodies all the most famous people and events from the year and consistently draws viewing figures of around 90 per cent of the population.

As the clock ticked down to midnight at the end of what had been an unusually tumultuous year for the country, an Icelandic comedian named Flosi Eiriksson sang a song about the cases. Dressed in a police uniform and singing with a German accent, there was only one person he could be impersonating.

Underpinned by a jaunty beat, fake-Schütz swaggers up to the camera while waggling a police baton and sings:

> *Now we have crazy criminals that try to trick the police*
> *We capture in no time*
> *Everyone who is suspected of this crime*
> *And we bring them here to this dank hole*
> *We bring them here to confess!*
> *We bring them here to confess!*

In the background, a group of morose prisoners stand in cells, rattling the bars of their cages with cups, while in front of them three women holding truncheons dance to the music and interject after each verse with the chorus 'Ja, ja, ja' (or, in English, 'Yes, yes, yes').

When Flosi does the German accent his face contorts and he hisses the verses out of the corner of his mouth:

To confess is good for the soul
The police are quick to pull out confessions
We get everyone to confess before New Year's
(Yes, yes, yes)
We get everyone to confess before New Year's
(Yes, yes, yes)
Here dwell the people that have fought with the system
Though if we search carefully we'll find that something is
   missing
Yes, we need a specialist in this black hole
(Yes, yes, yes)
We need a specialist in this black hole!

Although the sketch held little comic value for those involved in the case, it got to the heart of what Schütz, the 'specialist', had done. He had been in Iceland for six months and in that time he had found the final suspect and tied together the disparate confessions and witness statements. The 'crazy criminals' had been caught.

By then, Erla had been released. When she walked out of prison she could not believe how incomprehensibly big the world seemed. Aside from excursions to look for the bodies, she had barely been outside for nearly eight months. The horizon seemed so far away, and she found that she couldn't see anything from a distance. It was all blurry. At first she thought it was because her eyes needed to adjust to the brightness, but later she learned that her eyesight had been permanently impaired from having nothing to focus on inside her cell.

She had made and retracted multiple statements saying she had been a witness to the attack on Geirfinnur, but, by now, it was clear she had not been actively involved in it. It was almost exactly a year since she had first been arrested for the postal fraud.

Erla was blamed less for having been in the vicinity of Geir-finnur's murder than for having accused the Klubburinn Four. It was this latter detail that most disturbed people. While Saevar was an unknowable quantity who could be categorized in people's minds as a monster, there was something about what Erla had done that offended people's sensibilities more keenly, perhaps, even than murder.

Was it because she didn't share Saevar's otherness? Yes, she had spent a few years in the US as a child and, yes, in her late teens she had dressed like a hippie and taken drugs, but she was also the daughter of two Icelanders and the half-sister of one of the country's most-loved sports stars. The vitriol towards her was magnified for many reasons, not least because the names seemed to have originated with her. But it was also because it felt like an inside job. She had betrayed her family. She had betrayed the community. Her father, Bolli, whom she had always felt closest to, looked her in the eyes and called her 'Judas'.

On 2 February 1977, Karl Schütz called a press conference. Dressed in a brown tweed suit and flanked by translators, he presented his findings. Pinned to a board behind him was a picture of the Hafnarbudin café and a mock-up of the car that had been driven to the dry dock. In front of him was the 'Clayfinnur'.

Over the course of an hour, Schütz told the assembled journalists what had happened. Schütz spoke in spurts so that his translator could keep up. 'In a historic press meeting,' reported *Dagbladid* on 3 February, 'the solution to the mysterious criminal case was finally revealed.' It had all been a misunderstanding: a smuggling deal gone awry.

The premise of the rendezvous in Keflavik had been established at Klubburinn two days before. Saevar and Kristjan were there to steal wallets from inebriated clubgoers. Saevar introduced himself to Geirfinnur as Magnus Leopoldsson and the two men discussed the possibility of doing a deal on some homebrew. However, Saevar never intended to buy the alcohol, but to steal it once Geirfinnur had shown him where it was.

Two days later, an extraordinarily convoluted trip to Keflavik took place. A pair of investigators, Sigurbjorn Vidir Eggertsson and Ivar Hannesson, had painstakingly measured the journey as accurately as possible in a Volvo owned by the police.

Saevar, Erla, and Saevar's mother went to see the documentary about a volcanic eruption at Kjarvalsstadir in central Reykjavik, one of four consecutive showings that night, and then left at 8.40 p.m. in Erla's Land Rover. They drove to Saevar's mother's home to drop her off: she was diabetic and needed to get home in order to eat a hearty evening meal.

They drove to Erla's home, where they changed cars and got into a light blue Volkswagen they had rented from Geysir Car Rental the previous day. No rental contract was signed, said Schütz, but the employee was given 5,000 kronur, along with the promise that Erla would clean his apartment as part of the payment. A former employee of Geysir Car Rental had been interviewed on 21 December 1976. He could remember renting Erla and Saevar a car without a contract.

At 8.58 p.m. Erla and Saevar drove to Gudjon's house at Asvallagata, arriving at 9.08 p.m., but he was not at home. They found him with some friends in Lambholl at Starhagi, in another part of Reykjavik, at 9.15 p.m. Gudjon then drove Erla and Saevar to Vatnsstigur to meet Kristjan. Sigurdur Ottar Hreinsson, Kristjan's cousin, arrived in a van. He had come to help with the smuggling deal. They set off in convoy for Keflavik at 9.32 p.m. Sigurdur Ottar confirmed in a statement taken on 14 December 1976 that this had taken place. He repeated this claim under oath six months later.

Gudjon drove and Saevar sat next to him. Kristjan and Erla were in the back. Saevar said Geirfinnur seemed reluctant to come – they might have to get 'rough' with him if he didn't bring what he had promised. They arrived in Keflavik at 10.07 p.m., which was later than they had intended. Geirfinnur was not there. He had already come to the café and returned home.

Saevar went to a kiosk to phone Geirfinnur, but then decided against the idea. There were people spilling out of a nearby cinema and he feared he would be recognized, and so, instead, Kristjan made the call from the Hafnarbudin café. Geirfinnur's son picked up the phone and heard a voice he didn't recognize. He passed it to his father – 'I was already there. OK I'll come back' – and then Geirfinnur headed out into the evening, ignoring the requests from his son that he come along.

They picked up Geirfinnur at the café and drove to the dry dock. It was dark, raining, and there was only one source of light: a single spotlight hanging above the dry dock. This was one of the reasons why the various statements kept changing so much – it was difficult to see clearly. Saevar asked Geirfinnur to give them the homebrew, but Geirfinnur had misunderstood: he thought it was he who was buying alcohol from them. Saevar took out 70,000 kronur to induce Geirfinnur to hand over the goods.

At that point Geirfinnur tried to leave but, before he could escape, Gudjon grabbed him. A fight broke out and Geirfinnur was beaten to the ground. 'Kristjan listened for a heartbeat while Saevar searched for a pulse,' reported *Morgunbladid*, 'and their verdict was unanimous: Geirfinnur was dead.'

There was no alcohol to transport and so Sigurdur Ottar drove back to Reykjavik in his van. Saevar, Kristjan and Gudjon transferred Geirfinnur's body into the back of the blue Volkswagen – by the left seat so that he leaned against the window – and then wrapped his head in a coat. They drove back to central Reykjavik and stored the body at Kristjan's grandmother's house at Grettis-gata 82. They put it on a wooden bench and wrapped it in faux leather. Meanwhile, Erla hid in a storage room in Keflavik and hitchhiked home the following morning.

Two nights later, Erla, Kristjan and Saevar drove the body to the red hills at Raudholar. En route, they bought a five-litre petrol can. They dug a shallow grave and put Geirfinnur's body in it. The corpse was set on fire.

Although a cadaver had not been found, Schütz said, it was clear from the testimonies that he was buried at Raudholar. He declared that the investigators had excavated a large part of Raudholar but ground frost had prevented them from conducting a more thorough search. 95 per cent of the evidence, said Schütz, was confessions. He concluded by saying, 'As we criminal investigators like to say, this case is beyond reasonable doubt.' Finally he praised the Icelandic police force: 'I have never met such hard-working police officers – nor ones who are paid so little!'

It had been one of the most extensive criminal investigations ever undertaken in Iceland and one of its most expensive. The

Secretary of State wouldn't confirm the cost, apart from to say that millions and millions of kronur had been spent. Newspapers the next day 'invited' readers to compare two pictures on its front cover: a picture of Kristjan's face and the clay head.

Criminal cases in Iceland did not use a jury, so there was no possibility of prejudicing jurors before the trial went to court. But it is testament to the power wielded by Schütz during his six-month stay in Iceland that long before the suspects had been prosecuted he was declaring them guilty to the media. He returned to Germany three days later.

On 16 March 1977 the charges against the defendants in the Geirfinnur case were filed. The charges in the Gudmundur case had already been made on 8 December 1976. Three judges – Gunnlaugur Briem, Armann Kristinsson and Haraldur Henrysson – took over custody of the case, and criminal court proceedings began on Monday, 3 October 1977, at 9.30 a.m. Kristjan strode into the drab courtroom wearing aviator glasses and a pilot's shirt, his white polo neck slung over his shoulder.

Witness statements had already been taken in court before proceedings began. A scraggly-haired, bespectacled man called Gunnar Jonsson had been flown over from his home in Torremolinos, a resort town in the Costa del Sol, to testify that he had been at Hamarsbraut 11 and seen a fight in which someone fell on the table. He said this man could well have been Gudmundur.

Elinborg Rafnsdottir and Sigridur Magnusdottir, the two women who were driving out of Hafnarfjordur when they saw Gudmundur, had also been summoned to give evidence. In a police line-up, they identified Kristjan as the man who stumbled drunkenly with Gudmundur in the road. Both of them said they couldn't be confident, but he looked like the man they had seen. It meant Kristjan met Gudmundur near the club in Hafnarfjordur and took him back to Hamarsbraut 11. He had been the man in the yellow shirt.

Saevar, Kristjan and Gudjon were charged with killing Geirfinnur. Multiple witnesses had been called to confirm different parts of the story – a man who had seen Saevar at the cinema saying he was going to Keflavik, the former testimony of Sigurdur Ottar (the van driver), and the people who drove Erla home the next morning.

Proceedings lasted twenty-nine hours in total and concluded at 8.30 p.m. on Friday, 7 October. On 19 December 1977, the sentences were pronounced. All six were found guilty. Saevar and Kristjan were sentenced to life for killing Gudmundur and Geirfinnur; Tryggvi was sentenced to sixteen years for killing Gudmundur; Gudjon was sentenced to twelve years for killing Geirfinnur; Erla was sentenced to three years for perjuring the Klubburinn Four; and Albert was sentenced to fifteen months for obstruction of justice. There were a range of other charges, among them arson and theft, and perjury for Saevar and Kristjan, too.

Tryggvi, dressed in a pinstripe suit and a floral shirt unbuttoned to his stomach, beamed at the reporters as he was led away in handcuffs by investigators.

In West Germany, the subheading of Frankfurt newspaper *Abendpost-Nachtausgabe* read: 'German Spy Hunter Saves the Icelandic Government'. Schütz had solved the criminal cases that had threatened to bring the country to its knees. Iceland's Ministry of Justice declared that the nation's nightmare was over.

In many ways, it had only just begun.

INTERMISSION

The entire prison population of Iceland fluctuates around the 150 mark. Every one of its inmates could fit onto two double-decker buses. Iceland's prison system is so tiny that convicts routinely live at home until a cell becomes available. Some of them wait for half a decade.

Saevar, Kristjan and Tryggvi were imprisoned at Litla-Hraun, Iceland's highest-security prison, located fifty kilometres southeast of Reykjavik. It is a few kilometres south of Selfoss, where Saevar and Erla had defrauded a post office in 1974.

Originally built as a regional hospital in 1926, Litla-Hraun's function was changed in 1929, infuriating those from the neighbouring fishing villages who had volunteered to help in its construction because they thought their work would benefit invalids rather than inmates.

The chain-link fence that surrounded the prison was not difficult to climb, but the prospect of anyone fleeing was slim. There was nowhere to run to. Whenever inmates did scale the fence, they were caught within a day or two. Prisoners spent their days working on the grounds and making number plates for cars.

Although cells in Litla-Hraun were reserved for Iceland's worst criminals, there was still plenty of scope for recreation. The prison had a pool table, a TV room, and a yard where inmates could play football. Musicians frequently visited to put on shows, and one of them, named Tryggvi Hubner, lent Saevar his guitar. Saevar and fellow inmate Runar Thor Petursson formed a band while incarcerated: its name was Fjotrum, meaning 'Shackles'. They were given leave to record an album, *Iron Bar Rock*, at a recording studio named Glora.

Despite this leniency, Saevar was still treated as Litla-Hraun's most dangerous inmate. When a theatre company visited the prison to put on a play, Saevar was brought in by three guards and seated separately from the rest of the prisoners. The guards kept watch on him throughout the performance to ensure he did not incite trouble.

Gudjon was treated more favourably. Instead of being sent to Litla-Hraun, he served his sentence nearly 200 kilometres north of Reykjavik at Kviabryggja prison. Convicts at Kviabryggja were not expected to reoffend. Established in 1954 as a facility for those who had not paid their child support, there were no bars on the windows, and the fence surrounding the prison was low enough that inmates could vault over it with a running jump. Prisoners were not locked in overnight.

Located on a large patch of farmland, the prison warden dressed and spoke like a farmer. He believed in the importance of the prisoners doing a full day of work on the land. Gudjon says he enjoyed his time there. He and the other dozen inmates worked all day, processing fish for export or carrying out manual work around the farm, and in the evenings he could read his books.

After his release, Gudjon moved to Copenhagen to study the-
ology. When he returned to Iceland he decided to become a priest.
He visited all eighty homes in the area to meet his parishioners
and drank three cups of coffee at each one. He got the job. Residents of Snaefellsnes in the country's northwest came to his
pillar-box-red church to receive the Eucharist.

There was no women's prison in which Erla could serve her
sentence, and so she was sent to Akureyri, Iceland's second-largest
city, in the north. Erla made her own way there and was met at the
airport by the police. She was taken to a tiny prison that adjoined
the police station. It had enough capacity for nine inmates. Her
cell faced on to the road and sometimes Akureyri locals shouted
at her from the street outside.

Erla was released on 9 August 1981. All she could think about
was getting on the plane. Her daughter was on the other side.
She had prepared for days to have the right things to say and the
right present to bring. When the plane landed at Keflavik, Erla
ran to the terminal to find five-year-old Julia waiting there with
a bouquet of flowers.

Her life in Iceland remained difficult. Either she provoked
curiosity or she was despised. She struggled to find work. Former
friends no longer spoke to her. One day in the street a smartly
dressed woman walked up to her and spat in her face, then
continued walking without saying a word. Erla went to live in
Hawaii.

After their release, Kristjan, Tryggvi and Albert all got on with
their lives. Albert worked in construction, Tryggvi found a job
in a ship factory, and Kristjan drifted in and out of employment,
eventually returning to prison for five years after he physically

assaulted his wife. None of the suspects spoke publicly about the cases. Except for one.

In newspaper articles written after his release, Saevar agitated for the reopening of the cases. Icelandic society, he claimed, had been misled. In 1983, the Klubburinn Four had been awarded substantial state-funded settlements of around 200,000 kronur each, and Saevar demanded similar compensation. Few people paid attention. It is not so unusual for guilty people to proclaim their innocence. When he complained about rough policing methods, he was told that things had moved on since the 1970s. If anyone was deserving of tough treatment, then it was the person responsible for two deaths.

For those whose lives had been destroyed, Saevar's lofty pronouncements about his innocence were infuriating. While the others who had been convicted settled quietly into the community, or moved away to start new lives, Saevar would not let the cases go. He kept on pulling off the plaster and exposing the wound to the air.

It had been the same when Saevar was in court. Before the final sentence was handed down, Saevar had taken to the stand to defend himself. It was a highly unusual thing to do. The verdict had already been passed and there was nothing to be gained from standing before the judges. It felt like an imposition, somehow, upon those who had suffered; a shameless gesture from someone who had lost the right to exercise his will so brazenly.

Dressed in a black velvet suit, a crisp white shirt and white boots, Saevar stood at the lectern. Seven bespectacled judges stared at him. Photographers from all the major newspapers lined the sides of the court.

Saevar paused for a moment to compose himself. He unfolded a crumpled piece of paper from his jacket pocket. Then he explained why he thought the court had reached the wrong conclusion. He ended with a quotation from Socrates. 'The hour of departure has arrived, and we go our separate ways, I to die and you to live. Which of these two is better only God knows.' He returned to his seat.

The camera bulbs cracked and white lights flickered around the perimeter of the courtroom.

6

DROWN THE RAT

The prospect of drowning within sight of shore has long troubled the popular imagination in Iceland. As fishing grew in importance towards the end of the nineteenth century and into the twentieth, deaths at sea became more common, in some years constituting as much as two-thirds of total accidental deaths. For those on land the only sign that disaster had struck would be the bodies that came in with the tides.

Stories testifying to the importance of learning to swim were widely shared. In the 1930s, a boat transporting four farmers and a rowdy cow capsized in a fjord and the only survivor was the farmer who had been taught to paddle to safety. Swimming education was made mandatory in 1940 and, soon after, pools began to appear all over Iceland, their saunas and hot tubs heated by siphoning the piping-hot water from the country's geothermal core. In warm countries the pool is where you cool down, but in Iceland it is where you warm up. Their popularity is immense.

The soul of Reykjavik is its pools. There are two close to the downtown area, and a handful more dotted around the outskirts of the city: the oldest is Sundhollin, a beautiful pre-war indoor swimming pool with the tiling from the original changing rooms still intact; the hippest is Vesturbaejarlaug, located in the west side of the city; but the best is Laugardalslaug, one of Iceland's biggest, which has two large outdoor pools, a waterslide, and a row of seven hot tubs.

In a country without village greens, town squares or pubs, the pool is where people go to be with people. A few enthusiasts don swimming caps and do lengths, but for the majority of Icelanders it is a place to meet up with friends after work, to argue with strangers about politics, or to soak in the warm water and stare into space.

There is much to enjoy about being in a large bath with people you don't know. Undressed and divested of anything that might gesture towards status, everyone is on the same level. When politicians want to canvass votes or to listen to the concerns of their constituents, they do the rounds of the pools. To be sat eyeball-to-eyeball with a stranger in their swimwear sounds awkward, but the opposite is true: there is not a trace of self-consciousness. Being with people in this way, up close, is humanizing.

By spring 2017 the filming of the documentary was finished and I had come to live in Iceland to continue my research, living for some time in a guest house downtown before moving in with a friend on the west side of Reykjavik.

When I enter Laugardalslaug one bright Saturday evening in April, it is packed. There are dozens of people pressed together into each tub. Although privacy is respected, the pools also compel interaction. Walking down the steps into the water as bathers shuffle aside to create space feels like entering someone's living room.

In one, a tattooed teenager tells his friends that he has heard that Icelandic rapper Emmsje Gauti is playing a secret set that night at Hurra, a popular bar downtown. In another, a large group of old men talk animatedly about whether there should be a levy on tourists coming into the country. The boisterous, good-natured group grows in number as they call across to people they recognize to bring them into the debate. I answer someone's question about what brings me to the city and suddenly the whole tub is discussing the disappearance of Geirfinnur.

Reykjavik is a buzzing, artistic, metropolitan city, but in some ways it is still the same gossipy fishing village it was in the 1970s. There is a phrase here that 'When three people know, everybody knows'. Sometimes, when I phone people to ask for interviews, they are already aware that I'm in town. Strangers send me emails with suggestions about the cases. I get texts from Saevar's sister: 'Have you spoken to Haukur Gudmundsson? He knows that Saevar was not in Keflavik'; and 'You guys should be careful. I wouldn't like anything happening to you'; and 'Saevar told me everything'.

The more time I spend researching the cases, the more I begin to feel what the investigators might have felt before Schütz came along: like I am chasing my tail. At night in my room I read about the disappearances until my head spins. In news articles from before the investigation began, I see the same names of politicians and police officers and become suddenly convinced that I can trace some greater design, some overarching narrative that ties everything together, before realizing, as I trawl through my jumbled notes the next morning, that I am manufacturing conspiracies from coincidences.

If the story had stopped with the convictions, then there would
be little reason to investigate the cases further. That the disappearances of Gudmundur and Geirfinnur are still being debated
in newspapers, on chat shows, in parliament, and, of course, in
Iceland's swimming pools, is a result of the discoveries made in
the years that followed.

At the swimming pool steam rises from the surface as the
conversations carry between the tubs and I think about something one of Saevar's lawyers once said: 'Find where the rumours
start – that's where it all begins.' I sink my head into the water
and away from the smoke.

'I was twenty-eight years old, it was January '96, and I get a phone
call from a guy who presents himself as Saevar Ciesielski,' says
Sigursteinn Masson. 'And, of course, everyone in this country
knew that name. Just the name would give you a bad feeling.'
The first thing Sigursteinn noticed upon meeting Saevar was how
small he was for a murderer, and how thin.

I go to meet Sigursteinn at his place of work in the old harbour area in Reykjavik. It is stormy and the sails of the whaling
boats moored to the jetty slacken then tauten in the wind. White
Iceland gulls veer in diagonals overhead. In the middle of a row
of darkened huts advertising boat trips to see puffins and the
Northern Lights is one shack not yet closed for the night. Next to
the door is a picture of a cartoon whale, a speech bubble coming
out its mouth saying: 'Meet us, don't eat us!'

Formerly a television journalist with Channel 2, the first pri-
vately owned television station in Iceland, Sigursteinn is now one of
the country's leading anti-whaling campaigners. He is tanned and

lean, and he welcomes me into his office with a firm handshake. Inside it is dark except for a small seating area towards the back and a desk lamp that illuminates papers and books spread out on a table. The suck of the wind whistles against the sides of the hut.

Sigursteinn speaks about the cases with a fervour that, despite its intensity, remains under his control. Although he often becomes visibly emotional, jabbing the table with his finger to emphasize his point, he never relinquishes his command of the granular details. On one occasion, the second time we meet, he says something about coming after anyone, in either a journalistic or legal sense, who misrepresents the truth of what happened, and I am left in no doubt that, although we are talking hypothetically, inaccuracies on my part will not go unnoticed.

His work has been devoted towards difficult causes: mental health equality, disability rights, opposing the powerful whaling industry in Iceland. And when Saevar approached him in 1996, long before Sigursteinn's career as a campaigner had begun, he was, in many ways, the kind of journalist the country had been waiting for since two men disappeared in mysterious circumstances in 1974.

When Sigursteinn was a boy, his mother would point out the red hills of Raudholar and tell him Geirfinnur's body was hidden there. The story of Gudmundur and Geirfinnur was so deeply embedded into the collective consciousness that it had become like the myths of trolls and hidden folk that cling to the Icelandic hills. For someone who had been just a child during the investigation, the idea of discovering anything new was absurd.

Although Sigursteinn was initially reticent to examine the cases, Saevar persisted, arriving at Sigursteinn's doorstep with hundreds of pages of documents from the Supreme Court verdict. Due to the sheer length of their sentences, the cases had been automatically appealed to the Supreme Court in 1980. Most of the convictions were shortened. The Supreme Court ruled that there had been no intent to kill either Geirfinnur or Gudmundur. Both instances had involved brutal attacks resulting in a fatality but neither could be classified as murder. Saevar's sentence was reduced from life to seventeen years. It was still the longest handed down in Icelandic legal history.

Sigursteinn's interest was piqued after he began to read through the papers Saevar brought to him. It seemed there was a disparity between the information in the reports kept by the police during the investigation and the narrative put forward in the Supreme Court. A lot of details were absent from the latter. Sigursteinn agreed to help and started to work on a documentary.

In the summer of 1996, after more than six months of research with the documentary's co-writer Kristjan Guy Burgess, Sigursteinn learned there was a plan to demolish Sidumuli prison, the facility at which those accused in the Gudmundur and Geirfinnur cases had spent the majority of their custody between arrest and sentencing.

More in hope than expectation, Sigursteinn contacted the Ministry of Justice to ask whether they could film some of the dramatization sequences for the documentary in Sidumuli. To his surprise, permission was granted. It was one week since the prison had closed, and as they walked through the entrance, the last prisoner was being escorted out. Sigursteinn, director Einar Magnusson and a carefully selected cast of lookalikes, many of whom were working for free, began their work. Einar Magnusson had sold his car to help fund the project.

Their first move was to lock up the actors. The cells were tiny and bare, with just a bed, a table and a wooden chair bolted to the floor. The absence of windows made it difficult to tell whether it was day or night. 'These young actors were so shocked,' says Einar Magnusson. 'I always feel really bad when I remember us doing this.' They were left there for three hours. Some cried and knocked on the doors from within their cells. Come the end, they were begging to be let out.

On the third day of filming, Saevar came to assist the film crew with the reconstruction. Freshly shaven, his brown hair down to his shoulders, it was obviously not easy for him to be back in Sidumuli. It was just as he remembered right down to the guard who accompanied the team as they walked around the prison – and inside his old cell Saevar could still find the marks on the wall that he had once stared at as an inmate. He pointed these out to the long-haired actor playing a twenty-year-old version of himself.

Sidumuli was a place that loomed large in the minds of those who served time there. Former internees recall how, starved of visual stimulation, their hearing became hyper-attuned to the sounds emerging from adjacent cells: the rhythmic inhalation and exhalation of an inmate doing press-ups; the distant murmur of guards conversing in the common room; the guttural scrape of chains dragged along the floor by a prisoner who had mis-behaved. Throughout 1976, as the pressure to find a solution intensified, the prison's narrow, green corridors incubated a par-ticularly febrile atmosphere.

Hlynur Thor Magnusson, a mild-mannered prison guard who worked in Sidumuli and who now lives in a small retirement home in the picturesque Westfjords region, describes how, during the investigation, Sidumuli was like another world. 'It was very tense, like at the beginning of a soccer game.' Gudsteinn Thengilsson, the prison physician, takes this further, recalling how, when Saevar and Erla were in custody, the feeling sweeping through it was akin to a wave of terror.

In the months leading up to their filming at Sidumuli, Sigursteinn and his colleagues had been learning all about how the suspects had been treated while in custody. This was why they were surprised when the Ministry of Justice allowed them to film on site. 'I don't think the authorities realized what information we had acquired during our months of research,' says Sigursteinn. 'Nor what sort of re-enactment we were planning to film.'

The day after Saevar's visit to Sidumuli, Sigursteinn and Einar Magnusson started to film the abuse scenes. In newspaper articles written after his release, Saevar had maintained he had been tortured, although this was difficult to prove as there were not many people who would corroborate his claim. According to Saevar, one of the chosen methods of punishment was called 'the stretching'. They would handcuff his hands to the chair and his feet to the bed, and then stretch him out across the floor.

As the actor playing Saevar screamed and writhed on the ground, the prison guard came over and said, 'No, no, that is not how we did it!' and then proceeded to demonstrate to the astonished crew the actual method that had been used; a method which was, somehow, even more brutal.

During a break between scenes, Sigursteinn and the prison

guard visited the room in Sidumuli that separated the prison guard facility and the cells. Lined along a high shelf in the corner, Sigursteinn noticed some old books. At that moment the director Einar Magnusson entered and calmly inferred from Sigursteinn's meaningful eye contact that the prison guard should be distracted. Proclaiming that there was something in one of the cells that he needed help with, Einar Magnusson drew the guard away, giving Sigursteinn the chance to pull a chair to the shelf and rifle through the books. On the spine of each volume was written a different year. They were the prison logs. Inside each book was a record of the day-to-day goings-on in Sidumuli prison. Judging by their appearance, some hadn't been opened for decades.

Almost immediately Sigursteinn could see that the logs corroborated many of Saevar's claims. There were so many details that had been impossible to confirm. The prison logs changed this. 'They were the breakthrough,' says Einar Magnusson. 'Everything we had been hearing about from Saevar came true. It was like someone who has been flirting with Christianity suddenly seeing Jesus Christ walking on water.'

From reading the logs, what was immediately apparent was the contempt in which Saevar was held. One entry, written on 26 April 1976, reports that Saevar could be heard crying loudly in his cell. Someone will return soon, writes the chief prison guard Gunnar Gudmundsson, to 'try the bastard once again'. During July 1976, Jon B. Sveinsson, a fellow prison guard, notes that Saevar refused to take some medicine because of his heart condition: 'We have been told by a doctor that there is nothing wrong with his heart [. . .] But it is my opinion, and that of others as well, that there is no heart in Saevar Marino Ciesielski.'

Elsewhere, Saevar is described as a 'scoundrel', and as someone to be 'torn down'.

Taken in isolation, a negative reference to Saevar might be dismissed as a misjudged barb; understandable, if not excusable, in the context of the horrific crimes he had confessed to. But taken together, they contribute to the sense of a warped atmosphere in Sidumuli. 'They treated me worse than an animal,' Saevar once said about his time in custody. It was as though Saevar was being dehumanized to justify the measures used against him.

Saevar seemed to provoke a particularly strong reaction in his inquisitors. He was mouthy, physically small, and regarded as the ringleader of the group. Hlynur Thor Magnusson recalls how his colleagues 'despised Saevar absolutely', becoming increasingly infuriated with his contradictory and imprecise statements. Compared to Sidumuli's usual inmates, whose misdemeanours were made comprehensible by the clear causality of their motivation – substance abuse, a flash of anger, money – the unique dislike Saevar inspired was bound up with his apparent detachment from the events, his crimes made all the more chilling because they seemed unmoored from any discernible motive. They felt like he was playing a game with them.

Hlynur remembers the transformation among his colleagues, men and women whom he had worked with for years and whom he knew to be kind people. Gunnar Gudmundsson, the chief prison warden, had always seemed a sweet, elderly man but, during the period of the investigation, he became a different person.

The first room on the right when you entered Sidumuli was the interrogation room. It was dark except for a bright light that hung above the table and two chairs in the centre of the room. Kjartan

Kjartansson, another Sidumuli guard, remembers standing in the corridor outside the interrogation room. Suddenly Gunnar Gudmundsson strode past Kjartan and into the room. He closed the door behind him. A lot of noise came from within. Kjartan looked at the other guards alongside him. Why was no one opening the door to see what was happening? He opened it. Gunnar and Saevar were inside. Gunnar seemed relaxed. Saevar, though, was visibly terrified. Gunnar told Kjartan to close the cell door immediately. Saevar had been shouting out, 'Calm down, Gunnar, calm down!'

Sleep was a battleground, a war waged upon Saevar in the early hours of the morning as he attempted to find some rest. Notes kept by Saevar during custody describe a two-month period in which the lights were kept on in his cell every night, a claim later confirmed by another prison guard – himself a former electrician – who had tinkered with the wiring to ensure the light switch no longer functioned. When Saevar tried to put a knitted hat over the bulb, he was prevented from doing so.

Next door to his cell was the common room, and sometimes, at night, his hearing sensitive from weeks in isolation, the guards would bang rocks against the walls to keep him awake. One prison guard, speaking in 1979, claimed one of her colleagues had insisted Saevar couldn't go to the toilet unless he was naked, and that another guard had 'worked Saevar over' by turning him upside down and shaking him.

It was common knowledge among the guards that Saevar was afraid of water. In notes Saevar wrote in 1977, he recalls how, one night in the summer of 1976, two guards came to his cell and announced that, if he did not accompany them, he would be removed with force. Saevar was taken to the small room in

Sidumuli where the prisoners washed. Attached to one of the walls was a steel basin.

When Saevar realized what was about to happen, he fought to free himself, but the guards grabbed him by his shirt collar and put a rag in the bottom of the sink to block the drain as it filled up with water. They lifted Saevar's legs and pushed his head down into the basin, keeping him submerged to the point of suffocation before pulling him back up. Where had he taken the boy Gudmundur? Who else had gone to Keflavik to see Geirfinnur?

Skuli Steinsson and Gunnar Marinosson, two of the prison guards on duty that night, both said they knew nothing about the incident. When Skuli was questioned about it in court in March 1977, he described Saevar's account as absurd. He said there was one instance where Saevar had refused to take a shower and so Skuli had forcibly taken him to the washroom. But then Saevar had closed the door, taken a shower, and that had been the end of the matter.

However, Hlynur Thor Magnusson, although not himself on duty that night, later said that he had heard his colleagues talk about how they had employed this tactic to break Saevar. It was for his benefit, and the nation's, too. 'Those guards who were doing it,' says Hlynur, 'they enjoyed it. They were proud of it. They laughed about drowning the rat.'

The prison logs confirmed that each of the guards named by Saevar were working on the night in question. It was the only time that month they did.

The brutal treatment tallied with what Jon Bjarman, the prison priest, had witnessed when he was present in the interrogation room on the night of 4 May 1976, the day after Erla had been

apprehended for a second time. In a series of letters written to the
Ministry of Justice in the late seventies, Jon Bjarman describes how
Saevar and Erla's arrest had precipitated an unnatural situation in
the prison, and that suspects had been kept in a state of constant
fear. When Saevar refused to behave in the way the investigators
wanted, he was, Jon Bjarman writes, physically assaulted:

> Eggert [N. Bjarnason] grabbed his hair, jerked him back
> and forth so that he nearly fell to the floor, and intimidated
> him. Later, when Saevar protested something, Gunnar, the
> chief prison guard, walked over to him and slapped him.
> The interview ended in chaos when Erla got hysterical and
> started to scream; then they called two prison guards, who
> dragged Saevar to his cell.

Most of the prison guards and investigators in the room initially
denied knowledge of the incident. Years later, they admitted that
it had taken place. It was justified on the grounds that Saevar's
behaviour had been 'reprehensible'. The incident caused such a
commotion that, the following day, Magnus Leopoldsson asked
the guards whether drunk people had gained access to the corridors of Sidumuli. At night, through the walls of his cell, he had
heard screaming.

These were all incidents that Saevar raised before the Supreme
Court trial in 1980. Among the twenty-six books containing case
notes for the court was one filled with Saevar's allegations of abuse.
Although the judges acknowledged that Saevar was 'unlawfully
mistreated', they did not accept it could have had an effect on the
verdict, in part because the key confessions had been made before

these incidents took place, and also because of the imprecision of the testimonies.

The guards, the Supreme Court judges contended, had overstepped their bounds, but it made little difference to what had been confessed to. They were intent on cracking the cases that had disturbed the nation.

Thordis Hauksdottir first met the man who would become the father of her children after a night out on 17 June 1988.

The dance was over and it was raining. As Thordis prepared to brave the elements, a small, dark-haired man appeared by her side. He offered to give her something to protect her from the rain and a ride home. She accepted, and in the days that followed he would call her to see if she wanted to spend time with him. In the beginning she wasn't interested, but he persevered, finding out what time she finished work and arriving after her shifts were over so they could chat and get to know one another better. Later that summer, they started to date.

Their relationship developed quickly. Although only twenty-four years old, she had always got along better with older people, and her new boyfriend seemed an old soul, marked by life in a way incomparable to other young men she had met. They had a natural affinity for one another and, as they grew closer, she came to love idiosyncrasies of his, like keeping notebooks filled with his favourite thoughts and phrases. Sometimes he would rearrange all the furniture in her apartment to change the ambience.

Thordis remembers the first time she heard her boyfriend's surname. It was a few weeks into their relationship, and they were sitting in a restaurant when a woman pointed at him and shouted,

'That's Saevar Ciesielski! That's Saevar Ciesielski!', as if she were drawing people's attention to a wild animal. Thordis knew he was called Saevar, but he had kept his surname a secret.

At the restaurant that evening, Saevar explained to her that he was one of the people who had been convicted for killing Gudmundur and Geirfinnur. Thordis was a decade younger than Saevar and had been a child when the cases were in the news: she hadn't realized that the man she had started to date was Iceland's most notorious criminal.

Impromptu heckling in Reykjavik eateries was unpleasant, but more difficult to navigate was her mother's insistence that she think carefully before entering into a serious relationship with Sacvar. Life, without question, would be harder. Although Thordis cared about what her mother had to say, this was a piece of advice she chose to ignore; she was prepared to deal with the consequences of being in a relationship with him.

In the years after his release in 1984, Saevar was viewed as nothing less than evil incarnate. Whenever he applied for a job he would be rejected, usually with no explanation, although some of his potential employers told him it was because he would be bad for business. No one wanted their pipes fixed by a convicted killer. Stable accommodation was as much of a challenge as stable employment, and even after Thordis and Saevar had their first son together, Hafthor, in 1989, they were evicted from their home.

These were the obvious drawbacks of being a pariah in a small community. Worse was the insidious feeling of being constantly on show. It was, of course, hardly surprising that many people felt uncomfortable seeing Saevar walk freely through the streets of Reykjavik. Sometimes Saevar would have fun with this, and loudly announce his arrival when he walked into cafés, pre-empting any whispers of 'It's Saevar Ciesielski!' that could reduce a full room to a hush.

At night, Thordis would be awoken by Saevar twitching and murmuring in his sleep as he dreamed of the nights he had spent in Sidumuli. She would calm him down, soothing him by telling him that he was not in prison anymore. Sometimes he would jerk from his reverie, his face shiny, his eyes wild, and be momentarily convinced he was back in his windowless cell, where the unblinking bulb made the night indistinguishable from the day, and the walls reverberated with each bang of the rock.

In 1993, Saevar and Thordis decided to leave Iceland with their two young boys, four-year-old Hafthor and two-year-old Sigurthor. Life there had become exhausting. Saevar had started to drink, too. Prior to his arrest in 1975 he did not touch alcohol, but during his time in prison he developed a taste for the way a few glugs from the bottle could draw his thoughts from the cases for an evening.

Following his release he repeatedly went sober, but these spells rarely lasted more than a year or two. Sometimes he stole away to low-lit bars in downtown Reykjavik without indicating when he would return. Every such occasion felt to Thordis like a betrayal. She asked him how he could do this to her when she was standing by him. He replied that he needed to meet people to show them he was not the person they thought he was, but for Thordis this justification, although sincere, was a fig leaf with which to cover his growing struggle with alcoholism.

Their new destination was Boulder, Colorado. It was a chance to start afresh, to raise their boys and be a normal family. They felt able to be themselves. The people were friendly, the landscape was big and open, and they took long walks through the Rocky Mountains. The children learned English and played in the quiet streets. There was not much of a bar scene, so any temptation Saevar might have had to drink was diminished and, anyway, the cases felt distant now they had left Iceland. Saevar found employment as a floor layer and Thordis took him from job to job in a battered white Cadillac they had bought on the cheap.

Late at night the ring of the telephone would interrupt their new sanctuary. A reporter from a newspaper in Iceland had succeeded in tracking them down, and the time difference between the two countries meant calls often came in the small hours of the morning. Saevar would retreat into the furthest part of the house, and as he delved back into the recesses of his memory, he would drink.

After a year, their visas expired and the family returned to Iceland. For Thordis, life in Colorado had provided a glimpse of what their lives would be like away from their warped existence in Iceland. She wanted to stay. But for Saevar, that same experience had made him dwell upon what life *should* be like in Iceland, and had fortified his resolve to prove his innocence. His determination to clear his name was now absolute. Thordis knew that if he plunged back into the cases it would lead to the end of their relationship.

Saevar began to work towards making an official request for a retrial. He attended rehab to curb his drinking, and devoted his time to gathering evidence to present to the Supreme Court. Thordis helped him with his petition, smoothing out the spelling mistakes caused by his dyslexia until the sentences flowed. Hafthor, their son, recalls his parents working together at the kitchen table, documents spread out in front of them. He doesn't remember a specific moment when his parents told him about the cases, but he always knew that something 'really dark' had happened to his father. It was like he had been born into it.

On 23 November 1994 Saevar went to the Ministry of Justice and requested he be pronounced innocent of any involvement in the Gudmundur and Geirfinnur cases. He produced a 120-page file criticizing the investigation that had led to his conviction. In 1995, his bid was rejected. 'I just couldn't believe it,' says Thordis. 'I think we both had a nervous breakdown. We had put so much hope on it – to have a real future, to be normal people like everybody else.'

She walked over the street to the Prime Minister's house in the centre of Reykjavik. It was the middle of the night. She banged on the door and was let in. She spoke with David Oddsson, the Prime Minister, until the early hours of the morning about the possibility of the state paying for a lawyer to represent Saevar for another bid.

But Thordis's premonition about the end of her relationship with Saevar proved correct. The day following the rejection, Saevar started to drink. She did not think he would be able to save himself from his battle with the system, and she did not want the cases to take her and the children down with him.

Thordis took the boys and went to live with her parents. At first, Saevar did not seem to realize she was serious. He told her that they had been gone long enough and it was time for them to come back. He had always said that he would not marry Thordis until his name had been cleared, but now they had separated before that could happen. Although they remained on good terms, and Thordis continued to support his fight, she never went back to him.

When Saevar arrived on Sigursteinn's door in 1996 with thousands of pages of court documents, he was a man whose life revolved around the cases. 'If I live for anything,' he said in an interview with Sigursteinn, 'it is for these cases to be reconsidered.'

On 30 January 1996, the same month Saevar approached journalist Sigursteinn Masson, Ragnar Adalsteinsson was appointed to help Saevar in his second bid for a retrial. Gruff-voiced, with rimless rectangular glasses and a gentle manner, Ragnar was one of the country's best-respected human rights lawyers. Ragnar, Saevar and the documentary team worked together to gather more information about the cases.

The more Ragnar read, the more he found that the judgements put forward for both the Gudmundur and the Geirfinnur cases were riddled with contradictions and inconsistencies.

Take the two young women who had driven past Gudmundur and the man in a yellow shirt.

The narrative presented to the court was that Kristjan, supposedly the figure in the yellow shirt, had led Gudmundur back to Hamarsbraut 11. But when Ragnar read through the statements made by Elinborg Rafnsdottir and Sigridur Magnusdottir, he saw they had actually said the reverse: Gudmundur and the man in the yellow shirt had been walking in the opposite direction from Hamarsbraut 11.

Sigursteinn and Kristjan Guy Burgess tracked down the two women and filmed an interview with them. Both blonde, brightly dressed, and wearing nervous expressions as if they were about to be told off, they explained that part of the reason why they had picked out Kristjan from a line-up was because they had seen pictures of him in the newspapers. Their memories of a night from so long before were hazy, and his was the only face they recognized.

The man in the yellow shirt had been slight, and was noticeably smaller than Gudmundur. Yet Kristjan was a large man, a good few inches taller than Gudmundur, and heavy-set. When Elinborg and Sigridur told police that Kristjan was much bigger than the man they'd seen accompanying Gudmundur, they were told Kristjan had ballooned in weight because of the regular meals he was receiving in prison.

Irrespective of this detail, their statements were already highly questionable. Neither agreed about who was at the wheel, about what they had seen, or about where they had been driving. The statement taken from Sveinn Vilhjalmsson, in which Gudmundur drunkenly slipped in the road, seemed to discredit the notion that the man in the yellow shirt had even stayed in the company of Gudmundur after Elinborg and Sigridur had driven off.

Ragnar received a phone call from Kristrun Jonina Steindorsdottir and Thordur Orn Marteinsson, the couple that ran Althyduhusid, the nightclub Gudmundur had visited on the night he disappeared. By coincidence, they lived at Sudurgata 40 in Hafnarfjordur, which was on the corner of Hamarsbraut 11.

After the last of the revellers left the nightclub, Kristrun and Thordur cleaned up for an hour before going home to update the accounts. The streets near their house were quiet. It was the same no-man's-land Erla traipsed through in the grip of her depression. They had lived at this address for years and were able to mark time from the sounds of passing cars. When a deluge of vehicles went by, it meant the staff at the hospital next to Sudurgata had finished their shifts. The two of them worked – as many do in the regions of Iceland that benefit from cheap, environmentally friendly geothermal heating – with the radiators on and the windows open.

Kristrun told Ragnar that if anything had happened that night, they would have noticed. Both Kristrun and Thordur were adamant they had not heard anything unusual: not a car driving to Hamarsbraut, not a commotion in the streets, and certainly not the tremendous amount of noise that would have accompanied someone being beaten to death in a drunken altercation.

The same applied to the married couple living in the flat above Erla and Saevar. The walls and floors were thin, so much so that Erla could hear their footsteps above, but they said they had never noticed any noise corresponding to the events purported to have taken place in Hamarsbraut 11. The family who lived opposite in Hamarsbraut 12 echoed this sentiment.

Gunnar Jonsson, the scraggly-haired witness to Gudmundur's death, flew over from Spain for an interview with Sigursteinn. Nearly two decades on from his testimony to the criminal court, Gunnar now told a very different story.

Gunnar said that his claims of ignorance about Gudmundur Einarsson had been rebuffed. When he insisted that he had no idea what the police were talking about, he was led towards his confession. Much of his testimony had been obtained in a corroborative meeting with Albert, in which Albert described what had happened and Gunnar simply agreed. The only reason he could describe Hamarsbraut 11 was because, as soon as he had arrived from Spain, he had been taken there to familiarize himself with the flat.

When Gunnar Jonsson was brought before the judges in court, he was seemingly unable to recognize the people he had supposedly witnessed killing Gudmundur. In a darkly farcical moment, relayed by Tryggvi's lawyer Hilmar Ingimundarson to a *Morgunbladid* journalist, the presiding judge announced, 'Bring Tryggvi Runar before the court!' Tryggvi was brought in by the bailiffs. The judge turned to Gunnar Jonsson and asked, 'Who is this man?' To which Gunnar replied, hesitatingly, '. . . Tryggvi Runar?'

Gunnar told Sigursteinn, on camera, that he was certain he had not been witness to a murder.

Ragnar's masterstroke, though, was in discovering a small note from a taxi driver working in Hafnarfjordur at the time. The existence of this note among the police files was seemingly accidental. On 26 February 1977, police officer Hellert Johannsson had called in on a Hafnarfjordur taxi service to question two of its drivers. Hellert wanted to know whether they remembered driving to Hamarsbraut 11 on the night of Gudmundur's disappearance.

The nature and specifics of the Gudmundur story made it likely that taxi drivers would have been able to remember the night in question. Gudmundur had been seen drunkenly attempting to hail a ride home. When it later transpired that he had disappeared, drivers who had been working that night would have wondered whether they passed the boy in the snow and did not pick him up.

Neither of the drivers recalled going to Hamarsbraut 11. But one of them stated that he and his colleagues did not drive during the later part of that night because there had been too much snow on the road. The large storm that swept through the southwest that night had dumped snow more than half a metre deep around Hafnarfjordur.

Taxis in Iceland are not like taxis in most other countries. In England, a deluge of snow forces almost all vehicles off the road, but in Iceland, where snowstorms are frequent, taxis are fitted with winter tyres and snow bumpers to equip them for the unpredictable weather. For Icelandic taxi drivers, being able to drive in challenging conditions is their livelihood. It takes a storm of colossal proportions to stop them.

If taxis could not operate on the roads that night, then it was highly unlikely Albert could have driven to the lava fields down the snow-covered, sunken dirt tracks while transporting three grown men and a corpse in his beaten-up Volkswagen. It wasn't just unlikely; it was preposterous.

The Supreme Court narrative for the killing of Geirfinnur also appeared to be peppered with errors.

In the Geirfinnur case, Kristjan was held to be the 'Clayfinnur'. But the person who was best positioned to see the man's face – a shy, middle-aged woman with curly blonde hair called Gudlaug Jonasdottir – was not consulted during the making of the clay head. There was no eyewitness testimony to corroborate Kristjan's presence; on the contrary, Gudlaug said he had not been the man in the café that night. She knew Kristjan, and would have recognized him.

When Gudlaug was summoned to the police station on 25 October 1976, she had been taken to a line-up. Kristjan stood in front of her, alongside a range of police academy students of similar age and height. Gudlaug said that none of them resembled the man she had seen enter the café. Asta Gretarsdottir, the young woman who had stolen a brief look at the caller, said the same.

Although Gudlaug affirmed that it had not been Kristjan, the criminal court judges interpreted her testimony differently. 'Kristjan Vidar might have come and made a phone call that night,' reasoned the judges, 'without [Gudlaug] noticing him, since many people were allowed to make phone calls on that evening.' But this conclusion did not make sense. The judges seemed to be suggesting that Kristjan might have sneaked into the café earlier, at a time that did not fit with when Geirfinnur had received his phone call at home, and made a different phone call to Geirfinnur. It undermined the entire narrative used to convict the suspects.

One by one, witnesses withdrew their testimonies: the drivers who had transported Erla; the witness to Kristjan walking back to Vatnsstigur; Sigurdur Ottar, who had driven the van to Keflavik. Some of them seemed to have been caught out by the length of time between the disappearances and the investigation: one of the car drivers *had* given a lift to Erla but it had been on a different night. Others, like Sigurdur Ottar, seemed to have been pressured towards making a statement. His lawyer, Robert Arni Hreidarsson, said that when he had tried to withdraw his client's testimony, he was told he could not do so. Sigurdur retracted his confession in court on 13 October 1977, but his original statement was used. At the abandoned building that Erla had broken into, there was little to indicate that anyone had forced entry or spent the night there.

Next was the matter of the convoluted journey to Keflavik. Sigurbjorn Vidir, one of the two investigators who reconstructed the drive in a police Volvo, testified in court that, on the evening

he and Ivar Hannesson had done so, it had been dry, with no snow
on the ground. But on the evening of 19 November 1974, when
Geirfinnur disappeared, the roads had been in a very different
condition. They had been slippery with ice.

The Volvo in which the police had conducted the test drive
had double the horsepower of the Volkswagen purportedly driven
by the suspects. Sigursteinn and his camera crew squeezed into
a Volkswagen and re-enacted the route themselves. It quickly
became apparent that, even leaving aside the difference between
the speed of the cars, the investigators' timeline for the journey
from Reykjavik to Keflavik was absurd.

Not only had the investigators not factored in sufficient time
for walking from the volcano documentary to the car, or for
waiting to come out of the cinema, but the drive itself would
have had to have been unrealistically well executed. The only way
Erla and Saevar could have driven from the film with Saevar's
mother, dropped her off, switched from a Land Rover to a rented
Volkswagen, met up with Gudjon and Kristjan, and then arrived
in Keflavik in time to phone Geirfinnur before half past ten, is
if they had thrown Saevar's mother out of a moving vehicle and
teleported between the different cars.

Erla and Saevar had supposedly gone to Geysir Car Rental and
hired a Volkswagen without signing a contract. This claim was
made plausible by the fact that an employee at Geysir Car Rental
had been fired at the start of 1976 for renting out cars without the
necessary paperwork and keeping the money for himself. When
the employee came before court on 20 June 1977, however, he
asserted that he had not begun his scam practice until 1975, the
year after Geirfinnur disappeared.

The Criminal Court judges recognized this difficulty, noting the witness couldn't say for sure whether he had rented a car from Geysir Car Rental to Erla and Saevar, yet both their verdict and that of the Supreme Court used the Geysir employee's testimony as one of the building blocks in the narrative of the evening. It had been a strange conclusion to draw in the first place. Erla had recently acquired a Land Rover. The Land Rover was in good working condition: it had been bought, second-hand, five days before Geirfinnur disappeared. Why would she take the trouble of renting a car?

As with the Gudmundur case, it was the Icelandic weather that provided the most satisfying refutation of the court's conclusions. On the night of Geirfinnur's disappearance the temperature was minus 4 degrees Celsius. The following night, it was minus 4.7 degrees. And on 21 November, when they supposedly buried the body at Raudholar, it was minus 10 degrees. The frost on the ground was so hard that they would have needed a pneumatic drill to get beneath the top layer. The story that clung to the red hills of Raudholar was pure mythology.

'I didn't know what had happened to Gudmundur and Geirfinnur,' says Ragnar. 'But I came to the conclusion early on that this did not happen like the Supreme Court believed it happened.'

When the judges took over the cases on the basis of a narrative that had the suspects stowing Gudmundur's body in the lava fields and burying Geirfinnur at Raudholar, police officers were still digging up gardens in Reykjavik in their ongoing search for a corpse.

During the autumn of 1996, Sigursteinn Masson, the journalist working on the documentary, began to suspect he was being followed. 'My imagination just went wild,' he says. 'I was wondering: "How far are they willing to go?" I was coming to realize how scandalous this case was, how much it had served the interests of powerful people. So I understood that they were willing to go very far to stop me. And I would have been foolish not to think so.' In his rear-view mirror, the same car followed slowly behind.

On one occasion he decided to confront his pursuers. He pulled over at the crossroads by the Melabudin grocery shop in west Reykjavik. The car behind him stopped close behind Sigursteinn's vehicle so that he was unable to see the number plate. Sigursteinn peered into his mirror. The two figures in the front seats were covering their faces with their hands. In other circumstances, Sigursteinn would have found it funny. But he was beginning to fear for his safety.

Sigursteinn was fired from his job. 'Channel 2's Newsroom upended because of Sigursteinn Masson's dismissal', read the headline on the front cover of Althyduhladid on 26 September 1996. 'This is a farce.' One of Sigursteinn's colleagues is quoted in the piece as saying Sigursteinn had been fired without any warning or valid reason. Sigursteinn thought he knew why, telling the press it might be because the programme director at Channel 2 also happened to be the son-in-law of state prosecutor Hallvardur Einvardsson who had played an active role in investigating the cases.

Paranoid and exhausted, Sigursteinn had a nervous breakdown. He was involuntarily checked into a psychiatric hospital for a month and a half, and after that went to Texas for six weeks. When Sigursteinn returned to Iceland in January 1997, he had been diagnosed with manic depression. Instead of thwarting the completion of the project, though, Sigursteinn says his breakdown enabled him and his colleagues to fly under the radar and finish the film.

According to Sigursteinn, Channel 2 offered to pay a significant amount of money to broadcast the film on a station that put out just a couple of hours of programming per day and was only broadcast in Reykjavik. He felt like they were trying to bury the documentary. Instead, he took it to RUV, the state broadcaster.

The film, *Adfor ad Logum* (or *Executed by Law*) was played in two parts over the consecutive nights of 28 and 29 April 1997. The police reported that the streets were silent when the films were being shown. It made front-page news throughout Iceland, and Sigursteinn discussed the issues it raised with journalists and Hallvardur Einvardsson on RUV. Thordis phoned Sigursteinn, a man she had never met, to say, '*eg elska thig*,' which is a term in Icelandic that signifies something more profound than love. These were the only words that could capture the depth of her gratitude.

It was now impossible to ignore the fact that something had gone wrong with the investigation. *Adfor ad Logum* was the most comprehensive argument yet that the Supreme Court narrative was flawed. A Gallup poll was released the following week suggesting that distrust of the courts and the police had hit an all-time high.

Before the verdict was returned, Saevar told a reporter from RUV: 'Everything was done to put the guilt on me – I don't know why. Maybe because I have a foreign name. I was treated like an animal. I want to regain my respect, and I insist that I will be acquitted and the case retried.' When he speaks, his head quivers. He is fierce, energetic, focused. The reporter asks, 'Are you optimistic that there will be a retrial?' and Saevar replies, 'If it won't be done now, then it will be done later.'

On 15 July 1997, the seven Supreme Court justices came to the decision that the conditions for reopening the cases had not been met.

The judges conceded, as had been previously recognized by the Supreme Court, that Saevar had been mistreated in prison, and that the warden and the guards had made improper comments about him. But this had happened after Saevar confessed to being complicit in the disappearance of Gudmundur Einarsson, and after he implicated four other men in the disappearance of Geirfinnur Einarsson – and there was therefore no justification for reopening the cases.

Ragnar argued that the prison logs alone should have been enough to warrant the reopening, not to mention the multiple glaring flaws in the investigation, but the judges disagreed. Only a 'minority' of the points put forward by Ragnar fulfilled the necessary conditions of reopening the cases. It must be remembered, wrote the judges, that the Supreme Court found some serious flaws in the investigation in 1980, but those flaws were not believed to hinder the proceedings or its verdict. These matters had already been considered.

The judges stated in their report that the onus was upon Saevar to prove that the Supreme Court's ruling was wrong. Outside court, Ragnar, dressed in a blue-and-grey suit, his face lined with fatigue, told the assembled media that this was a misinterpretation of the law. It was a demand made by the Supreme Court without legal authorization. The judges believed it so important to maintain the myth of the infallible judicial system that they were willing to go very far in interpreting the law unfavourably for the individual and favourably for the judicial system.

For the makers of the documentary, the lack of response was infuriating. 'Nothing happened,' remembers Einar Magnusson, the director. 'Everybody was silent. Even though everybody accepted what was shown in our documentary, nobody came forward to say "This is not right"!' David Oddsson, the Prime Minister, made a powerful speech in the Althing about the cases, but this was not cause enough for their reopening. Saevar held a rally in Austurvollur Square, which hundreds of people attended. A left-wing MP named Svafar Gestsson made a speech, and the comedian Steinn Armann told jokes, but in the wake of the rejection Saevar seemed deflated.

In an interview with RUV in July 1997, Saevar sits in a lush garden and, squinting into the sun, tells the interviewer that he had staked everything on the retrial. Even though Ragnar's court fees had been covered by the state, working to get the cases reopened had bankrupted him.

'Saevar was just a cat from the street,' says Siddo Stefansson, an old friend of Saevar's. 'He had no money, no connections, no power, no nothing. When you have nothing, and you are fighting against a big power, it's like coming up against a rock. You take up your teaspoon. And you don't stop knocking. That was what Saevar did. And if you keep knocking, then the rock will crack.'

In the eyes of the investigators and the courts, Saevar was Charles Manson and Rasputin rolled into one, the hippieish killer peddling drugs and strange ideas, come to charm Iceland's daughters and murder its sons. He was the embodiment of anxieties about drugs and loose morals in living, breathing form. But so much of what was thought about Saevar was distorted through the prism of a Machiavellian nature that never existed.

Being outside society's norms, and, at times, outside the law, appealed to him. On some level he was seduced by the idea of being a criminal. He walked around Reykjavik with a black briefcase and professed a love for Al Capone. He took pleasure in claiming to know more than he did, especially to people in positions of authority, and the result was to make the investigators think he was more dangerous than he actually was.

In truth, his criminal aspirations were those of a naïve teenager. He wanted to put LSD in the water supply and rob banks on horseback. These were schemes dreamed up in the communes as ways of sticking it to the man. Prior to his arrest for the postal fraud and drug smuggling, arguably his most prominent crime had been stealing a massive fish and then parading it around Reykjavik harbour to the amusement of his friends.

Viewed in the context of his supposed psychopathy, Saevar's sobriety carried a degree of calculation, a way of exerting control over others. Yet those who knew him say he simply didn't like alcohol and liked to keep his mind clear to think and paint. He didn't even like caffeine. Very few countries consume as much coffee per person as Iceland, but Saevar never touched it. He preferred milk.

Saevar had been set on the wrong track since childhood. Only much later in life was he was diagnosed as having ADHD by a Danish psychiatrist, but as a boy his disinterest in class and obstructive behaviour towards teachers were viewed as symptomatic of potential psychopathy. He had learning difficulties, partially caused by complications from surgery as a boy, but instead of receiving the help that might have come his way if he was born in a later era, he was moved between six different schools, diagnosed as possibly psychopathic and sent to Breidavik.

The necessity of resisting those who tried to grind him down was sparked in him by his father, nurtured at school, and then confirmed in an abusive institution. By the time he was put into custody in Sidumuli, he was already the type of character who did not easily give in and who would respond strongly when he detected negativity towards him.

The prison logs demonstrate the single-mindedness of the guards and the investigators to make Saevar confess. 'The prison guards were absolutely convinced that the prisoners were guilty,' says Hlynur Thor Magnusson, 'and that Saevar was the boss of the crimes and that these people were murderers.' But Saevar was an unusually strong character. Something unrelenting in his personality refused to break. He fought the investigators and the prison guards every step of the way and they hated him for that.

The investigators, convinced he was a master criminal, interpreted his deceit as further evidence that he was concealing something. They assumed he was playing with them and, at times, they were right, but perhaps not for the reasons they thought. Disillusioned by their continued refusal to accept his denials, he would send them searching for non-existent clues. He directed the investigators to a hill he had dreamed about, and they ripped it up with heavy machinery. They dragged the lake at Thingvellir after he told them Geirfinnur was buried there, even though he knew this was untrue. It was a way to wrest back a modicum of control in a situation that had grown increasingly absurd.

Saevar's faith in Iceland's judicial system remained consistent. He took the unusual step of taking to the stand in Reykjavik's criminal court, and again in the Supreme Court, to convince the judges of his innocence. In custody, when he tried to get letters out to the Ministry of Justice, they were dismissed as fake and further proof that the prisoners were communicating with one another. Inside the letters, Saevar attempted to draw government attention to what was taking place in Sidumuli. These weren't attempts to deceive. They were cries for help.

The force of will that infuriated those who interrogated him in Sidumuli was the same characteristic that drove him continually to assert his innocence after his release. Fundamentally misunderstood, but also underestimated, his refusal to give in both condemned him and kept his hope alive.

Saevar campaigned for another retrial in 1999, but by then he was beginning to lose his battle with alcohol. Although Saevar had bouts of sobriety where he would work on the cases – often with the help and support of his new partner Soley – as time wore on, the drinking took hold, and he ended up having no fixed address. Everybody knew who he was, so it was easy for him to get free drinks. Ragnar noticed that on the few occasions that Saevar visited him, he was intoxicated.

Hafthor, Saevar's eldest son, says the most difficult thing was watching this whole process in slow motion. Even though Saevar was no longer capable of fighting the system in any practical sense because he lived on the streets, he could not let the cases go. The will was still present, but all the momentum had dissipated. Just as Thordis had predicted, the cases were breaking him. Years spent campaigning for justice without receiving any concession from the state was tearing him apart.

'I'm very well known and some people are afraid of me,' Saevar once said in an interview. 'It is bad to be a marked man – you can't wash it off easily. Life is, of course, all about living a good life, and I feel like I haven't been allowed to. These cases have always stopped me. I have a certain syndrome because of this.'

Saevar became a fixture on the benches in Austurvollur Square and the bars around downtown Reykjavik. Once again, just like in the early 1970s, it was difficult to pass through the centre of town without bumping into Saevar Ciesielski.

He would sit, drunk, in the corner of bars and heckle any politician, police officer or judge unfortunate enough to stray into his line of sight. He had his nose broken repeatedly, and his body, which had always been slim and limber, started to hunch. His face, bloated from booze and weathered from exposure to the elements, gave him an almost monstrous appearance. It was as if he were assuming the physical shape that people had always believed his guilt deserved.

Although most people had mellowed towards him by now, the spectre of the cases still lingered. Victor, one of Saevar's sons with Soley, had to change schools after a teacher grabbed him because of who his father was. Victor and his sister Lilja felt compelled to take their mother's surname to circumvent further abuse. Thordis would bump into Saevar sometimes in the street, and he would tell her they should never have left Colorado.

A video filmed in 2008 shows Saevar confronting a room of journalists. He is dressed in a blue jacket and a bucket hat, and he has a bristly goatee. Just from looking at him one can tell that the past decade has not been kind. Whereas he was always a slight man, his body has filled out and he looks older than his fifty-something years. His good looks have gone, his hair is lank, and his face is puffed up from drink.

The journalists lean against the walls, the expressions on their faces suggesting a combination of discomfort and amusement. Saevar looks around the room. 'Who the *fuck* do you think you are?' he says, gesturing towards them with the index finger of his right hand. 'I suffered for you.' One of the male journalists smirks in response and the woman next to him looks down at the ground.

Now Saevar turns his attention, so he is looking just past the camera, giving a clearer angle onto his battered face. His beard is thick and rough, and his bloated nose is crooked in the middle. His expression is rigid with anger.

'I am going to tell you one thing,' he says. 'Life isn't that simple. Why did you have to attack me like that when I was a young boy?' He thrusts his thumbs with force into his chest and then in a hoarse roar: 'Why did you have to attack *me*?'

A few months later he moved to Copenhagen, back to Christiania, where he and Erla had once escaped when they were barely adults.

In the autumn of 1984, just as Saevar was being released from prison, Milton Friedman, the guru of free-market economics whose ideas were already vigorously being put into practice by Margaret Thatcher in the UK and Ronald Reagan in the USA, visited Reykjavik to debate with three Icelandic economics professors.

Veering between scorn and incredulity, Friedman attacked the egalitarian values espoused by his sparring partners. Asked pointedly by a floppy-haired academic as to whether he was against the free education of children, Friedman began to respond and then, suddenly irritated by the premise of the question, interrupted himself mid-answer and barked, 'There is no "free education". What are you talking about, "free"? You mean nobody pays for it?!'

Friedman's support of freedom of choice above all else, delivered in typically brash style, did not sit well with the academics lined up across from him, but there was at least one person watching for whom Friedman's way of thinking made for a refreshing change. David Oddsson, who was the mayor of Reykjavik at the time, and who would welcome Thordis into his prime-ministerial lodgings a decade later, viewed the Icelandic government as out-of-touch and old-fashioned, a nanny state from a bygone era: in what other European country was beer restricted and television banned on Thursdays? He and his supporters in the right-leaning Independence Party believed government intervention should be reduced and power given to the individual. For Oddsson, a man who would define mainstream Icelandic politics for the next two decades, Friedman's splenetic rejection of the country's values was exactly what was needed: it was time for Iceland to look to the free market to bring greater prosperity and independence.

Charismatic, driven, and supported by a group of loyal disciples, when Oddsson became Prime Minister on 30 April 1991 he revolutionized the Icelandic economy. Over the course of his fourteen-year premiership, Oddsson made it his mission to emancipate Iceland's economic system and target the inflation that had blighted the country for decades, in turn encouraging the sort of freewheeling individualism that made Iceland a hub for financiers. On his rare Friday afternoons off, he wrote short stories.

Regulation was cut, state banks such as Landsbanki, the institution established to help fund Iceland's nascent fishing operations, were steadily privatized, and corporate income tax was slashed in half. A country that had begun the century as one of the poorest in Europe became, by the end of Oddsson's tenure in 2004, a global player on the international market, and the country's so-called Venture Vikings, heralded in the media both home and abroad, were its new pioneers.

Ambitious Icelandic investors snapped up shares in everything from Russian alcopop suppliers to British high-street chains, many of them mining the imagery of the Sagas to associate their aggressive manoeuvrings with the spirit of their Viking descendants. The sudden entrance into foreign markets was described as 'utras', a Saga-era term for a rapid attack, while some financiers claimed to be making 'strandhogg', a word denoting a coastal raid. Oversized statues of Norse warriors, private jets embossed with the hammer of Thor, and yachts displaying names such as *Thee Viking* and *Mars* were the new trophies for Icelandic entrepreneurs profiting from the newly liberated economy to become colossally rich. It was the Saga age rebooted, romantic nationalism 2.0, the daring of Ingolfur Arnarson and the first settlers channelled into triumphant venture capitalism.

Iceland, too, became richer: the personal wealth of Icelandic families tripled between 2003 and 2006. A web of cranes spread across Reykjavik. For international financiers accustomed to cutting deals in New York and London, conducting business in Reykjavik made for a beguiling change. They jetted into the Icelandic capital to stay in the plush, newly constructed hotels and discuss business in geothermal pools. Success was toasted with private helicopter rides over lava fields lit up by the mid-night sun.

Millions of UK citizens put their money into Icelandic sav-ings accounts, attracted by the generous interest rates and the impression that Iceland's financial sector was cool, flexible, and topped off with that all-important dash of Nordic reliability. But Iceland's wealth was an illusion. In a country with dwindling fish exports and little industry outside of aluminium smelting, the country's rapid growth was debt-financed, its riches borrowed money.

In early 2008, when stock prices fell and the Icelandic krona tumbled in value, cautionary voices were drowned out by proc-lamations about Iceland's economic miracle. Olafur Ragnar Grimsson, the floppy-haired academic who had argued onstage with Milton Friedman, was now President, but instead of beating his old socialist drum, he vociferously supported the country's economic revolution. It was a transformation that encapsulated the shift in the nation's political landscape; even former leftist professors had become enthusiastic cheerleaders for Iceland's financial sector.

For many in positions of authority, it was clear that Iceland's economy was on the brink of collapse. But the person who ran the Central Bank, the person who was, in essence, responsible for raising the red flag at the out-of-control expansion of the financial sector, was, from 2005, David Oddsson. To draw attention to the enormous bubble would not only dent investor confidence, it would undermine much of what he had put into action during his tenure as Prime Minister.

Of course, to lay the blame at any one person's feet would be unfair. Oddsson publicly criticized the way financial institutions had been turned into money-making machines for entrepreneurs, and he claims to have cautioned the government, repeatedly, about the difficulties that the Icelandic banks faced. Swept along by the euphoria of Iceland's booming economy, warnings of imminent collapse went unheeded.

It was a system in which everyone had become complicit. The financial sector could do no wrong. 'There was an atmosphere in Iceland two or three years before the crash,' the former editor of *Morgunbladid*, Styrmir Gunnarsson, reflects, 'where you could not criticize the bankers. To do so would be seen as envious or as political.' The only comparable period in modern Icelandic history, says Styrmir, was the hysteria surrounding the Geirfinnur case: 'As a nation we had become somehow brainwashed.'

On 6 October 2008, the bubble burst.

Bank assets had grown to almost ten times the country's GDP. The three largest banks, Landsbanki, Kaupthing and the third, Glitnir, named after the gold-and-silver hall owned by the Norse god of law and justice, together owned debt worth more than 14 trillion krónur. Iceland's banks had borrowed more than $250,000 per Icelandic citizen.

Oddsson appeared on the evening news, his tone stern and paternal, to assure citizens that they would not be made to pay. They did. The Central Bank defaulted, the banks collapsed, and the Icelandic government was forced to borrow billions of dollars from the International Monetary Fund to bail the country out. Many families discovered their savings had been swallowed up overnight.

The myth sustained by the Venture Vikings had unravelled. Protesters broke into the home of the banker with the hammer of Thor emblazoned upon his jet and erected a banner that read 'WE WERE NEVER ELECTED TO ANY OFFICE, YET WE RULED EVERYTHING'. Viking effigies were hung from his balcony.

People took to the streets of Reykjavik, gathering in the square outside parliament each week to bang kitchen implements in the so-called 'pots and pans revolution'. Protesters pelted the Althing with *skyr*, the Icelandic yogurt, until its grey stone walls were streaked white. In a sketch on *Aramotaskaupid*, the New Year's Eve comedy television programme, comedian Jon Gnarr coined the phrase '*Helvitis fokking fokk*' (or 'Goddamn fucking fuck'), and the slogan soon appeared on signs and T-shirts outside parliament. Tear gas was used to break up protests for the first time since the anti-NATO protests in 1949. By early 2010, unemployment had risen from 2 per cent to 8 per cent.

The British government drew criticism for placing Iceland on their terror list to freeze deposits made by UK citizens into Landsbanki, but it was the Independence Party who drew the fiercest ire. Angry protesters called for new elections and jostled politicians as they entered parliament. Fake kronur worth nothing and decorated with Oddsson's head were handed out at protests. Oddsson employed bodyguards.

These protests possessed an extra edge, an anger that became more acute as citizens woke up to the staggering dimensions of the financial crash. Although Icelanders are used to cycles of boom-and-bust, their economy built upon the rhythms of the fishing seasons and subject to the whims of destructive geological processes, this was a disaster of a different complexion. It was man-made. The Icelandic people had been betrayed by an unsympathetic government that now refused to take responsibility.

From Copenhagen, Saevar was watching developments in Iceland with disgust. Arni Hallgrimsson, a tourist visiting Copenhagen, was walking through Christiania and asked one of his companions, 'Why do people come here?' Suddenly a gruff voice overhead replied in Icelandic, 'I will tell you about it.' Through the branches of a tree above him, Arni could see someone's toes. They were gnarled and swollen from having been in the cold. A pair of hands parted the branches and out peered the unmistakable face of Saevar Ciesielski.

Saevar told Arni, 'I can tell you that Denmark is a much better society than Iceland.' Arni said, 'Iceland is sinking,' and Saevar replied, 'Iceland is already sunk.' Arni offered Saevar some money and asked him if he would be insulted by a small donation. Saevar said, 'No, probably not,' in a tone, according to Arni, full of 'irony, regret and hopelessness'. They shook hands and bade farewell.

Life was fine in Copenhagen. No one knew who he was. He lived in social housing and he had a room with a bed and a desk. There was a place where he could shower.

On a bright day in early July 2011, Saevar went to a newsagent near Christiania. As he came out of the shop, he tripped over. He had been drinking for days and he fell heavily, hitting his head on the pavement. Saevar was taken to hospital, and on 12 July 2011, six days after his fifty-sixth birthday, he passed away.

Back in Iceland, Saevar's son Hafthor remembers being telephoned with the news. 'It was hard. But there was also a sense of release. He had been in a really bad condition before that.

I kind of knew that this would happen somehow, I expected it in a way. Still it was a pretty heavy blow. I just remember putting on Eric Clapton and some of the songs I remember us listening to together.'

Saevar Ciesielski's funeral took place in Reykjavik Cathedral on 2 August 2011. In attendance were MPs, artists and musicians, with members of Reykjavik's homeless community also crammed into the aisles. Erla, Thordis and Soley, Saevar's ex-partners, sat on the same bench at the front. Runar Thor, the musician Saevar met in Litla-Hraun, played 'So Long, Marianne' by Leonard Cohen. The priest Orn Bardur Jonsson quoted a passage from Halldor Laxness's classic historical novel *Iceland's Bell*, in which the protagonist of the book's first part, Jon Hregvidsson, escapes to Denmark after being wrongfully accused of murder by the Icelandic authorities.

On the news, the coverage of his death was characterized by regret, and was entirely inappropriate for someone charged with killing two men.

Saevar's death came amid fierce anti-establishment sentiment in the years following the economic crash. An electoral shift to the left ushered in the end of the Independence Party's long dominance of parliamentary politics. Jon Gnarr, the comedian whose slogan had captured the imagination of the protesters outside parliament, swept to victory in the Reykjavik mayoral elections on the back of a campaign whose central pledges included a polar bear for the zoo, free towels in swimming pools, and 'all kinds for the unfortunates'. The bankers who bore some responsibility for Iceland's bankruptcy were sent to Kvíabryggja prison, where Gudjon had served his sentence. Committees were created to scrutinize allegations of historical abuse in facilities such as

Breidavik. Victims of systematic maltreatment were discovering that their accusations were being looked at afresh.

It was the right time for a more critical assessment of issues that remained unresolved. Now was the moment for the cases to be reappraised. And if the courts wouldn't do it, another method needed to be found.

7

DAD'S PLACE

Kristin's baby was born prematurely, and her minute body, with its tousle of dark hair and tiny features, can be cradled in a pair of cupped hands. When she sleeps, the air draws in and out of her mouth so softly that it is difficult to tell whether or not she is still breathing. But when she wakes up, her brown eyes alert with unknowable intent, the room is in thrall to her presence.

We rig lights in the sitting room and set up the camera. Kristin is understandably distracted. She chit-chats and brings us coffee, but her gaze continually wanders to the pram to check that her baby sleeps soundly. Her partner watches us from a doorway. He looks exhausted.

Kristin moves into position for the interview and the cameraman pulls focus on her face. She is blonde and powerfully built. Her English is flawless. There is something no-nonsense about Kristin when she describes details personal to her, so that the facts of her life are presented as if they had happened to someone else. This is what transpired, she seems to be saying, make of it what you will. Only later in the story, when her absorption in the narration of her memories is total, does it become possible to detect the tightness at the edge of her jaw as she clenches her back teeth to prevent the emotion from showing on her face. Her detachment is not due to disinterest. It is her last line of defence against the emotions that stir in her when she speaks about her father's life

Just before the camera operator presses 'record', Kristin takes her baby outside to the balcony and leaves her in the pram to nap.

Kristin's first memory of her father is visiting him at his home when she was five years old. She called it 'Dad's place'. They would go there on Sunday mornings, her and her mother, the bus winding its way through the pale browns and greens in the southwest of the country until the spray from the sea began to speckle the bus windows, and the white immensity of Litla-Hraun rose upon the horizon.

Everybody knew Kristin there. 'How are you?' they would ask, and, 'Are you going to finish the picture that you drew last time you were here?' The one rule that Kristin had to follow was that she would never walk alone in the building without her father's permission.

In his room there was a bed, a stereo and a fridge. Bodybuilders grinned and flexed in the pictures that lined the wall. The windows were covered in bin bags and when she asked him why, he replied that he didn't want her to see the bars.

It didn't feel like a prison to Kristin. The guards were always friendly and she enjoyed seeing her dad. She was allowed to play with the other children who were visiting their fathers. They would throw frisbees to each other down the long corridors. Later, when her parents got married, they had their wedding reception there.

Each Sunday evening, when visiting hours were over and Kristin boarded the bus to return home, she knew her father would already be locked in his cell. It was a strange thought. He was in prison and it was not his fault. She had never been told this specifically, but the idea had seeped gradually into her consciousness, from conversations heard through half-closed doors and muffled voices on the end of telephone lines, until it became just another part of her understanding of the world.

Tryggvi was released in 1982, when Kristin was seven. The same week he came out of prison, one of Kristin's teachers turned to her in the middle of a lesson. 'Well,' the teacher said, 'it looks like your dad, the murderer, is coming home.' It was the first time Kristin had been told what her father had been found guilty of.

'Murderer'. The word stayed with Kristin. It was chilly and unfamiliar, and felt far removed from how she thought of her father. But people in the neighbourhood seemed perturbed by the prospect of his release. He must have done something; otherwise why were people so scared? The two ideas – that prison was for bad people, and that her father was a good man – butted against each other inside her head.

When her father was released, it felt like the atmosphere around Kristin changed. Overnight a barrier appeared between her and her schoolmates. Neighbours forbade their children from going to her house. That was fine. She learned to be on her own. If they didn't want to play with her, then she didn't want to play with them. It made it easier to see who was who.

As she moved into adolescence, Kristin felt embarrassed about who her father was. If asked, she would keep her answer vague. In a country as small as Iceland, disguising the identity of your father is a challenge. For Kristin, it was like chess. She had to be a few moves ahead in every conversation about her upbringing, alert to the possibility of shifting position before someone posed the question 'Who is your father?' He's not from here, you wouldn't know him. It was the question that made her feel most ashamed. Ashamed because of the confusion it provoked in her; ashamed because she was associated, however distantly, with something as unthinkable as murder; and ashamed because she betrayed her father, her father whom she loved deeply, on each occasion that she lied about him.

Tryggvi was meticulous about the things he could control. No one was allowed to touch his alphabetically ordered rock and roll record collection. There was a particular pair of socks for each working day and he washed them at the weekend. He got a job at a ship factory.

Over time, attitudes towards him softened. He was a family man. He worked hard. His colleagues respected him. But although people warmed to him, even liked him, he was tarnished, forever, by what he had done. However generous he was, however kind, he could never be more than a reformed criminal striving to better himself. Everything was viewed within that context. Each casual conversation at work, or passing exchange in the street, was shadowed by his past. 'He's not so bad,' they'd say, 'he's a nice guy.' Yet he was always kept at arm's length, held slightly apart.

Sometimes this feeling, that his whole life was pervaded by the case, ground him down and he would drink. On those occasions, Kristin's father – the cheerful, energetic man who curled her hair before school and taught her to swim – would disappear. These were the only times she heard him talk about the case. He would get angry. At night, when she should have been asleep, Kristin would creep from her bedroom and watch through the banisters as his frustration poured out of him and he cursed the people he felt had wronged him: 'Orn . . . Erla . . . Saevar'. One Christmas Eve he smashed up the furniture in the sitting room. He was screaming like an animal.

When she was thirteen, Kristin went into the basement to explore the storage space where her parents kept their old junk. Among the debris she found a battered suitcase. Its clasps were broken and its red colouring had faded to a faint orange. Inside, there were a dozen A4 ringbinder notebooks filled with her father's slanted handwriting. Kristin took three of them up to her room.

Kristin leafed through the notebooks. They were diaries that her father had kept while in prison. For the next few nights, she read them in bed. Although she was too young to understand a lot of what he wrote, she was thrilled to have access to a part of her father's inner life that had always been kept off-limits.

Each time she took them out of their plastic wrapper, she felt excited at the prospect of learning something more about her father. They seemed to contain so much of him that was both utterly recognizable and completely alien. What struck her most was the repetition. The ins and outs of his daily routine were listed in precise detail, from what he ate at lunch to the amount of push-ups he did, as if by delineating the mundane facts of his days he could imbue them with purpose. Either that or he was trying to keep a grip on his sanity.

There were angry passages too, where he would write the same words over and over again, in a tone, insistent and despairing, that made him feel unfamiliar to her. The truth needs to come out; lies have been told about me, and I can't stand it much longer. Repeatedly he asserted his innocence.

On the cusp of going to the criminal court in 1977 he writes: 'Yes, finally I have reached my main goal, to tell the truth in court. But it has taken a long time. I would have never expected, 15 and a half months! If I had expected this I would have never confessed [. . .] I thought that if I confessed, I would get out while the case was in court. I didn't want those two years Orn Hoskuldsson threatened me with if I didn't confess.' A few weeks later he writes that he does not need to be afraid, because 'I am innocent, and justice always prevails in the end'.

Kristin returned to the basement a few weeks later to borrow more of the books, but they were no longer in the orange suitcase. Outside, in the garden, she found a metal container with the blackened remains of what had once been the diaries. He had burned them. Kristin couldn't ask him why he had destroyed them because to do so would reveal that she had sequestered some for herself. Instead, she hid the three diaries she had already taken, which covered her father's time in custody between 25 October 1976 and 21 November 1977, and never spoke of their existence to her parents.

Kristin passes me the diaries. I am briefly filled with the same vertiginous sensation I sometimes get if I am standing at the top of an escalator or holding a sharp object near someone I care about. Might I tear the diaries up? Their sentimental value is, of course, immense. But there is more to them than that. These thin volumes – flimsy, insubstantial somehow – are key, Kristin hopes, to bringing about her father's exoneration.

Kristin gave birth to her first child when she was sixteen years old. Tryggvi was there to help deliver the baby. He cut the umbilical cord. Kristin named her son after her father.

Whereas Kristin had grown up with the case, her son was shielded from it. When there was news in the press, Kristin and the rest of the family would surreptitiously keep him away from the magazine rack at the supermarket. Although most of his friends knew about the disappearances, even writing about them in sociology classes in school, he did not. Somehow they just never came up.

Tryggvi and his young namesake formed a very close bond. Always ebullient, and in possession of an ability to put everyone around him in a good mood, he was his grandson's hero. They would drive around Reykjavik in a beaten-up Suzuki, buckets of paint piled on the back seats for Tryggvi's job as a house painter, and make jokes out of whatever they saw through the car windows.

Kristin started working for the Icelandic Ministry for Foreign Affairs. She travelled to different countries around the world, to Slovenia, to Morocco, to Canada, always taking with her the diaries – still wrapped in the same plastic holders as when she found them. They had become a piece of her dad's history, like an old picture or a well-worn shirt, and she wanted to keep them close.

In spring 2009, she received a call from her father. He was ill and wanted her to come home to see him. Kristin thought he was being melodramatic; after all, he still sounded his usual, upbeat self. But when she spoke to her mother it was immediately clear she should return to Iceland straight away. Tryggvi had oesophageal cancer and the doctors had detected it late.

Kristin visited him in hospital daily. Although his face was pale, almost the same hue as the pillow, his hair had retained some of its orange lustre. He tried to disguise it, but he seemed to be in a lot of pain.

One afternoon, when they were alone, Kristin told her father she had hidden away some of his diaries and that she had carried them with her ever since. There was so much unsaid in that moment. The diaries were never something he wanted his daughter to see, dredged as they were from the depths of the darkest period of his life and filled with all the anguish of an imprisoned man in an impossible situation. They had always been something to be kept as far away from her as possible. He had never wanted her to think of him as a prisoner or, worse, a criminal. He just wanted to be her dad.

Kristin apologized. What should she do with them now? Tucked up in the hospital bed, he looked so small that he was barely recognizable. 'Nothing,' he said. 'When the time is right you will know what to do with them.' Kristin's mother came into the room and the conversation moved on to something else. The next day, on 1 May 2009, Tryggvi passed away.

Following his death, Kristin could not get the diaries out of her head. Was there a way she could use them? Could they be important? They were certainly important to her. But did they have significance beyond a daughter trying to understand her father?

It was not until December 2010 that Kristin's son Tryggvi found out about his grandfather's past. He read an article about the Gudmundur case in a newspaper. He was eighteen years old. His feelings were complicated. He felt like a fool for not having known, but he also recognized that, by not knowing, he had given his grandfather a relationship untainted by the case.

Talking about it today, Tryggvi, now in his mid-twenties, says he would give up anything in his life to have a conversation with his grandfather about what he went through as a young man entangled in a murder case.

In 2011, two years after the elder Tryggvi's death, Kristin's mother, Sjofn Sigurbjornsdottir, granted an interview to a television journalist named Helga Arnardottir. Kristin came along too and, for reasons she didn't quite understand herself, brought the diaries with her. When the interview was finished, Kristin decided to show them to Helga. She wanted Helga to see something of her father. That felt important somehow.

On the cover of the first book that Helga took were the words 'This is the diary of an innocent man'. Helga had to leave to file her report, but a few hours later she phoned Kristin back. She had been in touch with her editor and they wanted to do a story on the diaries, specifically to take them to London so they could be analysed by a leading forensic psychologist, and native Icelander, named Professor Gisli Gudjonsson.

Gisli is a world expert on false confessions. He has served as an expert witness on many high-profile criminal cases, particularly in Britain, where his testimony has proved instrumental in clearing the names of, among others, the Guildford Four and the Birmingham Six. His writing on false confessions has been influential worldwide. He was awarded a CBE in 2011.

Helga phoned to explain to him what she had found. Gisli suggested she fly to London immediately and show him the diaries.

Kristin was faced with a tough decision. Either she could ask for anonymity so that it would not be known how the diaries had been found, or she could go to London and, for the first time, publicly associate herself with her father once the news broke about the diaries. Most of her friends knew who her father had been, but there were still people at work and at her son's school who had no idea she was the daughter of one of the men convicted for killing Gudmundur. She felt like a teenage girl again, dodging questions from schoolmates and hiding a part of who she really was. She made the decision to go with the diaries.

Less than seventy-two hours after meeting each other, Helga and Kristin boarded a plane and flew to London.

They landed at noon and Gisli picked them up at Heathrow Airport. He cheerfully asked Kristin about how she found the diaries and why she had kept them. Kristin felt anxious. For some reason, she was scared that Gisli would think she was lying. The whole trip was a mistake. She longed to be back home.

It puzzled her that she felt this way. She knew her father was innocent. It had informed so much of how she had lived her life. But it was this thought that made the stakes higher. If Gisli said that the diaries were meaningless, that her father was still guilty, then that would mean she had lived a lie. The thought had not entered her mind until she was sat in the car with Gisli. If he dismissed the diaries, then everything that her teachers and neighbours had said to her when she was a seven-year-old girl would turn out to have been true.

They arrived at Gisli's house, and Gisli took the diaries and went into his office. He closed the door behind him. Kristin and Helga waited in a small, circular sitting room. The windows were tinted green and went from the floor to the ceiling and curved above them in a dome. Gisli's wife was in the kitchen, cutting up strawberries and tossing the stems into a bowl. Kristin found that she was shaking.

Gisli came out of his office. His expression was inscrutable. He drank some tea and talked about the weather. Kristin wanted to scream, 'Who cares about the weather? Tell me something, anything. Is everything going to be OK? Do I need to go home and rethink my life?' But she didn't say anything. She smiled and drank from her mug while her insides churned.

Gisli returned to his study for another hour. He came back out into the sitting room after an hour. Kristin poured more tea from the pot. Gisli turned to Kristin. In light of these diaries, he said, there are grounds for analysing whether the confessions made by your father, upon which the whole case against him rests, were unreliable.

Gisli did not say he was innocent – he was in no position to say anything like that – but for Kristin it was just as close. There had never been a body. There had never been a crime scene. There had never been a motive. Just confessions. If it could be proven that these were coerced, that meant there was no remaining evidence against her father.

Something loosened in Kristin then, and she began to cry. Most of all, she felt relief. For the first time, she could say with pride who her dad was.

The interview is over and the camera operator begins to turn the equipment off. Kristin stays where she is for a moment. We shuffle around, unloosening stands and folding up tripods. It has started to snow and she goes outside to fetch her daughter.

In October 2011, Helga broadcast a documentary about Tryggvi's diaries. Saevar's death in July had caught the media's attention, and his family, along with Erla, had spoken forcefully on television about the failings in the investigation. There was anger and distrust towards those in authority in the aftermath of the financial crash. The stage was now set for a reappraisal of the cases.

After receiving a petition signed by 1,190 people, Ogmundur Jonasson, the Minister of the Interior, formed a working group in October 2011 to review all the documents in the Gudmundur and Geirfinnur cases, particularly with regard to the police investigation.

Ogmundur Jonasson was born on 17 July 1948, seven years before Erla and Saevar, and had watched the cases unfold for most of his adult life. He has a solemn, dignified demeanour, and when he says things that he does not mean or that he has not phrased as precisely as he would like, he has the presence of mind, earned through decades of television interviews, to ask for the question to be repeated so that he can have another attempt at saying it exactly right.

When Ogmundur heard that it would be expensive for Saevar's body to be transported back from Denmark to Iceland, he contributed funds. He is visibly embarrassed when asked about this, and moves the conversation to less personal ground, stating that he wishes the steps taken in 2011 were taken much earlier, when Saevar had still been alive.

'But this is not something that we are doing for him,' he says. 'We are doing this for justice. And a society that wants to be based on law must be able to reconsider its actions if there is reason to believe that they are wrong.'

The working group set up by Ogmundur consisted of lawyers Arndis Soffia Sigurdardottir and Haraldur Steinthorsson, and psychologist Dr Jon Fridrik Sigurdsson. Both lawyers were young in order to preclude the possibility of them having a connection with the cases.

It was now widely believed that Sidumuli had been a nightmarish place, and that there were major errors in the investigation and in the court judgements. But as the judges in both the criminal and Supreme Court had made clear, this did not necessarily affect the confessions. Maltreatment in Sidumuli had taken place *after* many of the key statements had already been obtained.

Besides, the incongruities and gaps in the judges' final verdict stood testament to the fiendish complexity of two cases that had produced over 10,000 pages of documentation. For those who maintained that the right people had been convicted, this tangled web of confusing and contradictory statements indicated the machinations of a group of suspects who had tried to confuse the investigators with an array of misleading stories in order to disguise their own involvement in two murders.

Arndis 'Disa' Soffia Sigurdardottir was the lawyer selected to chair the working group. A former police officer, she also owns a guest house on a farm in the shadow of the Eyjafjallajokull volcano in the south of the country. In the arenas in which she had worked and studied – the police force and law school – the prevailing opinion had always been that, although there were flaws in the investigation, the correct verdict had been reached.

The first task for Disa and the working group was to gather together all the documents. The sheer volume of paperwork was enormous. They collected files from the police station, the criminal court, and the Supreme Court. At the National Archives in central Reykjavik the archivists loaded boxes of statements and police reports on to trolleys and trundled them to the office at the Ministry of the Interior designated for the working group. The boxes, when placed side by side, stretched for metres. The documents were in no semblance of order and, although the working group was established to study the cases for half a year, the process took nearly eighteen months.

Recognizing the role these cases had played in the Icelandic consciousness across the years, the working group set up a mailbox that citizens could contact them through. It was soon deluged: a mirror situation of 1974, when tip-offs pertaining to Geirfinnur's fate had poured in.

Their initial objective was to establish the best possible overview of how the investigation had developed. With this database in place, the working group could then determine exactly how many times the suspects had been interviewed, how much access they had to legal counsel, and how long they had been detained in custody.

Very early on in the process, alarm bells began to ring. Disa had begun the task of sifting through the documents knowing very little about the cases, but it was soon apparent to her that something had gone seriously wrong. The means of gathering the confessions had been nowhere near as clear-cut as she had been led to believe.

There had been little contact between the suspects and their legal counsel. During 180 police interviews Saevar's lawyer had been present 49 times, while Erla's representative had only been present for three of her 105 interviews.

Reports contained in the prison logs demonstrate that, repeatedly, lawyers for the suspects were denied permission to speak with their clients. At one particular juncture, the judge, Gunnlaugur

Briem, stated that certain lawyers were under no circumstances allowed to communicate with their clients and that this ban would continue for a few days. It lasted more than a month.

What Disa found more shocking was the length of custody. In keeping with many criminal justice systems around the world in the 1970s, the Icelandic judiciary used prolonged detention during investigations of serious crimes in order to obtain confessions. Custody could be extended repeatedly. Some of the suspects had been kept in solitary confinement for a staggeringly long period of time.

Monotony degrades the mind. Even a rat kept in a maze and compelled to find its food in the same place, day after day, will alleviate the tedium by using different routes to reach its meal. Bereft of environmental stimulation or the opportunity for social interaction, isolation impairs the ability to maintain attention on one's surroundings. Just a few days of solitary confinement can shift the pattern of the human brain into an abnormal configuration characteristic of stupor and extreme disorientation.

There are not many credible experiments that meaningfully explore solitary confinement, primarily because the effects upon any test subject, either human or non-human, are so deleterious.

In one infamous experiment conducted by Harry Harlow in the 1950s, monkeys were kept inside a chamber from which they could not escape. After a couple of days the monkeys began to self-harm, walk round and round their cages in circles, and rock back and forth for long periods in a state of profound disturbance. It was termed the 'pit of despair'.

In 1951 Donald O. Hebb, a psychologist at McGill University in Montreal, analysed the effect an extremely monotonous environment had on test subjects, in this case college students. After lying down on a comfortable bed, the test subjects were fitted with plastic visors to limit their sight, gloves and long tubes along their arms to restrict their touch, and U-shaped pillows around their heads, like the ones used by passengers on planes, to block off any small sounds that might reach them from beyond the walls of their cubicle. Their only daily interaction with other humans was when food was brought to them or when they were taken to the toilet.

To begin with, the subjects passed the time by thinking about the experiment, their studies, and any personal problems that had been bothering them in the preceding days. Some counted upwards from zero until their concentration slipped. Others just let their mind drift. Many would later say they soon ran out of things to think about. Within days, almost all the students experienced hallucinations.

Generally, these hallucinations started as basic shapes. Dots and lines appeared in front of them and, over time, these simple forms would start to become more intricate, developing into the type of repetitive design one might find on bathroom tiles or on wallpaper motifs. Soon these patterns developed into full scenes – much like a film being played in their minds – such as squirrels marching with sacks slung over their shoulders, eyeglasses walking up and down a road, and prehistoric animals in a jungle. One test subject could see nothing but dogs.

The hallucinations were not restricted to the visual realm. Many test subjects reported that they heard talking, or felt different sensations along their body, one going so far as to say he could feel pellets being fired against his arm by a miniature rocket.

At first, many of the subjects enjoyed these effects: it relieved the tedium of isolation. But soon it began to disturb them, interrupting their sleep and rendering them unable to focus on anything else. Many reported dissociative episodes, wherein they felt they were simultaneously inside and outside their body. 'My mind,' said one of the students, 'seemed to be a ball of cotton wool floating above my body.'

All of the test subjects were paid for their involvement. Many of them studied psychology and were enthusiastic about what they might discover through taking part. The experiment was devised to be six weeks long. No one lasted more than seven days.

Clearly the parameters of this experiment are not entirely analogous to prison conditions, not least because the sensory deprivation experienced by the students was more extreme than that endured by those in custody. But what the students suffered in isolation tallies with what experts have found when they have interviewed inmates about their time in solitary.

Dr Stuart Grassian, a psychiatrist who was on the faculty of the Harvard Medical School for over twenty-five years and remains a leading researcher on the effects of solitary confinement, has written extensively about how the deprivation of stimulation causes severe psychiatric harm. He interviewed prisoners who had been kept in solitary confinement at a maximum security prison in Walpole, Massachusetts. The aspect that struck him most was the consistency of the specific psychiatric symptoms reported by the inmates, including intrusive thoughts, overt paranoia and hallucinations.

Indeed, Dr Grassian concluded that the extensive perceptual disturbances experienced by an isolated person – be these brief illusions, like objects changing in size, or more lengthy hallucinations – are found almost nowhere outside specific neurological illnesses. Solitary confinement sent inmates into a kind of delirum.

Using the Sidumuli prison logs discovered by Sigursteinn, the working group were able to calculate exactly how long the suspects had been kept in solitary confinement. By the time the cases were sentenced at the criminal court on 19 December 1977, Tryggvi had been held in solitary confinement for 627 days, Saevar for 615 days, Kristjan for 503 days, Gudjon for 412, Erla for 241, and Albert for 87.

Sidumuli housed two corridors, one of which, termed 'the women's corridor', was far quieter than the corridor in which the other cells were situated. 'They got me with the silence,' Tryggvi once said in an interview with Icelandic journalist Thorsteinn Antonsson. 'I heard nothing, just as I was meant to hear.' After a few days in solitary confinement, Tryggvi experienced florid psychotic symptoms. He began to hear voices, male and female, sometimes arguing up close, other times murmuring in the distance, as if he could hear people talking at a party. The chatter was nearly ceaseless. He did not sleep for four days.

Tryggvi took much of his enjoyment in life from physical exercise and practical activities, and complained bitterly if bad weather caused the prison guards to curtail his fifty minutes outside. He worked out in his cell, often for up to four hours a day, to keep his mind and body sharp. But aside from meals, interrogations and exercise, there was nothing for him to do but sit on his bed and think. Cooped up in a cell, he was confronted with the idea that he might have been involved in Gudmundur's murder. The case preyed on his mind during the interminable hours in custody.

He maintained his innocence for seventeen days before he eventually confessed. He was subsequently kept in solitary confinement for nearly two years.

Saevar, too, was profoundly affected by his time in solitary. When Stefan Unnsteinsson, a journalist, managed to obtain permission to interview Saevar three weeks after he had come out of isolation, he saw a very different man to the one he had known as a teenager at parties. In recordings Stefan took with Saevar following his release, Saevar could barely string a sentence together. All of the urgency with which he usually spoke was absent. He seemed listless, stupefied. 'At that point Saevar was raving mad,' Stefan remembers. 'For those first weeks, it was like he was on an acid trip.'

Starved of human contact and left to stew in her thoughts day after day, Erla says she became so desperate to speak to someone that she would do anything just for a little attention. 'You become this helpless baby. It's like your mentality and intelligence shrinks and you're in this abstract world with no comparison.' Held in solitary confinement for over seven months, her grip on reality disintegrated: 'I was going crazy,' she says, 'wondering, "Did I ever even have a baby? Is that also my imagination?" Because I could swear that I feel that I do, but no picture is coming.'

The effects of solitary confinement continued to plague Erla. She recalls going to watch a film with her family, and how, almost as soon as they had taken their seats, the lights in the cinema came on. Erla's first thought was that perhaps the President was attending the screening and the film was being paused so he could find his seat. But everyone in the auditorium, including her family, was getting up from their seats and leaving the cinema. The film was over but they had barely sat down.

Her perspective of time continued to warp. One evening at her mother's house, Erla sat on the sofa while her mother Thora wound an alarm clock. Thora then retired to her bedroom, and Erla stayed seated, looking at a petrol station across the street. She thought about how she no longer needed to press a rubber button to go to the toilet. The alarm clock went off. Erla thought about how it was taking her mother a long time to work out how to use it. At that point, Thora came into the sitting room and said, 'Haven't you slept?' Erla had been there the whole night. Outside it was still dark and the first cars were arriving at the petrol station to fill up on their way to work.

During an interview conducted seven years after his release, Kristjan described his state of mind during custody. 'Of course, there was nothing but the wait. The days were all as one. Waiting for the next interrogation, wondering what I should say. But often the statements were laid in front of me fully written and I just had to approve them. In the cell one could do nothing but think. I grew into the walls. They were green. I stopped when I could not feel my body. I was just head. Head.'

After a year in custody, Kristjan began to hurt himself. A recent study examining nearly 250,000 incarcerations in New York between January 2010 and January 2013 found a strong correlation between self-harm and solitary confinement. Those who were held in isolation were 6.9 times more likely to hurt themselves. Only 7.3 per cent of incarcerations involved solitary confinement, but these inmates accounted for 53.3 per cent of incidences of self-harm.

In December 1976, Kristjan tried to kill himself by cutting his wrists. Karl Schütz wrote a letter to the judge Halldor Thorbjornsson advising that Kristjan be monitored carefully on account of his being vulnerable, unpredictable and one of the most important suspects in the cases. The following month Kristjan deliberately set fire to his mattress while in his cell. He was placed on continuous suicide watch for four-and-a-half months, the door to his cell left open so he could be constantly observed, day and night, by two guards at a time. Given sedatives to keep calm, he wandered the corridors like a zombie. Sometimes he would walk into walls until his face was covered in blood.

Drugs were administered to the suspects by Gudsteinn Thengilsson, the prison doctor, as well as by the guards. The dosages were far higher than would be administered in the present day. On a single day in October 1976, for example, Saevar was given as much as 75 milligrams of the anti-depressant Tryptizol, 10 milligrams of Valium, 5 milligrams of the sedative Mogadon, laxatives, and a form of codeine. The inmates took sleep medication and sedatives, the hypnotic Chlordiazepoxide to calm them down, Metoclopramide to prevent nausea, chloral, Belladenal, Nitrazepam. They were given injections to reduce their delirium, and, in some cases, to persuade them to tell the truth.

It was difficult for the suspects to distinguish between the different functions of the cell, the interrogation room and the court, and so, too, the roles of investigator, prison guard and judge. Investigators entered the cells at night to question the suspects. Guards were assigned to individual prisoners in order to befriend them and to extract information. Hlynur Thor Magnusson was the guard assigned to Erla. 'At that point in the isolation,' Erla says,

'Hlynur was so friendly to me. It was like water in the desert. Then years later it was such a blow, even all that time later, to discover that he didn't care.'

Tryggvi claims that prison guard Skuli Steinsson pretended to be his friend. He told Tryggvi that he was confessing to different crimes in his sleep. We can hear everything you are saying, Skuli told him. Tryggvi says they placed tape over his mouth so he would not blurt out secrets while he slept.

Confident the suspects they held in custody were dangerous and duplicitous, the atmosphere in prison was extraordinarily intense. Sidumuli was a topsy-turvy world where guards became trusted confidants, a conversation with an investigator doubled up as a cross-examination by a judge, and everyday citizens, even sports stars idolized by Icelanders, were cast in the role of devious dissimulators, bent on deceiving the police and the nation.

The working group found that the suspects had been interviewed many more times than the police reports indicated. Saevar was interviewed at least 180 times before trial, Kristjan 160, and Erla 105. There had been dozens of 'co-accused conformity confrontations' in which the suspects were brought together in a bid to harmonize their confessions.

The impression given by the Supreme Court verdict was that those involved in the cases had repeatedly changed their confessions in order to cover their tracks: they were, to borrow Karl Schütz's word, 'cunning'. But the working group's findings showed the opposite was true. The investigators appeared to have led the suspects towards changing their statements in order to conceal the blunders made during the investigation.

In their first confessions, both Kristjan and Albert claimed Albert had received a phone call from Hamarsbraut 11 on the night of Gudmundur's disappearance. But on 27 Februrary 1977, an investigator named Gisli Gudmundsson learned that in January 1974, when Gudmundur disappeared, the phone at Hamarsbraut 11 had been disconnected due to lack of payment. This new piece of information started to filter through the subsequent confessions. Now statements were made in which the phone call never took place.

The same applied to Albert's vehicle. In Albert's confession dated 23 December 1975, and Kristjan's confession on 28 December 1975, Albert drove to Hamarsbraut 11 in his father's yellow Toyota. But, in January 1974, Albert's father did not own a yellow Toyota. He drove a Volkswagen.

When the investigators discovered this fact, the statements once more began to morph. Albert originally claimed that he parked the Toyota with its rear backing on to Hamarsbraut, so that Gudmundur's body could be stowed there. But the Volkswagen did not have a boot. It had only a tiny storage space in the front. Now statements were made in which Albert drove there in a Volkswagen and parked it facing Hamarsbraut 11. Gudmundur's body was wedged against the back seats. The confessions adjusted to incorporate this new reality.

Trapped in a surreal situation in which nobody would believe he was not involved, Saevar tried to prove the investigators were synchronizing the confessions.

On 3 March 1977, Saevar mentioned Gunnar Jonsson as a witness to Gudmundur's murder. He waited to see whether the story would spread. It did. By the following week, Albert, too, had named Gunnar Jonsson, while others in custody had mentioned that a man named Gunni had been present. It was well over a year after they had been arrested and yet all of them inexplicably remembered Gunnar during the same week.

These sudden, simultaneous shifts across multiple statements do not imply that, two years on from Gudmundur's disappearance, the suspects all concurrently remembered the same minute detail about a phone, a car or a witness. What they do suggest is that the investigators, whenever they realized that certain details in the statements could not possibly be factually correct, guided the suspects towards confessions that *could* be verified.

There is perhaps no greater sign of the suggestive, and perhaps coercive, questioning employed by the investigators than the miraculous, instantaneous transformation that occurs across a range of statements each time a new piece of evidence is discovered.

The cumulative effect of prolonged custody, psychotropic drugs, and numerous lengthy interrogations without legal counsel was to break down the suspects. They were at the whim of investigators who had the power to repeatedly extend their custody and to interrogate them for months on end. As the cases progressed, the minds of the suspects unravelled and the statements became more and more disparate. At times, it seems they barely knew what they were confessing to.

Hlynur Thor Magnusson remembers Erla compiling a written list of all the different people she had seen in Keflavik in relation to Geirfinnur's disappearance. 'I was absolutely sure that what she was saying was just a fantasy,' he says. She was mentioning figures including a minister in the Icelandic cabinet and a well-known merchant from Reykjavik. 'She could just as well have named the President of Iceland as being the boss who had murdered Geirfinnur,' he says. 'It was so absurd.' At one point, she accused JFK.

The Reykjavik police maintained in their final assessment that the suspects had provided deliberately false testimony and fabricated a number of stories. It seems far more likely that the intensity of custody meant the suspects were willing to say anything to alleviate the pressure they were under. Confessions poured out of them as they tacked between denying their involvement and affirming whatever the police wanted to hear.

What had been portrayed in the media as the duplicity of the suspects was, in fact, utter confusion.

This was when Schütz entered the picture.

From the start there was an air of superiority about Schütz, as if the entire enterprise of finding the culprits was beneath his expertise. In his memoirs he implies that the killers of Gudmundur and Geirfinnur had just been thugs, nothing like the ideologues from the Baader-Meinhof group he had pursued while working in West Germany. Yet despite his impressive track record, he was not a murder investigator. His experience lay in neutralising political plots.

Schütz wielded authority over his task force, the suspects and the lawyers working on behalf of the accused. Pall Palsson, Kristjan's lawyer, recalls observing the room in which the task force worked. On the walls were typewritten copies of different testimonies made by the suspects, and connecting them were dozens of pieces of string. Pall had not seen this investigative technique used in an Icelandic police station and while he stood and admired the handiwork, Schütz bustled in and barked, 'Who is this man?'

A voice replied that he was Kristjan's lawyer. Schütz demanded: 'Out with him!'

When Disa and the working group scrutinized the timeline, they could see that Schütz's arrival in Iceland during the summer of 1976 brought a concerted focus to smooth out the inconsistencies across a series of contradictory and imprecise statements.

For the suspects, Schütz's entrance was akin to spotting a lifeboat on the horizon after months adrift at sea. Saevar has spoken about how Schütz stood in his cell and pronounced that not even during the Nazi period had men been kept in such conditions. Schütz brought him tobacco and writing materials. Saevar was pleased. It felt like dealing with a human again. But then, Saevar says, Schütz's tone changed. He told Saevar he was there to bring the cases to a conclusion and that Saevar would be sentenced either way. If Saevar was cooperative, he would get a few years; if not, it could be life.

Erla, too, longed for an outsider to join the investigation. It was a chance to summon the strength to declare her innocence. The first time Erla met Schütz is quite a moment. It is difficult to verify the details, but when taken in the context of the disintegration of order in Sidumuli, this behaviour, inappropriate in the context of a criminal investigation, has the disturbing ring of truth.

Erla says she was in her cell when there was a sudden loud noise and the door was flung open. The prison warden demanded she remove her clothes and put on the heavy blanket he threw to her. It was coarse, made from grey wool of a peculiar heaviness, and wasn't big enough to cover her whole body.

The prison warden returned, and Erla was taken to another cell where she sat and waited. She could hear a commotion: people moving around outside and talking in low voices. Finally the door opened. Erla came out into the corridor. Standing there was a small man. Erla remembers that he had the brightest blue eyes, just like a child, but that the rest of his facial features were old. Around his eyes were wrinkles and his neatly trimmed hair was grey.

So much in this story is disembodied – right down to the literal absence of a cadaver – that somehow it feels appropriate that all communication with Schütz came through a translator, putting even the most important conversations at a slight remove. Schütz stared into Erla's eyes and spoke in a language that she didn't understand while the translator followed in his wake. Erla remembers that Schütz offered to shake her hand but that she was holding on to her blanket. She had to manoeuvre a way of greeting him without dropping it.

A few days later, Erla had an opportunity to speak to Schütz properly. She said she wanted to tell the truth, and he replied that he was glad to hear it. She launched into a retraction, telling Schütz that the things she had said about her brother and Magnus and the other men had all been a lie, and that she didn't know anything whatsoever about Geirfinnur's disappearance. Then she burst into tears. She felt utterly ashamed.

There was silence. Erla says Schütz looked at her with his bright, blue eyes. 'Do you think I am an idiot?' It took her a short while to process what he had just said. And then: 'If you think that I came here to play games, you are mistaken.' She was taken back to her cell.

Police notes provide a startling insight into how retractions made by the suspects were dealt with, especially once Schütz had taken the helm. On 15 October 1976, Schütz writes that Erla had declared she had not been in Keflavik. Repeatedly she tries to retract her statement, and repeatedly she is admonished. She is told that other suspects had already confirmed her testimony, rendering her retractions meaningless. The interrogation was called to a halt and Erla became upset. 'She seemed to be becoming hysterical,' wrote Schütz, 'and she hit the table again and again and screamed, "Nobody here believes me."' Her retraction was dismissed.

On 27 September 1977, Kristjan tried to retract his statements in court. He was asked why he had made these confessions if he now wanted to take them back. He told the judges that the police officers had asked him to confess and he thought he was not allowed to refuse them. 'I and the other charged were interrogated together without a statement being taken,' he said, 'and we were made to help each other remember events that had not happened but that the policemen thought had happened.' This was dismissed.

In a letter written by Orn Hoskuldsson to the judge Gunnlaugur Briem, Orn notes that he had not taken any notice of Saevar's attempted retractions because he 'knew better'.

It is this double narrative, where the suspects, viewed as conniving, struggled to untangle themselves from a bizarre web of lies, their every denial interpreted as dissimulation.

In interrogations Schütz used a technique of his own devising called the 'Indian' method. It consisted of asking a defendant questions about the cases in a non-linear order, by jumping from one subject to another. The rationale was that, by asking questions in a jumbled chronology, the defendant would have to answer without thinking, thereby making it difficult to lie. In practice, it was extraordinarily disorientating. The investigators believed they had arrested the culprits and if they squeezed them they would yield. But there was no concealed master plan for them to uncover.

Schütz was fully aware there was no evidence aside from the confessions. In his weekly report to the Minister of Justice, he expressed doubt that he was following the correct course. It was part of the reason he became so obsessed with finding the bodies and a more reliable suspect. Notes from the police reports indicate how the German investigator worked on suspects in interrogations in order to persuade them to say what he wanted them to say. One interview, on 7 August 1976, begins with Schütz telling Albert he did not think he was a criminal. Then, suddenly, the pressure intensifies. In the police report, Eggert N. Bjarnason writes:

> Schütz was certain that Albert must know where he had taken the body. But Albert claimed he couldn't remember. Schütz didn't believe him. Albert claimed that he wished he could remember where they had taken the body and buried it. Schütz reminded Albert that soon, after an undetermined amount of time, a very thorough search for the body would be conducted, using heavy machinery. Such a search would be very expensive, and Albert would be responsible for that.

Here Schütz's powers of persuasion are on full show. He flatters Albert, reasons with him, and bullies him, burdening Albert with the blame for the numerous failed, expensive searches conducted in the lava.

Schütz had certain answers in mind that he would guide the suspects towards, be that about where the bodies were located or who had driven what car, and he rejected retractions or contradictions as lies. When Albert tried to say he didn't know the whereabouts of the bodies, he was told he was mistaken; when Erla said she hadn't been in Keflavik, she was scolded. Interviews with suspects were taken with the specific purpose, as written in the police notes, of 'reinforc[ing] confessions'.

As a foreign consultant, legally he was only allowed to oversee the cases. Subsequent to his arrival, however, the investigation was shaped in his image. Out of half-remembered evenings, snatches of dreams, and warped memories, Schütz spun a narrative so compelling that it convicted six suspects in court, as well as in the minds of the general public. There was no significant evidence of any wrongdoing, but he had woven together a story that convinced a nation. He had corralled the smoke.

None of this explained the most intriguing mystery at the heart of the investigation.

Even after the suspects had been convicted, many of them did not retract their confessions. Erla did not take back her testimonies in the Gudmundur and Geirfinnur cases until 1980. As late as Saevar's first bid for retrial in 1994, Albert and Gudjon had not retracted theirs. Some of the key confessions, Erla and Saevar's first Gudmundur statements for instance, had seemingly been made before any abuse had taken place in Sidumuli.

For those who believed the right individuals were convicted, these facts, perhaps above all others, proved the Supreme Court's judgement had been sound.

In October 2011, Ogmundur approached Gisli Gudjonsson, the forensic psychologist who had first received Tryggvi's diaries in autumn 2011, to request his participation as an expert on the committee. Using evaluative methods that had not been available during the trials in 1977 and 1980, Gisli and the psychologist Jon Fridrik Sigurdsson began to analyse the reliability of the confessions.

For Gisli, it was like his working life had come full circle.

Gisli grew up in Reykjavik and had once flirted with the idea of being a police officer. But while his twin brother joined the Reykjavik Criminal Investigation Police, Gisli took a degree in social sciences at Brunel University in London.

In 1975, when he was still an undergraduate, Gisli undertook a work placement as a detective in Reykjavik. Gisli interrogated a man with a history of alcohol-fuelled memory blackouts about whether or not he had stolen a purse. The man confessed to committing the crime. But when the police continued their investigation, they realized something strange: no purse had been stolen.

Gisli was left to reflect on how his suggestive questioning might have influenced the suspect. It was the start of a career that has seen him act as a forensic psychologist in hundreds of cases of false confession across the globe.

He had been present in Sidumuli when the suspects in the Gudmundur and Geirfinnur cases had been held in custody in 1976. Although he had not worked on the investigation, he had conducted lie detector tests with many of them as part of his MSc dissertation in clinical psychology. What interested Gisli was how each suspect made a detailed confession relating to their involvement in two murders, and yet not one of them could provide any reliable information as to where the bodies were hidden. It seemed to Gisli at the time as though these young people might have suppressed their memories of the crimes.

Over the years, many figures, including Saevar and Sigursteinn, had attempted to persuade Gisli to assess the evidence, but he had refused to be drawn into the orbit of the cases unless new material was discovered. To the astonishment of the working group, Gudjon also produced some diaries he had kept while held in custody, casually handing them over during an interview in late 2011. Now there were two sets of diaries to examine.

Gisli officially retired on 1 January 2012. But on 30 January he returned to Reykjavik, to the city where he had grown up and where his interest in false confessions had been sparked, to work on two cases that had been unfolding under his nose in Sidumuli when he was a young man at the start of his career, and which had been rumbling on in the country of his birth for the span of his working life.

8

MEMORY OF A MURDER

Confessions are convincing. Evidence can be tampered with, accusations can be fraudulent, but for someone to admit responsibility for a crime is uniquely persuasive.

There is so little incentive to confessing to a crime that it seems illogical for a confession to be anything other than honest. To confess is to unburden, to expose the soul's dark iniquities, to divulge an unpleasant secret to the impassive profile of the priest. If a scale were made measuring how believable we find people's claims about themselves, then on one end would be implausible brags about material wealth or sexual prowess, and on the other would be confessions, those admissions of a much darker hue, whose credibility is upheld by how poorly they reflect on the confessor.

Confessions consistently prove to be the most persuasive type of legal evidence. In a 1997 experiment conducted by Saul M. Kassin and Holly Sukel, mock juries were shown different descriptions of a murder case, either based upon eyewitness testimony of the crime, material evidence or a suspect's confession. Their findings suggested that those presented with the confession were far more likely to believe the suspect was guilty. Even in situations where the confession had been to some degree coerced, participants still found it to be the most convincing evidence when reaching their verdict.

In real-life cases, too, courts have acknowledged the unique power confessions have to change the outcome of a case. In the famous 1968 case of *Bruton v. United States*, George Bruton and William Evans were tried together in the aftermath of their having robbed a jewellery shop. The judge admitted as evidence a confession Evans had made to a postal inspector, in which he named Bruton as his accomplice. The judge told the jury to disregard this confession in the context of Bruton's case because it was inadmissible hearsay. Both men were convicted and Bruton appealed. The Supreme Court reversed the lower court's decision on the grounds that, although the jury had been instructed not to pay attention to Evans's confession, it would have impossible for them not to be substantially prejudiced against Bruton. Confessions, argued the Supreme Court, 'are probably the most probative and damaging evidence that can be admitted'. By virtue of it being heard in court, Evans's confession, although legally inadmissible, had corroded any trust that the jury might have had in Bruton's innocence.

Confessions often prove so compelling that even substantial evidence to the contrary cannot disprove them in court. Days after the Great Fire of London a French watchmaker named Robert Hubert insisted he was guilty of starting the blaze. He claimed he had thrown a fireball through a bakery window. The claim was significantly undermined, however, by three facts: first, he was too infirm to throw; second, the bakery didn't have a window; and third, he had been aboard a ship in the North Sea when the fire had started. Based on his confession alone, he was executed.

This is an example of a voluntary false confession. These are made without any apparent police coercion, perhaps due to the notoriety of the case, as a means of attracting attention, of protecting the real criminal from detection, or as part of an unconscious compulsion to make amends for a previous wrongdoing.

When a false confession is not voluntary, then it has been coerced. In most instances, the individual making the confession knows what they are admitting to is false, but their desperation to reduce the intensity of custody or interrogation becomes too great to bear. In the 1936 case of *Brown v. Mississippi*, a lynch mob descended upon three black farmers and beat them until they confessed to the murder of a white plantation owner named Raymond Stuart. As the whippings progressed the farmers adjusted the details of their confessions so as to conform to the demands made by their torturers.

False confessions are rarely provoked through such physical methods, but non-violent investigative procedures are no less exacting. Extensive custody, exhausting interrogations and lengthy solitary confinement are the psychological equivalents of the belt whips across the farmer's back.

There is a third type of false confession. It is called an 'internalized false confession'. These confessions are also coerced but are more intimately associated with the fallibility of memory than either the voluntary confession made by the Great Fire watchmaker or the confession lashed from the three farmers. These are perhaps the most convincing confession in a legal context because they are not always retracted in court even though they are false. This is because an internalized false confession is made when a person comes to believe they have committed a crime of which they are innocent.

We place faith in confessions because we consider memory a generally reliable archive. Although we might not remember going to the park with a friend last year, we would expect to retain a detailed recollection of something as intensely memorable as witnessing or being involved in a crime, and we would be impervious to any attempt to make us believe otherwise.

Experiments conducted by researchers specializing in memory and false confessions show this assumption to be flawed. There are few more troubling signs of the unreliability of memory than the ease with which false memories can be implanted. Test subjects have been induced to give detailed autobiographical accounts of a wide variety of 'memories' that they never actually experienced, ranging from being attacked by a dog to having tea with The Prince of Wales. Half the participants in an experiment from 2002 developed false memories of flying in a hot-air balloon as a child after they were shown a doctored image and interviewed about it three times.

An experiment conducted in 2015 went a step further: the forensic psychologists Julia Shaw and Stephen Porter successfully implanted false memories relating to committing a serious crime. After gathering background information from the parents of each participant, all of whom were students at McGill University in Canada, Shaw and Porter interviewed their test subjects about memories they had of real events from their childhood. They gently prompted the students to remember whether they had been involved in any criminal acts as teenagers. The tone of the questioning was not coercive, yet 70 per cent of participants developed false memories of committing a theft, an assault, or an assault with a weapon. They gave elaborate confessions, often adding further detail to their statements at each time of asking. All that was needed was an insistent suggestion from an authoritative source and the students soon generated highly detailed accounts of a crime that had never taken place.

Although fascinating, the implications of these findings are disquieting. We would like to think we would remember something as extreme as attacking another person with a weapon, yet these experiments suggest our memory, such a large part of how we constitute our own identities, can be easily tricked: that we can come to believe we have committed acts of which we did not think ourselves capable, and that our sense of who we are is as vulnerable to change as a distant memory we try to recollect.

When the Gumundur and Geirfinnur cases were in court in 1977 and 1980, no substantial research had been undertaken on the relationship between false confession and memory. Gisli Gudjonsson, along with his colleague James MacKeith, devised the term 'memory distrust syndrome' in 1982 to refer to the profound doubts people develop about their memory that can lead, specifically in criminal investigations, to these types of confessions.

Generally there has to be a reason why the suspect being interviewed or interrogated might distrust their memory. It could be that a lot of time has passed since the night in question or that the individual has a history of substance abuse. Perhaps they believe they have repressed something traumatic. Maybe they sleepwalk.

In most instances, the suspect will be isolated. Not exclusively the domain of solitary confinement, it is more meaningful to think of isolation in terms of a person being cut off from anyone other than their investigators. When a suspect is in custody the investigator can become inquisitor and caregiver rolled into one, the person who establishes the day's rhythm, from bathroom breaks to recreation time, while also representing the suspect's sole avenue out of their predicament. A lawyer is vital in diluting the effects of isolation. Otherwise, the investigator can become the suspect's entire world.

The tone of the interrogations is vital. The sense, either implicit or explicit, that the situation in which the suspect finds themself is serious and that continued denials will prove futile, increases the probability that memory distrust will develop. More insidious than the table-banging, coffee-swilling, good-cop-bad-cop routine championed by television police dramas, persuasive interrogation can be as simple as telling the suspect that there is a perfectly good reason why they cannot remember something. They were drunk, drugged, highly emotional, asleep. The blank canvas of a forgotten night becomes populated with suggestions made by the police or embellishments from a suspect encouraged to imagine what might have taken place.

At the heart of memory distrust is a failure to remember a distinctive detail. Let's say that a friend talks to you about a trip to a restaurant from a year ago but you cannot remember it. At first you think your friend is mistaken, but then they remind you about a rude waiter who refused to give you tap water. Suddenly, from this one detail, the memory fills out. You remember the waiter's face, the food you ordered, and what the room looked like. Daniel L. Schacter, a Professor of Psychology at Harvard

University, writes that rich and detailed visual imagery can be thought of as a 'kind of mental signature of true recollections': it is what makes our memories credible to us.

When you are unable to say, 'Actually I was at home watching the Highland Games,' it becomes much more difficult to reject the possibility you might have done something you cannot remember. Your ability to produce a convincing alibi might come down to whether you mentally encoded a banal detail from a night you never expected to have to recall.

In early February 2012, Gisli and Jon Fridrik began to assess the statements made by the suspects using the method that has become the gold standard for evaluating whether confessions are false. They wove together background information from the cases, police reports, court reports, individual testimonies, interviews with the defendants and witnesses, and the psychiatric and social history of the defendants to create as full a picture as they could of the investigation.

Ostensibly, the suspects had good reason to distrust their memories. The period of time that had passed between the disappearances and their arrest meant it was nigh on impossible for them to remember what they had been doing on the nights in question.

Crucially, each of the suspects found it plausible that they might be involved. Perhaps the most haunting aspect of the experiment conducted at McGill University in 1951, in which students lay down and had their senses restricted, was how amenable they became to ideas that were patently false. At different intervals, the test subjects were played a recording of a talk that strongly argued for the existence of supernatural phenomena. When the attitudes of the students were tested before and after, it became apparent that isolation had made them far more susceptible to the possibility that spirits existed. According to Woodburn Heron, one of the experiment's researchers, many of the subjects reported that, for several days following the test, they remained petrified they were going to see ghosts.

In the Gudmundur and Geirfinnur cases, everything the suspects were being questioned about possessed a degree of plausibility. Saevar was involved in suspicious activity, Kristjan and Tryggvi had committed crimes, and there were nights when Erla had no idea where Saevar was. All of the suspects have spoken about how different 'possibles' were presented to them by the police until they agreed; suggestions that were unlikely, but which they were not able to entirely discount. They could not say, with complete conviction, what they were doing on a particular night from two years back. Against this void a false belief began to take shape.

The night in the cells six days after Erla had been arrested is the foundation for the most crucial moment of memory distrust and internalized false confession in the Gudmundur and Geirfinnur cases.

On the evening of 19 December 1975, shortly after she was interrogated for the first time about Gudmundur Einarsson, Erla lay in bed and began to think about whether she might have witnessed something awful. It seemed highly improbable to her that Saevar might be mixed up in serious crime. But it was possible. She thought more about her nightmare.

It was difficult to distinguish between what she could remember from two years ago and what she had dreamed. Did something terrible happen in Hamarsbraut 11? Could Saevar have committed murder? Where did he go at night? Following six days of exhausting custody, during which she was desperate to be returned to her baby, these questions battered at Erla's resolve. That she signed a confession on 20 December implicating Saevar and Kristjan in Gudmundur's disappearance shows how a tiny doubt, which begins as a hairline fissure in whatever certainties you hold, can widen into a gap large enough for the phantoms of your unconscious mind to pour through.

Reading the confession in the present day, over forty years after it was taken, is bizarre. Maybe my interpretation of the statement has been coloured by Erla saying that she was pressured into making it. The final words on the page drift between the intensity of detail that we associate with authentic recollection and a level of imprecision that seems unusual in the context of such a startling and memorable occurrence. There is something slippery and unreal about the document, as if it very much evokes the difficulty of trying to remember something you have just dreamed.

The statement is moulded by the topography of her depression during those months at Hamarsbraut 11. She sleeps fully clothed because, as with the cigarettes, she cannot muster the strength to engage in basic tasks. Saevar, an intense personality who denounces her friends as fools, manages the situation, telling the others to stay calm, and controlling how Erla responds to what she is experiencing. Elements of the nightmare are folded in: the presence of Kristjan and another man; the noises heard from her bed; the missing sheet; the sense that the action is all happening off-screen. And throughout it all a curious lack of agency – she is frozen, nailed to the floor, and unable to move.

To Erla, her powerlessness is part of the police's attempts to make it seem as though something incredibly disturbing had occurred. She sees it as a dramatic device: her sense of detachment is supposed to imply trauma. This is one of the reasons that, for her, make it so obviously fictitious: it is the sort of device that is used in fiction, not in a criminal statement.

But whether this is a realistic depiction of how someone might respond to a traumatic sight is beside the point. The statement's value lies in its representation of Erla's mental state: it contains all the fears, neuroses, doubts and dreads that Erla had been accumulating during the months she had spent in the no-man's-land of Hamarsbraut 11.

Or maybe it is the other way round. Another way of thinking about it is that the story Erla tells about her life at Hamarsbraut has been adapted retrospectively in order to fit the confessions wrung out of her as a vulnerable twenty- year- old. It is hard to tell whether the odder parts about her nightmare and its aftermath, details vital to understanding her story yet difficult to verify, are so strange because they have the ring of truth or because she had to bend the story of her life to fit the startling details of the confessions.

Regardless, the statement conveys the paranoia that had been a small, but real part of her relationship with Saevar, and which was a vital component in her memory distrust. 'They really worked on convincing me what a rotten human being he was,' she says. 'They knew about the girls that Saevar had been with when he betrayed me in that way and they really got into that.'

She was resistant at first, assuring them that he wasn't the man that they thought he was. But she felt enough uncertainty about him to begin to be persuaded. 'They formed a crack in my mind,' she says, 'and they got in there and worked on it with questioning.'

The day after she made her statement, Erla says she was phoned by the police and told that Saevar had confirmed, in detail, everything she had claimed in her own statement.

In reality, Saevar's first Gudmundur confession, made seemingly before maltreatment in Sidumuli began, had been nowhere near as clear-cut as Erla was led to believe. On 22 December 1975 the police report states that Saevar denied any knowledge about Gudmundur. The opening section of Erla's statement was read to Saevar. Only after hearing part of Erla's account did Saevar say that he knew something about the disappearance. He told police a confrontation had taken place in the flat at Hamarsbraut 11 and ended with Gudmundur's death. He is not quoted verbatim. The statement merely summarizes the gist of what he supposedly said.

Oddly, the police report that contains the information about Saevar's 22 December 1975 confession has clearly been written in haste: there are pointless repetitions and it is littered with spelling mistakes. Neither Saevar's signature nor Saevar's lawyer Jon Oddsson's signature is on the document.

It is curious, too, that the police would not take a more detailed report from Saevar when, in effect, he was confessing to having witnessed a brutal murder. This first confession of Saevar's, perhaps the most important in the entire case in that it bolsters Erla's strange nightmare statement and implicates Albert and Tryggvi, two hitherto unmentioned men, should have been meticulously documented. Instead it is shoddily put together and different in appearance to other police reports taken during the investigation. It is the report's brevity that makes it suspect.

It is impossible to prove conclusively whether the statement is fraudulent or not, but what is clear, at the very least, is that Erla's testimony from the nightmare was presented to Saevar. Saevar did not independently confess to the same story as Erla.

While the police reports suggest Saevar confessed on 22 December 1975, Sacvar maintains that what appears to be his second statement, made on 4 January 1976, is actually his first. Saevar says investigators Eggert and Sigurbjorn Vidir had promised him he would be released if he stated he had been at Hamarsbraut 11 on the night of Gudmundur's disappearance. 'I wanted nothing more than to be with my girlfriend and my child,' wrote Saevar about the forces that compelled him to confess.

But having confessed on 4 January, he was not released. Instead Saevar was taken for a drive where, according to him, he was threatened and beaten.

Sunday, 4 January 1976

8.00 p.m.   Saevar was taken for interrogation.

10.00 p.m.   Orn Hoskuldsson arrived. [. . .]

11.00 p.m.   The trio [Orn, Eggert and Sigurbjorn Vidir] took Saevar for a car trip. Returned at 12.10 a.m.

12.15 a.m.   Orn, Eggert and Vidir left.

01.50 a.m.   Saevar was answered, he had thrown up and got a nosebleed and complained of chest pain.

08.00 a.m.   [. . .] Saevar was observed from time to time all night and is feeling better now, but didn't sleep until he started nodding off near the end of the shift.

This is the original Sidumuli prison log entry for 4 January 1976. Saevar, in a book he co-wrote with Stefan Unnsteinsson, describes a car journey that could be a description of that night. 'They drove me to the lava fields at Hafnarfjordur,' he wrote, 'where they claimed we buried the boy. They handcuffed me with my hands behind my back and struck me repeatedly, asking where we had taken the boy. I said they must be mistaken, but I couldn't take much. They said they were going to bury me in the lava fields [. . .] I was convinced that they were going to kill me.'

Saeavar's recollection gives the entry in the prison log a different complexion. Back in his cell, Saevar's battered body kept him up all night, his nose bleeding, his chest bruised. When Gunnar Gudmundsson, the prison warden, gave a version of this day's log entry to Saevar's lawyer before trial, both the 1.50 a.m. and 8.00 a.m. entries describing the nosebleed and the sleepless night were omitted.

Up until that point, Saevar had been resistant. If we take his 22 December statement to be a forgery, then he had held out for three weeks in custody without making any mention of Gudmundur. But on 4 January, with the promise of release dangled in front of him, he confessed to having been a witness to Gudmundur's disappearance. On 6 January, after the late night car trip, he confessed to more substantial involvement. On 11 January, when he was brought before Orn in court, he recanted, saying that he wanted to press charges for being forced to sign a testimony that he knew nothing about. But it was too late. The investigators had their confession.

When Erla heard Saevar had confessed to killing Gudmundur, her small misgivings became much larger. It is the key moment of memory distrust in Erla's confessions. The doubts she had been harbouring about Saevar found form. At that point, and for many years afterwards, she believed that what she confessed to might have been true. Her nightmare was real.

'I could not remember this in any normal way,' she says, 'All I had were images of things that were forming when we were talking about it. Just like when you are reading a story and you see it in your mind.' The nightmare was not an unconscious expression of a suppressed traumatic event. There was no truth concealed beneath its evocative imagey. Instead, this dream, which seemed to tap into her anxiety that Saevar might not be all that he seemed, became the foundation for a murder case. The nightmare then seeped into all the different statements about Gudmundur's disappearance.

Albert, the yes-man who quickly confessed to driving Gudmundur's body to the lava fields near Hafnarfjordur, had good reason to distrust his memory. He had used drugs in his teenage years and had difficulty distinguishing between past events in his mind.

From the moment Albert was arrested, he was left in little doubt that he was tangled up in something monumental. On 22 December 1975, the same night a statement was allegedly taken from Saevar in which he implicated Tryggvi and Albert, the investigators moved to apprehend the two men. But Albert was not in Reykjavik. He was on the other side of the country, in the pretty coastal town of Seydisfjordur in the east, preparing to celebrate Christmas with his fiancée and her parents.

The Reykjavik police contacted the magistrate in Seydisfjordur but he refused to arrest Albert without a warrant, so the investigators called the Ministy of Justice at midnight to arrange for Albert to be collected. A plane was chartered. Albert was picked up from Seydisfjordur in the early hours of the morning and immediately flown to Reykjavik. Although Albert had the legal status of a witness, his midnight pick-up was more in keeping with the kind of dramatic set-piece reserved for a high-profile mafioso boss.

Albert trusted that the investigators would only question him if there were grounds for doing so. This made it easier for him to accept that he must have been involved. Police reports show that, before he made his statement, Albert was informed that Saevar had implicated him in the disappearance of a young man. There were details he could remember: he often drove Saevar around; he had visited Hamarsbraut 11 in the past.

On 23 December 1975 Albert confessed he had information on the Gudmundur mystery. Carefully he explained how he had received a call from a phone that didn't exist and then driven to Hamarsbraut 11 in a car that had not yet been purchased. He says police led him towards certain answers: he could not remember, so the investigators remembered for him. When Albert was quizzed as to where Gudmundur's body was hidden, he answered 'yes' to every cemetery suggested to him.

Four days later, Albert went berserk. The prison log notes drily that 'Albert went mad for a short while. He broke his chair, which was not actually supposed to be there, so we had to put his hands and feet in chains.' He had been sentenced to forty-five days in custody.

In March 1976, a psychologist by the name of Geir V. Vilhjalmsson carried out a series of hypnosis sessions in order to 'direct [Albert's] consciousness back in time' and 'sharpen' his recollections. Hypnosis does sometimes aid criminal investigations. In the same year Albert was being hypnotized, a similar procedure brought about a stunning resolution to a strange case in the USA. Twenty-six schoolchildren and a bus driver were kidnapped by a group of masked men in Chowchilla, California, and incarcerated six feet underground in a quarry. It took them sixteen hours to dig themselves out. Miraculously, they were unharmed.

California State Police questioned the bus driver to see if he could provide them with any information. He couldn't remember anything. But when placed under hypnosis, he succeeded in summoning, from the depths of his memory, almost every single digit from the number plate on the hijackers' getaway vehicle. The owner of the quarry and his sons were arrested and eventually sentenced to life in prison.

Yet instances such as this are rare. There is little scientific proof that hypnosis is beneficial in criminal investigations. On the contrary, in a custody situation where a suspect already doubts their powers of recollection, hypnosis can muddle the source and chronology of their memory.

During hypnosis sessions Albert was compelled to travel, in his mind, down roads he might have driven to hide Gudmundur's body. He was taken on physical trips to multiple locations on the outskirts of Hafnarfjordur: to an aluminium plant, to the harbour, to a road next to the Sea Creature Museum. His statements changed week by week. As the investigators searched the lava fields, Albert's memory of where he had driven changed to fit wherever the next hunt for the body might be.

The associated police report states that, should the search prove unsuccessful, they could attempt to place Albert into a deeper hypnotic state to mine further information from him. But there were no buried memories to retrieve. The hypnosis just made him more and more confused.

Following his release from custody, Albert told the police, 'There is something wrong in my head. I know I took part in [Gudmundur's murder] and that I should be able to tell you everything, but even though I try, I have a hard time distinguishing between fantasy and reality.' He could not provide a single detail about the fate that had befallen Gudmundur, but the investigative method had left him convinced the answer must be somewhere in his mind.

Albert has never fully recovered from the investigation. Although he can rationalize that he did not have any involvement in the disappearance of Gudmundur, he will never be entirely sure. Albert said in 1997 he could no longer 'assert' that he was at Hamarsbraut 11 on the night Gudmundur disappeared. It is a haunting lack of conviction. Those endless drives through the dirt roads, in reality and in his dreams, had left him unsure of whether he had been involved.

The only figure from the working group whom Albert would speak to was Gisli. 'When I saw him in 2012,' says Gisli, 'he told me that he dreads the possibility that perhaps he *had* seen something. After almost forty years, the man still believes that perhaps there is something he witnessed that is going to come flooding into his mind and disturb him greatly. So to this day he is living in fear. Imagine living with the thought that perhaps you had witnessed a murder and having that in the back of your mind for forty years.'

At times, memory distrust seemed to have left the suspects brainwashed. Hlynur Thor Magnusson, who joined a number of the excursions out into the lava, recalls how sincerely the prisoners looked for the bodies. 'Kristjan *wanted* to find a corpse. He was really looking around and trying to remember.' Hlynur did not feel like Kristjan was trying to mislead the police. Broken by solitary confinement, he seemed convinced that he could help solve the mystery. He searched in the crevices of the lava fields for traces of something he thought he might have done.

Hlynur recalls being down one of the fissures in the lava when a shadow fell across him. He looked up and there was Kristjan. The police officer accompanying them was some distance away and so Hlynur was alone with Kristjan, a man who, in the words of the Reykjavik police report, could be gripped by a 'killing lust'. Hlynur says that if Kristjan had wanted to kill him, it would have been easy – there were plenty of large rocks that could have been thrown down upon him. Kristjan stood above him with his dark hair whipped up by the wind. 'But I was absolutely not afraid that Kristjan Vidar would do anything. This was not someone who wanted to cause me harm – absolutely not.'

In the National Archives in central Reykjavik there are some startling photos of Kristjan taken during the investigation. The police photographer clearly had an eye for a shot. They depict Kristjan at the dry dock, shortly after his suicide attempts, with the snowy mountains behind him and a cloud-streaked sky overhead.

He stares at a point behind the photographer. On the ground in front of him is a tangle of limbs and the hunched body of a beaten-up mannequin. There are numbered markers all around Kristjan, indicating where Gudjon and Saevar stood and where Geirfinnur fell. There is a car parked nearby, representing the

vehicle the suspects had driven to Keflavik. Kristjan's bell-bottom
jeans graze the ice.

The photos document a re-enactment of Geirfinnur's murder
carried out at Keflavik dry dock on 23 January 1977. Schütz had
organized this in order to examine how the defendants responded
when on location. 'Once you've enacted something, you're showing
them how they did it and it may reinforce that memory,' says
Gisli. 'It may have a damaging effect in the sense that, if it's false,
people may actually begin to think that it did happen like that.' In
another photo Kristjan glumly holds a police officer in a headlock,
physically acting out how Geirfinnur's death had happened. In
interrogations, corroboration meetings, alone in their cells, and
now in a re-enactment, the suspects ran through a story about
smuggling and Geirfinnur and a fight at the dry dock that eventually took root in their minds.

Although Kristjan is still alive, it was strongly recommended
that he should not be approached for interview in light of how
damaged he has been left by an investigation conducted when he
was practically a boy.

In terms of the intensity of the interrogations and the investigative methods employed, as well as the vulnerabilities of the
suspects involved, the Gudmundur and Geirfinnur cases were
something of a perfect storm for memory distrust and internalized
false confessions. The suspects were vulnerable, isolated, and in
a situation of incredible intensity where their guilt, it seems, was
often assumed.

The only one of the suspects who did not develop memory distrust was Saevar. As with the belt-beaten farmers, his confessions
seem to have been made to escape temporarily from the pressure

he was under, though he does not appear to have ever doubted his own innocence. The key confession he made in the Geirfinnur case on 22 January 1976, which served to confirm much of Erla's account, was squeezed out of him under considerable duress. On 19 and 20 January he was interrogated for six hours each day, and on the night of the twentieth a female prison guard was ordered by the deputy prison warden to keep Saevar awake. On 22 January Saevar was interrogated for ten-and-a-half hours. Parts of Erla's Geirfinnur testimony were presented to him and, despite having denied involvement up to that point, he consequently confessed to driving to Keflavik with Einar and Magnus.

The other five suspects, though, at times believed that they had either witnessed or been involved in a serious crime for which there is no substantial evidence of their involvement.

On 21 March 2013, the working group handed their 486-page report to the Minister of the Interior.

In their chapter in the report, Gisli and Jon Fridrik wrote that the confessions made by all six of the suspects were unreliable beyond reasonable doubt.

It is difficult, of course, to make claims about the reliability of statements from more than forty years ago, but in the case of Gudjon, it was possible to state that memory distrust had caused his confessions to not just be unreliable, but false.

The working group were able to make such a confident assertion because of the diaries Gudjon had kept while in custody. Gudjon's diaries differed from Tryggvi's diaries in that they started four days after his arrest. They documented over thirteen months in Sidumuli, their final entry dated 27 December 1977. They had not been opened for thirty-five years.

Gisli has worked on over five hundred criminal cases and he believes Gudjon's diaries are absolutely unique. 'It's the only case I know of,' says Gisli, 'where you've got detailed diaries of a suspect's mental processes which demonstrate, without doubt, his memory distrust and how it developed and progressed over time.' They provide a fascinating insight into how someone can come to believe they were responsible for a crime they probably had nothing to do with.

The diaries are very credible. Gudjon's entries correspond with the prison logs, the police and court records, and the detectives' handwritten notes, some of which had never been made available prior to the working group's being granted permission to examine them. On 7 December 1976, for example, Gudjon writes about a journey to Keflavik with the investigators, and in both the prison logs and the police report there is a description of a trip made that same day. On 30 December 1976, Gudjon mentions long conversations with an investigator named Gretar Saemundsson and describes himself as shaking so much he could hardly eat. The prison log corroborates this, detailing how Gretar spoke with Gudjon late into the night and brought him cakes to eat in his cell.

Gudjon was taken into custody on 12 November 1976. In the years leading up to his arrest, he had dropped out of university, his marriage had fallen apart, his father had passed away, and he had been arrested after it was discovered he had been smuggling hash from Holland. In spring 1976, his doctor had suggested it might be advisable for him to check himself into a psychiatric ward. On some days he was apathetic and lethargic, on others he worked himself up into a kind of mania during which he could talk for twenty-four hours without a break.

Initially, Gudjon denied all involvement. He asserted that he had no knowledge relating to the disappearance of Geirfinnur Einarsson other than what he had read in the newspapers. He told police that the reason a notebook listing major events in the case had been found in his room was because, after being initially interviewed as a character witness for Saevar, he jumped to the assumption – correctly as it transpired – that he would be implicated somehow. He wanted a record of the different news articles from the days surrounding Geirfinnur's disappearance in case he should ever find himself being questioned about it.

Six days after his arrest, he had a panic attack. He felt guilty but he was not sure what about. His doubts about his mental state in the years preceding his arrest undermined his certainty that he was not involved. 'For two years I have had the belief that I did not know anything about this case,' he writes on 22 November 1976, 'but now I am supposed to have been very much involved [. . .] What game is God playing with me? Am I mentally ill, or have been? I would admit to that. Many of the things I have done in recent years were madness.' His claims of ignorance were rebuffed: 'Nobody believes that I can't remember anything.'

After ten days in Sidumuli, his resistance broke. The notion that he was a murderer crept up on him in the solitude of his cell. 'The nights are the worst,' he writes. 'I wait desperately to fall asleep but it is slow in coming and I have intrusive thoughts [. . .] If only I knew if I participated in this or not.' When asked whether he had played a role in the disappearance of Geirfinnur, he replied that he did not think that he had but he could not be sure.

Excursions to the 'scene of the crime' reinforced in him the idea that he was somehow involved. After accompanying the police in a car journey to Keflavik, Gudjon started to speak in vague terms about driving there with Saevar. When questioned as to why he could not remember such an important event, he replied that the death of his father had left him depressed.

His diary entries reveal a man battling with his conscience. 'I deceive people, that's the way it is. I am always acting, I am an ill man.' He needles himself about past misdemeanours. He urges the Lord to give him guidance, even if that means just giving him strength to confess. He searches for atonement, praying to God that he gets 'a heavy punishment and preferably a long one', to alleviate the guilt and confusion that cloud his thoughts.

Gudjon began to rely on Gretar Saemundsson, the police officer assigned to him. 'Gretar came and implied many things,' Gudjon wrote, 'and thinks I'm in a bad position in the case. He even wants me to get used to the thought of being a murderer.' Gudjon got along well with Gretar. He found it difficult to discount the idea that Gretar might be right. Gretar brought him copies of *Der Spiegel* to read and the two men played chess together in Gudjon's cell.

On 30 November, a police line-up loosened Gudjon's grip on his sanity. Although he asserted that he had never seen Kristjan before, Kristjan was easily able to identify him from a line-up of eight men. This was proof that Gudjon could not trust his own mind.

But the findings of the identification parade were misleading. A police report shows that when Gudjon was initially brought in for interview, Kristjan had been moved from his cell so that he could watch Gudjon. It was a charade: Kristjan knew who Gudjon was because he had been taken to see him months before.

A key stage that can occur in memory distrust is known as

'reconstruction'. Once a suspect has come to accept that a certain event could well have happened, and that it is plausible that they either participated in or witnessed this event, they begin to construct their own memory of it.

Gudjon became increasingly determined to remember what part he played in Geirfinnur's disappearance. If the police said he had committed a crime then surely they had their reasons. Gudjon sat in his bare cell and willed the memory to come. He prayed to God. Night by night, he grew more convinced that he might be involved, his 'memory' of events becoming more detailed as he created in his head a version of Geirfinnur's disappearance. At one point, he even wrote a screenplay about the cases.

His diary entry from 7 December 1976, the day before he makes his key confession, reveals a man torn apart by weeks spent doubting his own mind. While most passages in his diary are written in clear, lucid prose, here he just lists his ailments, as if he can barely summon the strength to think in full sentences: 'I am so tired, cannot remember anything, have difficulties talking, cannot think, cannot, dread tomorrow, know that it will all be the same, don't remember, know nothing, then I will be deprived of my sanity. I am totally exhausted.'

The next day, on 8 December, almost four weeks after his arrest, Gudjon told police he participated in an attack on Geirfinnur along with Kristjan and Saevar. The confession is vague, elliptical in style, and – instead of asserting his involvement – he says he cannot rule out the possibility. It would form the foundation for his, Saevar's and Kristjan's convictions in court.

He writes: 'Now I hope the body of the man will be found in the next few days and then the nation can be relieved.'

At the end of December, Gudjon received an unusual visit. On New Year's Eve, 1976, a young Gisli Gudjonsson came to Sidumuli to record a lie detector test as part of a student project. Gudjon was asked whether he knew who was involved in Geirfinnur's disappearance. He replied, 'Yes.' Gisli repeated the question. Now Gudjon really seemed to think about what he was being asked. He paused. And then he said, 'No.' Direct, impartial questioning about the case appeared to sharpen his focus. Now he started to wonder: 'Did I really do this? Was I really there?'

That night in his cell, Gudjon wept. 'Where are these bodies?' he writes. 'How should I know? I have a headache. Feel terrible.' Two days later, he began to seriously doubt his involvement. Being posed neutral questions had shaken him from his belief that he might have been responsible. 'Should I maybe retract all I have said? [. . .] I feel like I'm tangled in some incredible web of lies, there is never any light, I never see a clear sky. Success is harder to swallow than failure. It will be great when this Geir-finnur case has been solved. There is something strange about it, especially I find the lack of memory to be strange, this has never happened to me sober, that I don't remember anything. What happened really, did I not go to Keflavik 19/11/74 but some other night?'

When Karl Schütz returned from his Christmas holidays on 4 January 1977, he was incandescent with rage. Schütz refused to countenance the possibility that his German-speaking star witness might retract his statement. Without Gudjon, the confessions relating to Geirfinnur were too contradictory, and the remaining suspects too untrustworthy. He wrote a letter of complaint to the Reykjavik courts and sent a copy to the Ministry of Justice. 'It was expected of Gudjon that he clear up the last issues that were in doubt,' Schütz explained. 'The whole investigative method used on him was aimed towards that.'

Schütz began to turn the screw. In his diary entry four days after Schütz's return, Gudjon writes that they 'are now coming harder at me, breaking me down by not talking to me, forbidding the priest to come, stalling letters and packages etc.'. Then he dismisses this as his own insecurity: 'you can get so paranoid and full of hate being isolated like this.' Less than a month later, on 2 February 1977, Schütz declared the case to be solved and promptly returned to West Germany. Gudjon was convicted of killing Geirfinnur that December. He did not retract his confession for nearly two decades.

I came away from my first meeting with Gudjon thinking maybe he knew what had happened to Geirfinnur. If he was innocent, then why wasn't he beating the table with his fists and declaring he had been wronged? He seemed ambivalent about whether he had played a part. It was off-putting.

However, as I spent more time with him, I began to realize that his avoidance of earth-shattering pronouncements was not an indicator of guilt but of temperament.

He is out of step with how we expect, or, perhaps, how we want, a victim of a miscarriage of justice to behave. He replies to questions from odd angles, he avoids assertions, and only after hours of probing will he definitively say he was not involved. When he was asked recently by Valtyr Sigurdsson, one of the Keflavik investigators, about whether he had been to Keflavik on the night that Geirfinnur disappeared, he replied, 'Is it illegal to go to Keflavik?' His offbeat sense of humour and aversion to answering with certainty anything that he is not entirely confident about do not lend themselves to emphatic denials of guilt.

With Erla, there is a sense that this case stalks much of her daily existence. Gudjon has responded differently to life after conviction. More than any of those who were accused in the case, he seems to want to forget all about it, and is faintly puzzled that people are still interested. I could imagine being a friend of his for years without finding out he had been handed a ten-year sentence for involvement in a man's death. He served his time and tried not to give it any more thought. He took the opposite approach to Saevar and moved away from Iceland as soon as he could. 'I chose me,' Gudjon once told Thordis.

He sighs when asked whether it has been difficult to live in Iceland after returning from abroad. Mildly exasperated by the question, he replies: 'Since I was released, I have never met anyone in my short, sweet life who has thought that I was guilty. Never. Never heard of anybody even.'

He later admits that some members of his parish in West Iceland refused to let him conduct a service for their family member because of the case. But eventually they relented. He ended up burying one of those men themselves.

The people of Iceland, he says, had to receive some closure to the Geirfinnur case. An answer had to be found. 'So here I was to clear up the case,' he says, 'and I'm sorry that I couldn't clear it up, but I tried.' Someone had to take the blame and it just so happened to be him. 'We did as well as we could,' he says. It is an astonishingly phlegmatic response.

He reads aloud from his diary ironically, mocking the emotional tone of the passages written by his younger self. It's a defence, of course, because reading these extracts is painful. But it is also because he does not recognize the plaintive voice of this fragile young man, trapped in the machinations of a stubborn investigation.

Gudjon believes that, once the investigation had started, there was no way back for the police and the judges. He remembers his relationship with Gretar fondly: 'We were the same age. We were both country boys. We had a very nice time together but maybe he went too far. Maybe I also went too far.' The state had invested too much, both politically and financially, to forget about the case. So they just kept on going. 'And they knew how we would be judged.'

'You get tired', says Gudjon, 'you answer the same questions again and again. You don't know if you are dreaming or remembering things that possibly could have been a part of what we were talking about from two o'clock until seven o'clock. And then you start again and you talk with the deputy until five o'clock in the morning. And he is asking you the same questions again and again. Where were you two years ago? You have no proof of where you were: you were at home taking care of your kids. That is all. And maybe you could somehow prove that you were by saying "I remember watching television!" But I didn't have a television. I was not that lucky. My wife was not at home. So you can't prove it. And the proof is on you, not on the police, because you are the guilty one.'

Gudjon did not retract his confessions for the next nineteen years.

He describes the story of Geirfinnur's disappearance as getting confused with his dreams. 'You get it all muddled,' he says. 'You say "yes" to something that really didn't happen. It is a false memory. It came like a short clip, like a movie into my mind. Driving a car, an old Beetle car. I had these short clips. But I never had a car like that.'

He still has memories of that same moment, like replays of an old film, in which he drives to Keflavik at night down the long, dark road that carves through the lava fields, to play his part in a crime that probably didn't happen, to be on time for an appointment he never made.

9

SCAPEGOAT

It is nine o'clock in the morning on 28 January 2016 and I am standing in the foyer of the Reykjavik District Court. The sun is two hours from rising. Downtown is busy with people hurrying to work in the dark. At the end of the corridor to my left is a large, bald man standing with his face so close to the window that his spectacles are almost touching his reflection. From where I am it is impossible to see if he is staring at something in particular or just staring. I try to match up his face with photos I have seen of Schütz's task force. Is that the representative of the judge who led parts of the investigation? Is that Orn Hoskuldsson?

A photographer from *Morgunbladid* arrives and starts taking pictures of the group of journalists assembled outside the court-room door. Discreetly, I ask him whether it is Orn and he confirms. I weigh up whether to go over. I have spoken with him before, briefly, on the phone. Well, not really spoken 'with' but 'at'. During both calls I outlined who I was and what I was doing and asked whether I could speak with him, his response to which was to politely decline and hang up. Does he accept that the investigation was mismanaged? Does he still think that the right people were convicted? He watches the darkness through the glass. Then he turns from the window and enters the courtroom. I feel relieved and then annoyed at myself for feeling relieved.

The foyer of the district court that morning is a cavalcade of figures from the past. There is Sigurbjorn Vidir Eggertsson, the stocky, ruddy-faced police officer who became Erla's confidant; Ragnar Adalsteinsson, Saevar's lawyer, looking exactly the same as he did twenty years ago, except his brown hair has now turned white; Hafthor, Saevar's son, and his younger brother Sigurthor, who looks just like his father when he was a young man. Disa, Jon Fridrik and Gisli arrive. Three years after the publication of their report, in which they concluded that the confessions made by all six of the suspects were unreliable beyond reasonable doubt, members of the working group are here to be questioned by the state prosecutor to help determine whether the cases should be reopened.

Erla arrives wearing a long black-and-red coat and an expression that suggests she would rather be anywhere else in the world. The suspects were allowed to call witnesses and so Erla summoned Orn Hoskuldsson, Sigurbjorn Vidir Eggertsson and Eggert N. Bjarnason. It is a strange moment for Erla. She does not feel hatred for these men, but there is an undeniable satisfaction to be taken in seeing them under scrutiny rather than her.

Orn took to the stand. Staring up at him were a gallery of faces from the past: the woman who confessed to postal fraud in December 1975; the man who came into Sidumuli as a young forensic psychology student to conduct lie detector tests; and someone who looked just like Saevar did when he was first arrested. Orn gripped the lectern as though it were taking all of his weight.

Ragnar put it to Orn that it was unusual for a pair of arrests relating to postal fraud to have evolved into a missing persons investigation The police report stated that Erla had been questioned because the detectives had heard that her partner could possibly be involved in the disappearance of Gudmundur Einarsson. Quite aside from the irregularity of questioning someone who has been in custody for an entirely different case, why had this happened in the first place? Where had this rumour begun? Orn stated that he was not obliged to answer that question, to which Ragnar replied that, in fact, he was. Orn said that he could not remember.

And so began the theme of the morning. Sigurbjorn Vidir and Eggert (via telephone) responded similarly. Questions were answered with 'I don't remember' or 'I don't recall'. They contradicted each other and prevaricated. At one point Orn said that he had let the police officers get on with it, but later Sigurbjorn Vidir claimed Orn had been in charge. 'I find it incredible,' says Gisli, 'that investigators involved in the biggest case of their lives were unable to provide information as to why they started the investigation in the first place.'

When asked whether he would have done anything differently if given the chance, Orn replied that, yes, there were a lot of things he could have done better. 'It was good to hear him say that out loud in a court of law,' says Hafthor. Looking up at Orn, Hafthor saw a tired, old man. He didn't feel hate or a desire for revenge. He felt sorry for him. It was a relief to realize that was how he felt.

On Friday, 24 February 2017, the Rehearing Committee announced that five out of six of the defendants would have their cases reheard by the Supreme Court: Saevar and Kristjan for the killing of Gudmundur and Geirfinnur, Tryggvi for killing Gudmundur, Gudjon for killing Geirfinnur, and Albert for his involvement in Gudmundur's disappearance.

It had been a freak winter with barely any snow, but on the day that the findings were announced, and over the weekend that followed, record-breaking quantities fell from the clouds over Reykjavik. The next six days were equally unusual: clear blue skies and not a breath of wind. Along the pathways by the small park in the city centre the snow was stacked into pillars. They stood like silent sentinels around the perimeter of the pond.

It was a moment to savour for those who had spent years petitioning for the reopening. Hafthor wrote a post online articulating the mixed emotions he felt upon learning the fight begun by his father had finally resulted in a meaningful response from the authorities. It is not possible to explain in words, he wrote, the experience of being born into this injustice. Congratulations, Dad, your struggle and resilience have finally brought about this result.

But one charge has not been reopened: the perjury. As it stands, Erla, Saevar and Kristjan will remain charged with accusing the Klubburinn Four of involvement in Geirfinnur's disappearance.

Of course, there is no denying that the perjury did occur, and that it had very real consequences for those falsely accused. Magnus Leopoldsson, Einar Bollason and Valdimar Olsen each spent 105 days in custody, and Sigurbjorn Eiriksson spent ninety. But given the reopening of the other cases, it seems illogical that the perjury charge won't also be reheard. In theory, Saevar and Kristjan could now be exonerated for killing Geirfinnur, but remain charged, along with Erla, of wrongly accusing people so as to cover their involvement in something they weren't involved in. If they had nothing to do with Geirfinnur's disappearance then why would they blame other people for it? The reopening of the Geirfinnur case renders the perjury motiveless.

In comparison to killing Geirfinnur, the perjury charge might sound insignificant. But in a pair of cases where only the most committed advocates of the Supreme Court's 1980 ruling now believe there were sufficient grounds for convicting six people for killing Gudmundur and Geirfinnur, the perjury charge, it seems to me, is what is important. Reputation is everything in a country where anonymity is impossible. By refusing to reopen it, the damage caused by the cases themselves – which on both a societal and personal level has been considerable – is being left with Saevar, Kristjan and, perhaps most of all, Erla.

In a display cabinet at the Digital Forensics Unit in Iceland's State Criminal Investigation Police headquarters is a small bust of a man who made a phone call from a café more than forty years ago.

A police officer humours me and opens up the display so that I can handle it. I cup its satisfying weight in my palms. This brown statue and its inscrutable stare holds the secret to how this all began. I meet its gaze for a while and try to imagine it is the face of a living person who came and made a phone call in Keflavik before slipping into the night.

The Klubburinn Four is the most important thing to understand about the Geirfinnur case – and the most convoluted.

Erla asserts that, from the start, the investigating officers wanted her to implicate the manager and the owner of Klubburinn – Magnus Leopoldsson and Sigurbjorn Eiriksson – in Geirfinnur's disappearance. When it became clear that she and Saevar did not know who Sigurbjorn Eiriksson was, she claims they steered her towards implicating Einar, her half-brother, and Valdimar, the brother of her friend. This created a connection between Saevar, a well-known crook who had been arrested for smuggling in the past, and the men from Klubburinn. It was possible Saevar would know Einar and Valdimar through Erla, and they, in turn, were more likely to know the men from Klubburinn because of their close similarity in age, and the fact that Valdimar also worked in the nightclub industry.

In short, Erla is saying that there was always intent to implicate the men from Klubburinn, and that she was led towards accusing Einar and Valdimar as a way of making that accusation more feasible. It was plausible that Saevar and the men from Klubburinn might have killed Geirfinnur during a botched smuggling operation, and by accusing Einar and Valdimar the connection between all these men became more plausible still. 'If this can be proven then it would be a whole new ball game', says Einar. 'I am not sure what I would do, but it will be a completely new thing. It's one thing to have four young people accuse you of something after they have been threatened, but if it came from the police in the first place – wow. I can only say wow. Then it is really serious.'

On the night of Geirfinnur's disappearance, a man walked into the Hafnarbudin café in Keflavik. A likeness was made of his face. Before the three-dimensional portrait was created, a sketch artist spoke with eyewitnesses in the café and produced between fifteen and twenty different drawings of the man they had seen. But one of the sketches originated from a different source. Magnus Gislason, the sketch artist in question, says the police handed him a photo of a man's face and asked him to draw it for them. This sketch was then selected as the basis for the creation of the statue. The photo the police gave Gislason was of Magnus Leopoldsson. That's why the bust looked so much like Magnus: the sculptor was working from a picture of his face.

Gudlaug Jonasdottir, the woman who caught the best glimpse of the man who came into the café, was not consulted during the creation of the 'Clayfinnur'. Long before Erla and Saevar were arrested, there seems to have been intent to implicate Magnus Leopoldsson in Geirfinnur's disappearance.

One of the members of the original Keflavik investigation was a customs officer named Kristjan Petursson. Square-jawed and with a predilection for tinted aviator glasses, Kristjan Petursson's memoirs give the impression that he saw himself as a James Bond-like figure, his remit seeming to extend far beyond that of a regular customs officer. He appears to operate in the margins of the Geirfinnur case in all sorts of strange ways.

The proposed connection between Geirfinnur, smuggling and Klubburinn had always been tenuous. The sum of the evidence that even remotely linked these elements together was that Geirfinnur had visited Klubburinn two days before he disappeared and that, in a separate incident, he had allegedly made an agreement with an acquaintance to distil some alcohol. It seems a precarious foundation for an extensive investigation into Klubburinn. But by 4 December 1974, a fortnight after Geirfinnur disappeared, the story was already in the press: one Icelandic newspaper ran the headline 'The Keflavik Police wish to speak with the man who spoke to Geirfinnur Einarsson at 12 a.m., Sunday, 17 November, at the nightclub Klubburinn.'

Iceland has such a small population that it is easy to read into coincidences. It is inevitable the same names will appear in relation to different cases. There simply aren't that many members of law enforcement. But what is worth signposting is that, when Klubburinn was first investigated for tax fraud in 1972, Kristjan Petursson worked as one of the lead investigators. So, too, was Hallvardur Einvardsson, the assistant state prosecutor who played an active role in the Geirfinnur investigation.

In early February 1976, just after the Klubburinn Four were arrested, Kristjan Petursson appears on television news on RUV and states that the Geirfinnur case is related to Klubburinn and alcohol smuggling. When the Klubburinn Four are released in May 1976, multiple newspaper articles call for more investigations into Klubburinn and cite Kristjan Petursson as the chief source. On 14 May 1976, in an article in *Visir*, Vilmundur Gylfason writes that, although Magnus and Sigurbjorn Eiriksson have now been released, Klubburinn's financial affairs remain in need of further scrutiny. Using the 'indisputably logical' arguments of Kristjan Petursson as his basis, Gylfason asks why various payments made by Klubburinn had not been more closely inspected, and demands their business interests be investigated as far back as 1966.

Time and again, it is Kristjan Petursson who is directing attention towards the nightclub, whispering in the ears of politicians, journalists and investigators, and fanning the rumours that played a part in a string of convictions.

Why would Kristjan Petursson have wanted to drag Klubburinn

into the case? Was he genuinely convinced its owners were involved? Or was his motivation political? Kristjan had links to the same Social Democratic Party politicians who accused Olafur Johannesson in parliament. Was this a way to undermine Olafur Johannesson's Progressive Party? The Progressive Party had covered for Klubburinn in the past and they owned property with them in Reykjavik. By connecting Klubburinn to the Geirfinnur case, some of the SDP's chief political opponents were brought into disrepute.

We can only speculate. There is no proof of what motivated Kristjan Petursson. When he was interviewed in 1996, fifteen years before his death in 2011, he dismissed as 'ridiculous' the suggestion that he was responsible in any way for linking the Klubburinn fraud case and the Geirfinnur investigation. He said that he had absolutely nothing to do with the construction of the clay head.

It has long been the contention of the authorities that not just the names of the men from Klubburinn, but also the narrative associated with Geirfinnur, originated with Erla and Saevar: either because it was a crime they committed or a story they fabricated in order to perjure four innocent men. But there is one statement in the police files that completely undermines this thesis. It could finally explain where the story about what supposedly happened to Geirfinnur began.

On 22 October 1975, nearly two months before Erla and Saevar were arrested on suspicion of committing postal fraud, a nin-teteen-year-old boy named Arni Sigurdur Gudmundsson came to Reykjavik police station. He believed that his father was involved in the disappearance of Geirfinnur.

When the police questioned Arni's father, a forty-two-year-old hospital worker named Gudmundur Agnarsson, he told the officers that he had been drunk and showing off. He wanted to look like a big man in front of his family by pretending he knew what happened to Geirfinnur. Gudmundur Agnarsson was mentally unstable and had spent some time in Kleppur psychiatric institute. When the police arrested him, he had reportedly been drunk for a week.

The yarn Gudmundur Agnarsson spun his family was that he had become acquainted with the owner of Klubburinn, Sigurbjorn Eiriksson. Sigurbjorn Eiriksson knew that Gudmundur Agnarsson had formerly worked as a ship mechanic and so he requested his assistance in collecting some smuggled liquor near Keflavik harbour. The men were supposed to be meeting someone named Geirfinnur Einarsson. Magnus Leopoldsson came too.

They arrived late. Magnus Leopoldsson made a phone call from the café. Geirfinnur arrived and then he and Gudmundur Agnarsson set out on a small boat to collect the smuggled goods.

Sorties were made from the dry dock to the sea, each time Geirfinnur diving in to retrieve the alcohol and Gudmundur Agnarsson remaining on board. On the third such trip, Geirfinnur did not resurface. Gudmundur Agnarsson waited there for four hours before returning to shore.

Gudmundur Agnarsson told his family that the men from Klubburinn had pressured him never to tell anyone about these events. They had given him a cheque for 70,000 kronur, he said, to buy his silence, but when his son-in-law and children asked to see it, he refused.

Gudmundur Agnarsson's story is, in detail, what Erla, Saevar and Kristjan confessed to the following year: it includes the same people, the same motive behind the meeting, and the same manner of Geirfinnur's death. I am not suggesting these similarities imply this actually happened. What I am suggesting is that the drunken ramblings of a middle-aged man wanting to look important in front of his family is the template of the future narrative put forward about Geirfinnur's disappearance, right down to the exact amount of kronur purportedly handed over by the assailants.

The Reykjavik police knew about this story: police reports show Gudmundur Agnarsson and his family were interviewed on two occasions by the investigators following Erla and Saevar's arrest. 'They always seemed to have a story in mind,' Erla has said. Saevar, too, felt as though the police were leading him towards a particular story: 'They were always going to put the case of Gudmundur on us and use it to open the case of Geirfinnur,' Saevar said in an interview in 1996. 'We didn't know Sigurbjorn Eiriksson in Klubburinn, Magnus Leopoldsson or Valdimar Olsen in any way [. . .] How were we supposed to create a story about these men? We didn't know them. What were we supposed to have been doing in Keflavik? [. . . The investigators] thought they knew exactly what had happened – I only had to confirm it.'

Gudmundur Agnarsson told the police that his tall tale was based on nothing more than the gossip of the time. The story the investigators may have had in mind when they interrogated Erla and Saevar came from the booze-addled brain of a middle-aged man who had been reading too many breathless articles about smuggling and Klubburinn, gangsters and clay heads, and had concocted a story to impress his kids. The case caused nationwide hysteria because it tapped into fears about organized crime arriving on Icelandic shores, but what no one realized was that the opposite was also true, that the case was confected from the same hysteria. The Geirfinnur story was pieced together from different rumours that had been floating around in the press. It was a nation's nightmare writ large in a criminal case.

It is difficult to know how several salient aspects of this story became incorporated into Erla and Saevar's confessions. The police may have believed there was truth in what the hospital worker said and then directed their questions towards the suspects accordingly. But the notion that the narrative about Geirfinnur's demise originated with Erla and Saevar as a way of perjuring others is significantly undermined by the fact that the story existed, in detail, months before they were arrested.

In the police report compiled by Eggert N. Bjarnason on 10 March 1976, he implies that Erla first started to talk about Geirfinnur on her own volition around mid-January. In fact, as early as 5 January 1976 – weeks before the authorities allege Erla first mentioned Geirfinnur – the Reykjavik police requested that the Keflavik investigators send them all the files they possessed on Geirfinnur. They were already lining up the Geirfinnur investigation long before Erla, or any of the other suspects, supposedly spoke about him.

Magnus acknowledges that the investigation seemed geared towards eliciting a confession from him, but this does not dilute his anger towards Erla. 'Innocent people don't confess to stuff like this,' he says. 'That is nonsense. There may be some sick people that might do that. But people that are sane don't confess to things that they haven't done, it is complete nonsense that people say that you would confess after a week or something like that. Then I must be special. It is incredible what experts are trying to assert.'

Although Magnus does actually strike me as being especially

strong-willed, one of those rare personalities, like Saevar in some ways, exceptionally resistant to the pressure of an onerous police investigation, the answer is surely more prosaic: he was thirty years old, came from a steady background, had a secure job and enjoyed a comparatively settled home life. He had regular access to his lawyer. The same applied to the rest of the Klubburinn Four. These men were older, occupied respectable positions in society and had people who could vouch for their character. Sigurbjörn Eiriksson was nearly fifty and had actually been a police officer when he was a young man. He was well prepared for the interrogation process. Einar remembers the police as being nice to him.

Even so, Einar found himself on the verge of confessing after just one week in custody. He developed a system of exercise and prayer that helped him stave off his doubts about his own involvement. Censored letters from his wife were brought for him to read and he asserts that if he hadn't had access to this correspondence, he may have been compelled to fabricate a story himself. 'I remember very clearly,' says Einar, 'that I was beginning to think "Maybe it's true, maybe I was there that night and I had a shock or something and it made me lock everything up inside me".' When Einar remembered his alibi he was taken to see if he could verify it, but when Saevar and Erla did the same their claims were dismissed as lies.

'When Erla began to wrongly accuse us she was not in custody, she was free, walking the streets like everyone else,' Magnus reminds us. But although Erla may not have been behind bars, she wasn't free. Even prior to her being placed in solitary confinement, she *was* isolated: from her mother, from the father of her child, and from any substantial legal assistance. Back at her mother's house, her phone ringing with people threatening her safety, the investigators became Erla's world. They were in regular contact with her, at one point sending armed police to her home to guard her overnight. She was under the impression that the father of her child was a murderer, and, most of all, she was desperate not to be returned to a cell in Sidumuli prison and separated from her baby.

With Saevar locked up, she began to rely on the investigators, came to trust them, and would say whatever she thought they wanted her to say. 'To let them down,' she says, 'that was the worst thing that could happen to me because if they turned against me, then I would be in custody and my life would be gone.'

In letters she wrote to the investigators while still in custody, the power they held over her is evident. She is desperate not to upset them, she suffers when they do not speak to her, she begs for absolution, and, most of all, she implores them to give her access to the one thing she most desires, time with baby Julia as the days tick down to her first birthday.

Yet however much the evidence seems to pull in the direction of police incompetence or worse, Einar and Magnus circle back to those moments when Erla sat in front of them and accused them of a crime they didn't commit. Their lives were severely impacted by the false accusations. There will always be a barrier to forgiveness, regardless of whether Erla was seemingly, by this point, ready to say anything to avoid being taken back into custody. It is an anger that cannot be explained away.

The perjury is a collision of so many competing factors. It is nobody's 'fault'. But that, it seems to me, is what the perjury charge is essentially about. 'Somebody has to pay the price,' says

Einar. In terms of the repercussions, it is no longer about the truth surrounding Gudmundur and Geirfinnur. It is about who should bear responsibility for all this pain.

'There is no proof that murder is at the core of the Geirfinnur case,' wrote a *Morgunbladid* journalist in February 1976, '[. . .] yet people think they know what is going on, and are never tired of drawing conclusions from their speculations [. . .] The public wants "action". A criminal is wanted. The mob wants its criminal, no matter whether his name is Barabbas or something else [. . .] Whether men are convicted without a reason, whether men are hanged without their guilt being proven, does not matter anymore. The criminal must be found and if he cannot be found, then he must be made up. This demand must be satisfied.'

This oddly prophetic column was written in relation to the Klubburinn Four shortly after their arrest, but it could just as well have been referring to Erla, Saevar and the rest of the suspects. By the time the case had sucked politicians and public figures into its vortex there was a need, a 'demand' even, for a resolution. Society had been left shaken by the accusations of organized crime and corruption. When the four men presumed guilty were proven innocent, someone had to take the blame. It is not just 'Who caused the unjust punishment of these four men?' It is 'Who whipped up this hysteria?', 'Who created this angry mob?', 'Who brought the big bad world to Iceland's door?'

Compared to, say, the UK, Iceland is noticeably egalitarian – in how many other countries could Thordis bang on the Prime Minister's door and be welcomed in for a midnight chat? – but its small population creates drawbacks when it comes to judicial responsibility.

In a country where it has been customary for former Prime Ministers to designate themselves governor of the Central Bank upon retirement from parliament, it is perhaps unsurprising that the so-called 'old boys' club' has remained a small but powerful part of Iceland's political and judicial reality. When Saevar petitioned for a retrial in 1997, Gudjon remarked that he was doing so twenty years too early: too many of the old guard remained in positions of power. Many of the judges who presided over the cases in 1980 still had substantial influence within the judiciary when Saevar and Erla were petitioning throughout the 1990s. The young investigators who once worked on the cases have consequently held some of the highest positions of state. A state prosecutor recently found herself compelled to step down from assessing the retrial because she was related to Orn Hoskuldsson.

It is a problem I encounter throughout my research: even legal professors I interview insist on going off record because they are connected by blood or marriage to people in the cases. After further stalled legal proceedings in recent years, Saevar's son Hafthor wrote online: 'Are we just waiting for someone to die?'

Surviving judges who presided over the Supreme Court appeals, like Ragnar Hall and Haraldur Henrysson, insist that everything they have to say on the matter is contained in their court judgements. 'I will not speak,' Ragnar Hall said to me on the phone. 'It has always been my principle not to comment,' says Haraldur Henrysson, 'and I am not going to break that principle.' Certain figures who move in the shadows, like Kristjan Petursson, have passed away, and so too has Karl Schütz.

I think back to Sigursteinn's story about the people following him in their car. Despite the story's dark connotations, the idea of his pursuers covering their faces with their hands had always made me smile. But they were smart to do so. It is difficult to affix blame upon systemic failings, an incompetently run investigation, and rumour-mongering, less so on an individual. In a pair of criminal cases where so much remains absent, right down to whether they should even be classified as criminal cases, those false accusations have a substance that is lacking elsewhere. They definitely happened.

From the moment Orn named Erla as the 'perfect witness', she became the face of the cases. Erla was rearrested on 3 May 1976 and confessed to having killed Geirfinnur with a rifle. It is obvious that the investigators did not put much stock in her confession. Erla wasn't formally questioned for another four weeks, and then for another two months after that. The cases were in such disarray that Orn tried to resign.

But her confession served another very important function. Although the membrane between Sidumuli and the Icelandic media was usually porous, this time it held tight. The news of her confession did not hit the press for a week, only receiving news coverage on 10 May, the day after the high-profile and humiliating release of the Klubburinn Four. The coinciding of their release with the news of Erla's first Geirfinnur confession was, at the very least, fortuitously well timed for the investigators. It distracted attention at the perfect moment. They had found their scapegoat.

On the front cover of *Dagbladid* in early 1976, just as the furore over the Klubburinn Four was reaching its peak, a heavily bearded Eggert N. Bjarnason stretches out his hand towards the camera in an attempt to stop the photographer from papping him. It is a gesture that feels oddly modern, reminiscent of celebrities in the nineties and noughties trying to deflect the attention of the press. There are still so many people covering their faces in these cases. Erla, on the other hand, has been visible.

It was December 1976, holiday season, and Erla had just been released from custody. Feeling dazed and disorientated after nearly eight months in Sidumuli, she went Christmas shopping with her mother. It felt as if everyone was looking at her. She had read that when prisoners get out of jail that's what they tend to think, but as Erla got to Laugavegur, one of the main streets running through the centre of town, and the thoroughfare got busier, it became impossible to ignore the fact that she was being stared at.

In the background, beneath the hubbub of people shopping, she could hear shouting. She walked with her mother towards the noise. As they approached, the street filled with people, and she could still not hear what was being called out. Then they saw a man in the street selling newspapers. He was shouting her name. Erla grabbed hold of her mother's hand and said, 'We need to get out of here.' Passers-by were giving him handfuls of kronur to buy newspapers with Erla's face on the cover.

She has had to be visible. From the young woman accused of perjuring her half-brother to the peroxide-blonde sexagenarian trying to clear her name, Erla's adult life has played out under media scrutiny. She has been sealed into these cases in people's minds. Equally, she has used the media cleverly at times, aware that keeping herself in the news means the possibility of her exoneration stays alive.

Interviewing Erla so long after the disappearances makes the idea of distinguishing what she really remembers difficult.

She acknowledges that her memories of events from more than forty years ago are, by their nature, imperfect. 'I am not going to remember something like I am watching it being filmed,' she says. 'I am going to remember it through the filters that go in here. I am sure that a lot of it is a matter of maintaining your mental health. We are not going to be aware of all the truth that happened.' The difficulty being, of course, that in an investigation where so much took place behind closed doors in the small hours of the morning, in which the police notes are sparse and the investigative protocol seemingly sparser still, so much of what we know is reliant on the memories of those who lived through it.

At times I find it impossible to suspend belief and to accept the level of specificity: does she remember the coat is red or does she remember remembering the coat is red? Distinguishing between memories and memories of memories becomes too slippery a slope to stand upon. But then there are moments when I can see, in the sudden stillness of her face, or the distant, uncomprehending expression in her eyes, that she is there, right there, as if forty years has rewound in an instant, and she is a young woman living it all again.

Parts of her story strike me as self-serving – how could they not? It is the same with anyone talking about something that happened so long ago. When she says that defecating in her bed after her nightmare reminds her of not reaching for her cigarettes it is almost too emphatic a psychological echo for it to be entirely credible. It may well have happened this way, but I can't help but feel wary about swallowing every detail when she knows how her childhood narrative, of teenage rebellion and of tricky familial relationships, maps on to the psychological nuances that led her to confess. It is the way her whole narrative coheres so perfectly that makes parts of it doubtful to me.

But only parts of it. The reason why her story fits together so well is because she has told it many times, and the details that I find questionably literary are a result of her having written a book about her life. It is a story that she has to be able to tell: in the absence of a coherent police narrative, it has become vital that she remember. There were four people in that interrogation room and Erla is the only one who will speak about it.

The investigators say they cannot remember what happened and don't agree on who was in charge. It was a long time ago and they have had little incentive to dwell upon the cases: the Supreme Court ratified the findings of their investigation. They have the luxury of forgetting. Erla, on the other hand, needs to remember. Her memories have helped to overturn the account that once held primacy. By telling her story, she has been able to pick away at a police narrative that has become more threadbare by the year.

A pair of forty-year-old cases that have produced thousands of pages of documents and there is not a single piece of substantial evidence that links any of the convicted to the disappearances. Instead, there is a mass of stories, an accumulation of statements that give different iterations of the same narrative, and which, through their sheer volume, give the illusion of a solid foundation upon which to build two criminal cases. An excess of detail in the absence of verifiable fact.

Peel back the layers of different confessions and there is nothing underneath. This has created the strange contradiction whereby nobody knows anything, and yet people remain convinced they know everything. Opinions on the cases are defined more by ideology than by evidence: they are a void onto which people project their own interpretations. Thordis once told me that the real monster in all of this was never Saevar, it was prejudice, and I think she is right. Ragnar Hall, the state prosecutor who rejected Saevar's request for a retrial in 1997, once said something revealing in response to questions put to him that Saevar and the others were likely to be innocent. He said: 'These were no choirboys.' It was the no-smoke-without-fire argument, as if the fact they had criminal pasts justified his judgement, regardless of whether there was sufficient evidence with which to bolster it.

Even today, when I interview people who believe that they were guilty, they invariably fall back upon the idea that these were 'no choirboys'. In a pair of cases devoid of any evidence of wrongdoing, it is perhaps unsurprising that stereotype still defines many people's stance. They were crooks, thieves, druggies, scum. One interviewee spits an Icelandic word ruder than the rudest English word imaginable in relation to Erla, as if this *ad feminam* attack somehow confirms Erla's guilt rather than exposing how little he has been paying attention to developments in the cases these past four decades.

Although none of the convicted were actively involved in politics, they embodied the global changes that seemed a threat to the fabric of society. There was a strange moment at the end of a press conference given by Karl Schütz on 2 February 1977 when Orn stood before the Icelandic media and said that the reason the youngsters had committed the crimes was because they were radicals and had negative views of rich people. It was what these young people represented that made it so difficult for them to be believed.

'It was just like in the 1600s,' says journalist Omar Ragnarsson, 'with all the witches and the burning. Same as with the Muslims now. It is an old story and it will happen again and again. There becomes a huge desire for a whole nation to take people and nail them. The community needed it – we had hippies, new music and women's rights. It was a divided nation. And so we got rid of the hippies and the rebels. We didn't want the revolution to destroy everything.' Who cares whether the witch floats or not? What is important is the feeling that something has been cast out.

When Erla returned from abroad and joined Saevar's fight to get the cases reopened, she gave a radio interview on a prime-time Saturday show. The interviewer, veteran journalist Broddi Broddason, told her that he was not happy to do it because he knew they were guilty.

Before the interview took place, the two went for a walk so that Broddi could get an idea of what questions to ask. Erla explained to him that her confessions had been coerced and that she was innocent. The walk lasted much longer than they had originally planned. As Erla was leaving, Broddi called her back. He was clearly troubled by something. You have to understand, he said, that this has always been our safe community and things have always been OK here. What you have told me is robbing me of that. And where does that leave us?

In that moment Erla understood the predicament she was in. 'This small place is safe,' she says, 'not like America and everywhere else where everyone is killing each other. We are so safe here. Now all of a sudden the authorities are the bad guys and this little Iceland family is not about to face that even here we are human.'

There are some pictures of the investigators after the Criminal Court verdict has been returned. They are grinning and shaking each other's hands. On their faces are expressions of jubilation and, more than that, relief. They believed they had cracked the cases. What they did is only comprehensible, if not justifiable, in the context that they were convinced of the guilt harboured by those they had arrested.

In a pair of cases where many key details remain frustratingly elusive, there is a lot of truth in the words 'no choirboys'. It is a painful irony that in trying to save the country, the police used methods that have been a source of shame ever since. The investigators seem to have taken the position that these were bad people and proceeded to work backwards from there. They buttressed a mistaken assumption with incidental facts, such as a visit to a popular nightclub or the number 31 from Geirfinnur's landline. They built a story out of a misguided belief. These young, small-time criminals who stood outside of mainstream society had been guilty from the moment they were arrested.

It is a cold, clear Saturday evening and I am walking down Laugavegur, the main street that runs through downtown, to meet Erla. The bars are packed with people taking advantage of the happy hour deals that make drinking in Iceland, where alcohol taxes are some of the highest in Europe, even vaguely affordable, and outside the most popular restaurants there are queues. I have been coming to Iceland for three years and even in that short period of time there has been a noticeable transformation. Iceland has become really, really popular.

It wasn't always this way. When legendary UK post-punk band

The Fall came to Iceland in 1981 the band were baffled by all the restrictions, including the ban on any music above 100 decibels enforced at venues by officials who used wads of toilet paper as ear plugs. The Fall's manager, Kay Carroll, remarked to *NME* journalist Colin Irwin: 'No booze, no trees, no telly, no cigarettes, and blokes walking around with toilet rolls sticking out of their ears – what kind of a place is this?'

Iceland was perceived by those who knew nothing of it as a provincial backwater characterized by miserable weather and unusual proscriptions. But by the nineties, the success of bands like The Sugarcubes and Sigur Rós had begun to forge a different image of Iceland in the minds of outsiders, one that was substantially augmented when The Sugarcubes' vocalist, Björk, embarked upon a solo career and became a global megastar. Björk's swooping, unpredictable vocal range tapped into Iceland's serene and explosive landscape, and her inventive videos and fusion of musical styles reinforced the idea of Iceland as beautiful, strange and unlike anywhere else in the world. Damon Albarn acquired part-ownership of a bar. Films like *Reykjavik 101* (and the book of the same name) showed off Iceland's wild terrain and even wilder nights. The legalization of beer above 2.25 per cent in 1989 helped too. Iceland was becoming the kind of place that people wanted to visit.

Two explosions, first of the country's economy in 2008, and then, two years later, of the volcano Eyjafjallajokull, brought unprecedented numbers of tourists to Iceland. When the volcanic eruption interrupted flights worldwide in 2010, the Icelandic tourist board anticipated a PR disaster. But instead of warding people off Iceland, the images beamed around the world of alien landscapes and powerful natural forces were a great advertisement for the country. The krona was cheap and so were the flights and tourists came in droves. Since 2010 tourism has increased more than 20 per cent each year. Between 2015 and 2016 it rose by more than 40 per cent. More Americans visit the country each year than there are Icelandic citizens. The Americans are pouring through Keflavik airport again but this time with a different purpose: to see the country's waterfalls and geysers.

Tourism has become the cornerstone of Iceland's economy and provides more jobs than any other industry, constituting more than a third of GDP. By April 2017, unemployment had fallen to 2.4 per cent and capital controls were loosened for the first time since the crash. Cranes have returned to the Reykjavik skyline. Outsiders arriving on Icelandic shores are now the nation's lifeblood.

The sudden influx has also brought difficulties. Iceland's infrastructure was not built to withstand millions of visitors per year. Roads have been worn down and tourist hotspots on the Golden Circle, a route that takes in some of the most spectacular locations in the southwest of the country, struggle to cope with the amount of visitors, especially when those guests bypass the ropes protecting the sites. Human excrement at places of natural beauty has become an issue of national concern and signs have been erected around Iceland to remind visitors that defecating at the base of a waterfall is not acceptable behaviour. At Thingvellir's historic Drowning Pool, once an execution site, park rangers in scuba gear fish out the coins thrown in the water by tourists.

Tourists have put a major strain on ICE-SAR, the rescue services. In 2015, four young British men had to be rescued on three separate occasions during the same trek as they tried to cross from

North to South Iceland on foot. A group of Americans having a picnic on a glacier had to be saved when the ice broke off and they started to drift towards the Norwegian Sea.

One particularly memorable incident occurred in the summer of 2012 when a female tourist went missing from a sightseeing tour near the Eldgja canyon in the south, only for the fifty-strong search team to realize at 3 a.m., after hours spent combing the landscape, that the woman they were looking for was actually part of the search party. She had not realized the person she was involved in a search for was herself. The Minister of Tourism, Industry and Innovation went on record to say that the country should not be trying to attract more tourists.

The unusual story of Huang Nubo, a Chinese billionaire who tried to build a hotel resort and golf course in one of the most desolate parts of northeast Iceland, demonstrates how tourism is seemingly being used to conceal the ulterior motives of those with a political interest in Iceland. The area is so barren that the Foreign Minister described it as a place where 'you can almost hear the ghosts dancing in the snow'. The sheep farmer who owns the land was quoted in the *New York Times* as remarking drily: 'Golf here is difficult.' Huang Nubo is reported to have a sincere love of Scandinavia, and it could well have been a successful venture. But his former occupation as a member of China's propaganda department caused the Icelandic government some pause for thought, especially when the business plan he offered up was less than convincing. The bid was rejected.

There is speculation that Chinese interest may be related to the fact that Iceland is a NATO member with no standing army. China's first trade with a European country was with Iceland in

2013 and, despite only having a handful of diplomats, it has built a huge embassy in Reykjavik that boasts the capacity to accommodate five hundred personnel. It has announced its intent to use the improved shipping routes off the Icelandic coast brought about by the melting of Arctic ice. Having a foothold in Iceland would be a strategic boon. The Cold War may be over but Iceland remains a prized asset in the geopolitical manoeuvrings of the world's superpowers.

There is no doubt that the massive increase in tourists has brought positives for the cases. People are fascinated by Iceland. It is a place people want to visit, learn about, understand. When the Icelandic football team returned from their UEFA European Championships heroics in the summer of 2016, the video of their rapturous reception by thousands of Icelandic citizens celebrating in unison with the so-called 'Viking Clap', on the same hill overlooked by the statue of the first settler Ingolfur Arnarson, went viral around the world. Television programmes such as the BBC's *Trapped*, critically and commercially successful films such as *Of Horses and Men* and *Rams*, and bands such as Of Monsters and Men – the first Icelandic group to get a billion plays on Spotify – have all turned worldwide attention onto Iceland.

When I tell Icelanders I am researching a book on the disappearances they often smile a small smile whose meaning it took me a while to work out. In part, I suppose, it is grim amusement that this story from so far in the past continues to provoke interest. But increasingly it seems to me that they smile because they know that international focus on a story that has destroyed dozens of lives has been fanned by Iceland's enormous popularity as a holiday destination.

A few days prior to my meeting with Erla, the committee returned their verdict that the perjury would not be reopened. There is a part of her, she says, that just wants to get on a plane and fly somewhere far away. Although she feels the pull of escape, there is no way she is going to leave. Her daughters live here, including a girl she adopted from South Africa. She has roots here. If she cut ties with Iceland, then a part of her would wither.

'I am doomed,' she says, 'I have to stay because I am part of this soil. But at the same time I need to get out.' During the 1980s she lived abroad, figuring she could escape to Hawaii and lounge under a palm tree until everything was OK, but she soon returned. Torn between her heart and her head, the energy she takes from her homeland and the exhaustion of constantly being on show, her relationship with Iceland is an uneasy one.

Wherever she goes in Iceland she is still seen in relation to these cases. A community that she values and wants to be accepted by has cast her out. Perhaps this is part of the reason why she puts so much stock in the spiritual. She feels like she has been cheated on earth, like she was never given the opportunity to really live her life, and that she is, in some ways, still that girl of twenty years old, alone in her cell, lying on her bed while images scroll through her mind of dark figures silhouetted against the blind and a cigarette drooping in the ashtray.

When she looks at pictures of herself from that time, she says, 'I always see this child and I still haven't been able to connect that this is the same person as sits here now. It's just so painful to see this child. I don't know if I'm supposed to get to that point of being able to experience that this is actually me. It's always somebody else. Often when I see it, I look away or I remember moments in isolation, or I think of my daughter like it was her in there. It's a really weird thing.' She talks often of an afterlife, not a Judaeo-Christian one, but something more mystical, where she will see Saevar again and they will laugh together about that crazy, horrible trip they took down on earth.

Saevar is buried near the house of his grandparents, where he spent many of his happiest months as a child. The graveyard is perched upon the incline of a sweeping valley next to a church. There is a wooden fence that runs knee-high around the perimeter.

Erla took Dylan and myself to visit it at the end of our drive around the southwest of the country. I hadn't thought about how going there would affect her, in part because it had been her who had suggested the trip, but also because looking back on their relationship, from the vantage point of more than forty years, it almost felt like something from a different life. But being at Saevar's grave is painful for her, perhaps more than she realized it would be, and she sits on a bench and starts to weep. Despite there being no one else in the graveyard, a dog appears, presumably the pastor's, and while Dylan films the headstone, it rubs its flank against the bench and puts its head in her lap.

Perhaps the most unsettling part of the entire investigation was the way in which the police exploited Erla and Saevar's relationship. At corroboration meetings between them, the police pressured Saevar to confess to the same description of events given by Erla. The two of them are described in police reports as confused, crestfallen, unable to understand what is happening. When describing one of these corroboration meetings, Saevar said: 'They didn't use duress or anything. They were just going to use love. They interrogated Erla in the morning and told her, tried to convince her that she would get out if she was able to make me admit that I was at Hamarsbraut. And then when I came for interrogation, Erla said, "Please do it for me, Saevar, say you were there."'

Broken down, terrified of being kept from her baby and convinced Saevar might have had something to do with Gudmundur's disappearance, she accused the father of her child of being involved in killing someone. How can two people ever recover from that? In the years following their release, although they could both rationalize that they were fellow sufferers, their experience in Sidumuli overshadowed them.

When they saw each other there was still a bond between them, especially when it came to sharing the upbringing of Julia, but it would take years, Erla says, for them to properly reconnect. They were not angry at each other. But their past was shadowed by such darkness that they could no longer communicate properly.

They continued to see each other intermittently. By the time Saevar was on the streets, maintaining a friendship was difficult. Sometimes he would come to her house. The bond they had forged all those decades ago by the red light still counted for something, despite the ugliness of what they had been through ever since. 'Because of my children and my family I was not able to have him in the home,' she says. 'There was just so much stuff that came with it. And so I would go downstairs and we would go to a corner in the apartment building and sit there for an evening and just talk about everything. It was freedom just sitting there.'

When my meeting with Erla is finished, we step outside. It is the evening of the first day of March 2017 and the sky is dark and speckled with stars. The moon is so low you feel you could

stand on a car roof and touch it. Suddenly Erla says, 'Look!'
and points back over my head. I turn and see in the sky a huge
shimmering oval, like an enormous mouth, muted green with
purple around its edge. I am surprised by how quickly it moves,
the circle breaking into a band of brilliant colours that whips up
and down like a scarf unfurled in the wind.

Erla is on her feet, a cigarette in her hand, and she is pointing
up at the sky saying, 'That is the truth! That there is the truth!'
What she is saying, I think, is that this natural event has an
inherent truth to it that her life has so often lacked. This beautiful
phenomenon, although made comprehensible by experts in solar
wind and plasma particles, is the whispering of some larger force,
the sky dance of a greater being. For her, it is truthful because
it is not of this earth, it is free from any falsehood or agenda; it
is inhuman.

EPILOGUE

OUT OF THIN AIR

At 4.30 a.m. on Saturday, 14 January 2017, twenty-year-old sales assistant Birna Brjansdottir exited Hurra, a bar in downtown Reykjavik. She bought food from a late night takeaway spot and began to walk home.

A series of CCTV cameras mounted at different points in the city centre captured footage of her walking along Laugavegur. Dressed in a black jacket and holding a falafel pitta, her gait a little unsteady, she headed in the direction of Breidholt, the suburb of Reykjavik where she lived with her father. Around 5.00 a.m., the cameras along Laugavegur lost track of her. Birna had disappeared.

The largest search and rescue operation in Icelandic history began the following day. More than seven hundred ICE-SAR members, eleven dogs and an array of police units searched the lava fields and craggy coastline around Reykjavik. Three days after she had disappeared, they found something: Birna's black Doc Martens by a dock in Hafnarfjordur. Oddly, the shoes had snow on them despite no snow having fallen in the area.

The following weekend her body washed up fifty kilometres

from Reykjavik on a black pebble beach near the bright yellow Selvogsviti lighthouse.

Acting in concord with local media, investigators spurred the public into action by showing CCTV footage of Birna's last hours and imploring anyone who had seen anything to come forward with more information. A red Kia Rio car could be seen in the CCTV footage of Birna and, when the police traced the licence plate, they discovered the car had been hired by some crew members aboard a Greenlandic trawler. The boat had been docked in Hafnarfjordur on the night Birna disappeared.

Iceland's Coast Guard sent a helicopter with six officers from Iceland's special forces, otherwise known as the 'Viking Squad', to intercept the Greenlandic boat, named the *Polar Nanoq*, which had just sailed off from Hafnarfjordur. Two men were arrested. One of them was released, leaving Thomas Frederik Moller Olsen as the chief suspect.

For those who lived through the Geirfinnur disappearance, it seemed, for a moment, like history might be repeating itself. Local newspapers took the unusual step of publishing pictures of the suspects, including their names, their ages and their jobs. On Facebook, people declared that these men were the faces of evil. 'I just thought – is this happening again?!' criminologist Helgi Gunnlaugsson tells me. The most high-profile disappearance in more than forty years, and once again outsiders were being tarred with criminal responsibility before anything had been substantially proven.

But whereas with the Gudmundur and Geirfinnur cases there were reams of confessions and no evidence, here the opposite was true. Despite his claims of innocence, the evidence against

Thomas Olsen was considerable. In a black bin bag on board the *Polar Nanoq* trawler, investigators found Birna's driving licence. It had Thomas Olsen's fingerprints on it. The police located CCTV footage of him buying cleaning products at 10.30 a.m. on the morning after Birna's disappearance. He spent forty minutes cleaning inside the red Kia Rio seen driving in the vicinity of Birna on the night she disappeared. Forensic analysis of the car found her blood beneath the back seat and around the steering wheel.

When Karl Schütz arrived in Iceland in the summer of 1976 he had scarcely been able to believe the paucity of training that the Icelandic police had received. He wrote a letter in October 1976 claiming that the investigators were so ill-prepared for interrogations that it would be easy for a suspect of reasonable intelligence to deceive them. The investigators, wrote Schütz, lacked the personal confidence and charisma to achieve results in difficult interrogations.

More than anything, these words reflect Schütz's warped attitude to police investigations, one in which the personal qualities of the investigator are prized above rigorous police work. But they also touch upon an important truth about the investigation: the Icelandic police had not been trained to handle complex murder cases. Schütz, for all his faults, brought a systematic approach to an investigation that, until his arrival, had been chaotic.

The Birna investigation, by contrast, was clear-headed, effective and well executed. Since the 1970s there has been a steady professionalization of the Icelandic police force. Officers are much better trained and more experienced in dealing with murder cases. In the Birna investigation, the police were able to use Thomas Olsen's mobile phone data to trace the route he had driven from

Reykjavik, where Birna was last seen, to Hafnarfjordur, where the car was parked. This evidence was used in court in September 2017, and proved instrumental in building up a narrative of Birna's last moments. Technological innovations and improvements in forensic analysis meant that investigators could gather evidence from a wider array of sources, reducing the reliance on confessions.

When it comes to criminal evidence, CCTV footage and DNA analysis have a substance and validity that memory, for all we rely on it, lacks.

Frequently the 1970s investigation pursued leads that, from our present day perspective, seem misjudged. A story leaked to the press in May 1976, detailing how police had sent divers to search for Geirfinnur's body near Grindavik harbour, based on a member of the public's dream: a woman had contacted the police to say she had 'seen' a clue lying at the end of a pier. 'They have chased mediums and clairvoyants for their help with investigating the case,' wrote *Dagbladid*, 'and it now seems that only coincidence will decide whether the Geirfinnur case will be solved or not.' The headline read: 'The Geirfinnur case: searching for a dream'.

They repeatedly found recourse to use psychics. Detective Njordur Snaeholm interviewed a woman who thought she knew Geirfinnur's location because she had received visions of where he was. Long after his work on the case had finished, the Keflavik investigator Haukur Gudmundsson flew to Jordan in the Middle East with Geirfinnur's wife Gudny to try to contact her missing husband.

A Dutch psychic by the name of Gerard Croiset was enlisted to help. Croiset, nicknamed 'the Mozart of Psychic Sleuths' by his followers, was one of the world's most famous contemporary parapsychologists. Iceland was not alone in its use of psychics. Croiset was used extensively by British police and was employed as far afield as Japan and Australia. He advised investigators during the search for Lord Lucan.

Croiset's first major success was in 1963 in his native Nether-lands when he assisted police in their search for six-year-old Wim Slee, a boy who had gone missing in Voorburg in South Holland. Croiset declared that his body would appear after twelve days in a canal. The Dutch police continued to search for the missing boy in vain, and then, exactly a dozen days after Croiset had made his prediction, the boy's body surfaced in a canal. It had been lodged beneath an object underwater.

For those sceptical of the utility of clairvoyance in murder investigations, Croiset's failures are more memorable than his triumphs. In 1957 in a town near Utrecht he informed a married couple that their missing son had drowned in a quay close to their home. Only after the parents had organized the funeral did the boy emerge from where he was hiding in a haystack. In 1966 he helped the South Australian police in a search for three children who had gone missing after a day at Glenelg beach in Adelaide. Croiset became convinced that they were buried beneath a large warehouse. The police could not dig up the building's foundations just because Croiset had told them to, but decades later it was excavated. No bodies were found.

Croiset arrived in Iceland in January 1975 and soon started to receive visions of Geirfinnur's fate. He was baffled that he could sense trees around the area where Geirfinnur went missing, because he had heard that Iceland did not have any trees. When asked whether Geirfinnur was dead or alive Croiset replied, unequivocally, that if the missing man were located where Croiset thought he was, then he was deceased.

Investigative methods have, of course, evolved considerably since Crosiet's heyday, and so, too, has the Icelandic legal system. What was unusual in the 1970s was that the representative of the judge and the prosecutor both took an active part in the investigation. When Orn Hoskuldsson questioned prisoners in their cells, they were being questioned by the same machinery of the state that would convict them in court. Often Hallvardur Einvardsson, the assistant state prosecutor, would be present for interrogations, further blurring the lines between the investigation and the prosecution.

But in a major structural reform in 1992 following a traffic incident in Akureyri in the north of Iceland, the judiciary and the executive were separated for the purposes of criminal investigations. Safeguards were introduced to prevent long stretches of custody. It is unlikely that there would be a repeat of the intense situation in which the suspects in the Gudmundur and Geirfinnur cases found themselves. Although Birna's disappearance provoked an emotional response from the Icelandic public, there was no sense that the Icelandic police force allowed the heightened pressure, comparable in intensity to the furore over Geirfinnur's disappearance, to affect their judgement.

Court hearings for the murder of Birna Bjarnsdottir began in September 2017. On 28 September 2017, Thomas Olsen was found guilty of her murder, and also of trying to smuggle twenty kilos of hash. He was sentenced to nineteen years in prison, the longest sentence since Saevar Ciesielski was convicted for the killing of Gudmundur and Geirfinnur.

The disappearances remain a mystery. As recently as June 2016, two men were arrested. They had been driving through Hafnarfjordur on the night Gudmundur disappeared. One of their ex-girlfriends had come forward to say that she was in the car with them when they knocked a boy down during a storm. She was dropped off at home and the two men drove away in the snow with the boy in the back seat. She did not know if it was Gudmundur but thought it could have been.

One of these two men, named Stefan Almarsson, was serving a sentence for a minor offence just before Erla and Saevar were arrested. Police reports indicate that it was Stefan who provided the information that tipped off the police that Erla and Saevar were responsible for the postal fraud. Stefan was then transferred from Litla-Hraun prison to Sidumuli on 18 December 1975 and released on 19 December, the same day Erla was first questioned about Gudmundur. It appears he was released earlier than he should have been. 'He was being compensated for something,' says Ragnar Adalsteinsson.

An interview with Tryggvi published in 1991 by Thorsteinn Antonsson suggests Stefan Almarsson may well have given the police more than just information pertaining to the postal fraud. Stefan was known to despise Kristjan. In the interview, Tryggvi claims that Stefan Almarsson, who was an old friend of Tryggvi's, had come up to him at a party and apologized for getting him involved in the Gudmundur case. 'He said he didn't mean to,' said Tryggvi. 'He had only wanted to get Kristjan into trouble. Can you believe that?'

There is a police report from April 1978 that adds further credibility to the idea that Stefan Almarsson could have been responsible for implicating them. That month, Stefan Almarsson told the Reykjavik police that the bodies of Geirfinnur and Gudmundur were buried at Grettisgata 82, the home of Kristjan's grandmother. The fact that Stefan allegedly disliked Kristjan, provided information that led to the solution of the postal fraud, and was giving tip-offs about the whereabouts of Gudmundur and Geirfinnur's bodies as late as four years after the disappearances, suggests he could well have been, at the very least, the origin of the Gudmundur rumour.

Stefan Almarsson was arrested in June 2016 and the case lit up the media once again, but he was soon released. In some ways it is similar to everything else that has happened in these cases: more rumours, more stories.

Has there ever been another criminal investigation where rumour has played such a central role? It is the defining quality of the two investigations, what drives them forward and where they both begin: rumours about Klubburinn, about smuggling, and about Saevar knowing more than he lets on. One of the most extensive criminal investigations in Icelandic history, and its origin is hearsay and tittle-tattle, its lifeblood baseless accusations and wild goose chases through the lava.

New discoveries are still being made. Astonishingly, in 2016, the journalist Jon Danielsson managed to uncover the most compelling evidence to date concerning Saevar's alibi. Again, this was something that Saevar had told the judges, something that would not have been difficult to investigate, should any of them have felt so inclined.

In letters written by Saevar in September 1977, he describes in greater detail his memories from the night he had spent watching a film about a volcanic eruption with his mother and Erla; the night that Geirfinnur disappeared. He had thought long and hard about that evening. After the film was over, he had gone to his mother's house and watched television. And he could recall what it was he had watched. It was a news report by a journalist named Sonja Diego, in which she talked about red wine fraud at a company in France.

Jon Danielsson dug through the television schedules and found 19 November 1974. At 10.25 p.m., immediately after the sports documentary Einar Bollason had been watching at his home, a television programme called *Heimshorn* was broadcast. It was presented by Sonja Diego and finished at 11.00 p.m. The final segment of the programme was seven minutes in duration and titled 'France's "Winegate"'. While Geirfinnur got into his car in Keflavik to drive back to the café, this evidence suggests Saevar was at his mother's house watching television.

It took almost forty years, but we now know the key alibis in the Geirfinnur case can be found on a single piece of paper: the television schedule on the morning of 19 November 1974.

Arguably more astonishingly, over the summer of 2016, a famous journalist and media personality named Omar Ragnarsson, one of Iceland's most revered national treasures, released a book about the Geirfinnur disappearance. He says he interviewed a couple fourteen years previously who said they had knocked Geirfinnur down in their car, panicked, and dumped his body in the lava fields. He did not name the couple and said that he never would. The publication of his book was akin to David Attenborough announcing that he knew the person who had killed Madeleine McCann but was not going to tell anyone who it was. Some journalists dismissed the revelations in the book as either unfounded or as a strange, misguided fiction, but he insists that it is true.

There is still a lack at the heart of this story: no evidence, no body, no motive, no connection between the disappearances. Nobody knows if they were even criminal cases: it has since transpired that the Keflavik police never traced the call from the café to Geirfinnur's home. The clay head was a complete nonsense, crafted from a picture of Magnus Leopoldsson and made to match the face of a man who might not have even been phoning Geirfinnur. Gudmundur could have died in a storm.

More than forty years ago two men vanished into thin air and people have been fabricating stories, rumours, statements and confessions out of it ever since. The cases, made up from rumour and hearsay, were as much a product of the hysteria they helped create; the confessions, used to convict an array of people, were stories that to this day remain mixed up in people's dreams.

ACKNOWLEDGEMENTS

Thank you to Rich Arcus from Hachette UK. An author could not ask for a better editor: his precision, verve for storytelling, and passion for the subject matter are present in every paragraph. Thank you to Juliet Mahony from Lutyens & Rubinstein for emboldening me to write a proposal and for being a constant source of support throughout this whole process – this could not have been written without her.

Thank you to Dylan Howitt, who conducted many of the key interviews upon which *Out of Thin Air* is based. Without his sensitive and thoughtful approach, this book would be much the poorer. Thank you to Margret Jonasdottir from SagaFilm who took the Icelandic-language interviews that featured in this book and gave valuable feedback throughout the writing process.

Thank you to Mosaic Films and SagaFilm for allowing me access to interviews and research gathered during the making of the documentary of the same name.

Thank you to my employers and colleagues for their flexibility concerning my time commitments as well as their encouragement of the project: Andy Glynne at Mosaic Films, Kavita Puri at the BBC, and Laurie Harris at Detour.

Thanks also to those who read versions of the book during different stages of the drafting process, in particular Helgi Gunnlaugsson, Gisli Gudjonsson, Jon Danielsson, Sumarlidi Isleifsson, Charlie Griffiths, Jasper Jolly, Camilla Adeane, Henry Adeane, Madeline Adeane, Pat Brooke, Helena Blackstone, Joe Dodd, Hugh Davies, and Dan Meththananda.

Thank you to Sigurthor Stefansson, Helga Luthersdottir, Tryggvi Brynjarsson and Tryggvi Hubner for their help at various stages during the writing process.

There have been many excellent English-language books written about Icelandic culture and history, and the ones that I found particularly useful were Gunnar Karlsson's *The History of Iceland*, Sigurdur Gyfli Magnusson's *Wasteland with Words: A Social History of Iceland*, Gudni Johannesson's *The History of Iceland*, and Kirsten Hastrup's *A Place Apart*.

And, most of all, thank you to the people who welcomed me into their homes to patiently answer my questions about their lives. I hope that I have done this sad and complicated story justice.

Any mistakes are, of course, of my own making.

ANNOTATED BIBLIOGRAPHY

PRIMARY SOURCES

Boyes, Roger, *Meltdown Iceland* (London: Bloomsbury Publishing Plc., 2010). Not just a fascinating insight into the effects of the financial crash, but also a rigorously researched and entertainingly written history of Iceland.

Gunnlaugsson, Helgi, and Galliher, John F., *Wayward Icelanders: Punishment, Boundary Maintenance and the Creation of Crime* (Wisconsin: University of Wisconsin Press, 1999). A particularly useful book for its analysis of Iceland's various proscriptions and bans, as well as for its potted history of prisons.

Johannesson, Gudni Thorlacius, *The History of Iceland* (Santa Barbara, California: Greenwood, 2013). Brilliant on the effects of the Second World War on Reykjavik and Keflavik and also on the Venture Vikings and the terminology used to describe their actions on the financial markets.

Karlsson, Gunnar, *The History of Iceland* (London: C. Hurst & Co., 2000). The most comprehensive history of Iceland written in the English language. Meticulously researched and forensically detailed, it was a valuable resource for specifics about Reykjavik pre-1970 and the aid Iceland received from the Marshall Plan.

Magnusson, Sigurdur Gylfi, *Wasteland with Words: A Social History of Iceland* (London: Reaktion Books Ltd, 2010). A brilliant, at times counterintuitive, read, it delves in much greater detail into the subjects of *kvoldvakas*, Icelandic identity, and the effects of Americanization on Keflavik.

SECONDARY SOURCES

Auden, W. H., and MacNeice, Louis, *Letters from Iceland* (London: Faber and Faber, 1937)

Byock, Jesse, 'History and the sagas: the effect of nationalism', from *From Sagas to Society: Comparative Approaches to Early Iceland* (London: Hisarlik Press, 1992)

Fairhall, David, *Cold Front: Conflict Ahead in Arctic Waters* (New York: I. B. Tauris & Co. Ltd, 2010)

Grassian, Stuart, 'Psychiatric Effects of Solitary Confinement' from Washington University Journal of Law & Policy, volume 22, *Access to Justice: The Social Responsibility of Lawyers / Prison Reform: Commission on Safety and Abuse in America's Prisons* (January 2006)

Gudjonsson, Gisli H., 'Delinquent Boys in Reykjavik: A Follow-up Study of Boys Sent to an Institution' from *Abnormal Offenders, Delinquency, and the Criminal Justice System* (London: John Wiley & Sons Ltd., 1982)

Gudjonsson, Gisli H., *Psychology of Interrogations and Confessions: A Handbook* (London: John Wiley & Sons Ltd., 2009)

Gudjonsson, Gisli H., 'Memory distrust syndrome, confabulation and false confession', Cortex (2016)

Gunni, Dr., *Blue Eyed Pop: The History of Popular Music in Iceland* (Reykjavik: Sogur Utgafa, 2013). Excellent account of the history of Icelandic pop music accompanied by great pictures and illuminating interviews with the key players from all the different music scenes.

Hafstein, Valdimar, 'The Elves Point of View: Cultural Identity in Contemporary Icelandic Elf-Tradition' in Fabula 41 n1-2 (2000)

Hastrup, Kirsten, *A Place Apart: An Anthropological Study of the Icelandic World* (Oxford: Oxford University Press, 2004)

Heron, Woodburn, 'The Pathology of Boredom' from Scientific American, Inc., 1956

Higgins, Andrew, 'Teeing Off at the Edge of the Arctic? A Chinese Plan Battles Iceland', New York Times, 22 March 2013

Irwin, Colin, 'The decline and Fall in Iceland', *Melody Maker*, 26 September 1981

Kaba, Fatos et al., 'Solitary Confinement and Risk of Self-Harm Among Jail Inmates' from American Journal of Public Health, March 2014, 104 (3)

Kassin, Saul M., and Wrightsman, Lawrence S., *The Psychology of Evidence and Trial Procedure* (Beverly Hills: Sage Publications, 1985)

Kissinger, Henry, *Years of Upheaval* (London: Simon & Schuster, 2011 reprint)

Kois, Dan, 'Iceland's Water Cure' from *New York Times*, 19 April 2016. Illuminating article on swimming pools in Iceland.

Laxness, Halldor, *The Atom Station* (Reykjavik: Second Chance Press, 1948)

Lewis, Michael, 'Wall Street on the Tundra' from *Vanity Fair*, April 2009

Moore, Tim, 'Iceland's tourism boom – and backlash' from *Financial Times*, 8 March 2017

Paumgarten, Nick, 'Life is rescues' from *The New Yorker*, 9 November 2015 issue. A particularly good article about ICE-SAR and the Geysir crash.

Schacter, Daniel L., *The Seven Sins of Memory: How the Mind Forgets and Remembers* (Boston: Houghton Mifflin, 2002)

Shaw, J. & Porter, S, 'Constructing rich false memories of committing crime' from Psychological Science, 26 (3), 2016

Smiley, Jane, *The Sagas of Icelanders* (London: Penguin, 2005)

Steinsson, Sverrir, 'The Cod Wars: a re-analysis' from journal of European Security, volume 25, 2016, issue 2

Sveinsson, Ottar, *Lost on the Glacier*. Ottar Sveinsson has written numerous books about Icelandic rescue missions. His account of the crash of the Geysir in 1950 has yet to be translated into English, but his research underpins much of the description of the death-defying rescue in Chapter 1 of this book.

Von Troil, Uno, *Letters on Iceland* (London: W. Richardson, 1780)

Wade, Robert H, and Sigurgeirsdottir, Silla, 'Iceland's meltdown: the rise and fall of international banking in the North Atlantic' from the Brazilian Journal of Political Economy vol.31, no.5, Sao Paulo 2011

Whitehead, Thor, *The Ally who came in from the Cold: A Survey of Icelandic Foreign Policy 1946-1956* (Reykjavik: Iceland University Press, 1998). Very informative account of the NATO vote in 1949.

Whitehead, Thor, *Island I hers hondum [Iceland and the Allied Military Presence]* (Reykjavik: Iceland University Press, 2002)

INDEX

NOTE

Please note that Icelandic names are indexed by their first name rather than by their surname